"This volume is a labour of love. The authors' commitment to, and experiences in, aid and development are charted with honesty and openness. They have in the process come to understand themselves and their motivations better. We, the readers, can benefit similarly by reading these thoroughly enjoyable, stimulating and often very moving accounts."

Sir Myles Wickstead, *Visiting Professor of International Relations, King's College London, UK and coordinator of the 1997 UK Government White Paper, Eliminating World Poverty: A Challenge for the 21st Century*

"A welcome volume masterfully edited and brilliantly and thoughtfully written by development practitioners from nearly 20 countries of their struggles and victories in their journey of development practice. The eye-opening and reflective work is a must-read for anyone interested in development issues."

Ashok Swain, *Professor of Peace and Conflict Research & UNESCO Chair on International Water Cooperation, Uppsala University, Sweden*

Dear Development Practitioner

In this book, influential development practitioners reflect on their careers by writing letters of advice to their younger selves. Sharing their successes and failures, the challenges and barriers they have encountered, and the changes and continuities within their work, these deeply personal accounts provide an invaluable window into the world of development practice.

The authors come from nearly 20 countries. They have held a rich mix of jobs across a range of sectors and organisational types, bringing a long-term perspective to the sector's contemporary challenges. The distinguished list includes a Nobel Peace Prize winner, senior figures in government and international organisations, those working at the frontline of humanitarian aid and civil society organisations, and those who might not even have thought of themselves as "development professionals", such as technologists and social entrepreneurs. Despite the differences, common themes emerge: the pursuit of meaningful change, the navigation of barriers, and the ongoing sense of hope.

This book will inspire those about to embark on their professional careers and remind new entrants and current development practitioners alike how much there remains to be done.

Simon Milligan is an Independent Advisor with more than 20 years of professional experience in development cooperation. As a consultant and "critical friend", he has been engaged by various governments, multilateral agencies, inter-governmental organisations, and non-governmental organisations. He has a particular interest in evaluative thinking, partnership-based approaches, and mentorship. He has a PhD in Geography from the University of Sussex, UK. Simon is an Adjunct Senior Lecturer at the University of Lund and teaches on Lund's Masters in International Development. He lives in The Hague, Netherlands.

Lee Wilson is an organisational anthropologist who has spent the best part of the last two decades striving to understand and drive change in a diverse range of institutional settings and cultural contexts. A particular focus of his work has been on innovative approaches to capacity building and culture change. When asked what he does professionally, he will probably tell you rather glibly that he works "to put the people back in to strategy". He has worked as an advisor to national and regional government agencies, international organisations, non-governmental organisations, research centres, arts organisations, and law enforcement agencies in Australia, Asia, the Pacific, and Europe. Lee has a PhD in Social Anthropology from the University of Cambridge and is an Adjunct Senior Research Fellow at the Centre for Policy Futures, University of Queensland, Australia. He is currently based in Geneva, Switzerland.

Rethinking Development

Rethinking Development offers accessible and thought-provoking overviews of contemporary topics in international development and aid. Providing original empirical and analytical insights, the books in this series push thinking in new directions by challenging current conceptualizations and developing new ones.

This is a dynamic and inspiring series for all those engaged with today's debates surrounding development issues, whether they be students, scholars, policy makers and practitioners internationally. These interdisciplinary books provide an invaluable resource for discussion in advanced undergraduate and postgraduate courses in development studies as well as in anthropology, economics, politics, geography, media studies and sociology.

COVID-19 and Foreign Aid
Nationalism and Global Development in a New World Order
Edited by Viktor Jakupec, Max Kelly and Michael de Percy

Critical Approaches to Heritage for Development
Edited by Charlotte Cross and John Giblin

Disability and International Development, 2nd edition
A Guide for Students and Practitioners
David Cobley

Researching Development NGOs
Global and Grassroots Perspectives
Edited by Susannah Pickering-Saqqa

South-North Dialogues on Democracy, Development and Sustainability
Edited by Cristina Fróes de Borja Reis and Tatiana Berringer

Dear Development Practitioner: Advice for the Next Generation
Edited by Simon Milligan and Lee Wilson

For more information about this series, please visit: www.routledge.com/Rethinking-Development/book-series/RDVPT

Dear Development Practitioner

Advice for the Next Generation

Edited by Simon Milligan and Lee Wilson

Routledge
Taylor & Francis Group
LONDON AND NEW YORK

Designed cover image: © Jasenka Arbanas / Getty Images

First published 2024
by Routledge
4 Park Square, Milton Park, Abingdon, Oxon OX14 4RN

and by Routledge
605 Third Avenue, New York, NY 10158

Routledge is an imprint of the Taylor & Francis Group, an informa business

British Library Cataloguing-in-Publication Data
A catalogue record for this book is available from the British Library

ISBN: 978-1-032-19803-3 (hbk)
ISBN: 978-1-032-19802-6 (pbk)
ISBN: 978-1-003-26092-9 (ebk)

DOI: 10.4324/9781003260929

Typeset in Sabon
by Apex CoVantage, LLC

Contents

Contributors

Lina AbiRafeh Global women's rights expert and gender equality advocate, and former Executive Director of the Arab Institute for Women at the Lebanese American University, based in New York and Lebanon

Brian Atwood Senior Fellow for Public and International Affairs at the Thomas Watson Institute for International and Public Affairs, Brown University, and former Administrator of the U.S. Agency for International Development

Ken Banks Founder of kiwanja.net and creator of FrontlineSMS, National Geographic Explorer, and recipient of the Eugene L. Lawler Award for Humanitarian Contributions within Computer Science.

Hannah Birdsey Chief Executive Officer of Investing in Women, formerly a senior executive with the Australian Department of Foreign Affairs and Trade

Anna Bwana Country Director of BBC Media Action in Tanzania

Harpinder Collacott Executive Director for Mercy Corps Europe and former Chief Executive Officer of Development Initiatives

Fernando Damazio dos Santos Programme Analyst on LGBTI Inclusion at the United Nations Development Programme

Bill Drayton Founder, Chief Executive Officer and Chair of Ashoka: Innovators for the Public

Leith Dunn Independent Advisor and former Senior Lecturer/Head of the Institute for Gender and Development Studies at the University of West Indies

Mark Goldring Director of Asylum Welcome and former Chief Executive Officer of Oxfam GB and VSO International

Bahey eldin Hassan Director of the Cairo Institute for Human Rights Studies

Lysa John Secretary-General of the CIVICUS World Alliance for Citizen Participation and former Head of Outreach for the UN Secretary General's High Level Panel on the Post-2015 Development Agenda

Petra Karetji Team Leader of the Australia-Indonesia Synergies and Collaboration to Accelerate Service Delivery Programme and former Head of the United Nations Global Pulse Lab Jakarta

Tawakkol Karman Chair of the Tawakkol Karman Foundation, Nobel Peace Laurette and Co-founder of Women Journalists Without Chains

Morten Kjærum Director of the Raoul Wallenberg Institute of Human Rights and Humanitarian Law, Sweden

Gabriele Köhler Senior Research Associate of the United Nations Research Institute on Social Development

Salmah Eva-Lina Lawrence Honorary Associate Professor, Australian National University, and Director of Systemic Change and Partnerships at the International Women's Development Agency and non-executive director of WaterAid Australia

Frannie Léautier Partner and Chief Executive Officer, SouthBridge Investment and former Vice-President at the World Bank Group and Senior Vice-President of the African Development Bank

Indrani Medhi Thies Design and technology researcher, author, public speaker and start-up mentor and former Principal Researcher in the Technology and Empowerment Group at Microsoft Research India

Mark Moran Independent advisor, author and researcher, Senior Industry Fellow at the Centre for Social Responsibility in Mining, and former Professor and Group Leader of Development Effectiveness at the University of Queensland

Julie Mundy Chair and former CEO of MSI Asia Pacific, Adjunct Research Fellow, Latrobe University

Suresh Nanwani Professor in Practice at the University of Durham, UK

Deepa Narayan Independent Advisor on poverty and development, and former Senior Advisor in the Vice-President's Office of the Poverty Reduction Group of the World Bank

Admiral Ncube Programme Coordinator of the Institutional Capacity Building Programme, Southern Africa Development Community Secretariat

Johannes Oljelund Swedish Ambassador to the Netherlands and former Director General for International Development Cooperation at the Swedish Ministry for Foreign Affairs

Jeffrey O'Malley Senior Advisor, LGBTI Inclusion, Africa, United Nations Development Programme

Dias Rahwidiati Senior Strategic Innovation Designer with CHÔRA Design and former Senior Strategic Communications Advisor Love Frankie

Adrian Schlaepfer Retired diplomat and former Assistant Director General of the Swiss Agency for Development and Cooperation

Irina Schoulgin-Nyoni Deputy Director-General and Head of Africa Department at the Swedish Ministry for Foreign Affairs

Ingrid Srinath Director, Centre for Social Impact and Philanthropy, Ashoka University

Fekitamoeloa Katoa 'Utoikamanu Minister of Foreign Affairs, Tonga and former Under-Secretary-General and UN High Representative for the Least Developed Countries, Landlocked Developing Countries and Small Island Developing States

Arthur Wood Founding Partner (Geneva) of Total Impact Capital and former Senior Vice President and a Leadership Group Member of Ashoka

Cara Yar Khan Senior Advisor, International Disability Rights, U.S. Department of State

Foreword

I have to admit that when Simon, one of the editors, asked me to write the Foreword, I was slightly overwhelmed at first. The first question that came to my mind was: "Who am I to write the Foreword to a book with authors who have years of experience in the field of development?" And this is a question that you might have been thinking about as well when you read my name at the top of the table of contents. Other than most of the others in this book (or the "expert" who usually writes a Foreword), I am still at the very beginning of my career within development. So, who is it writing to you, dear reader? I am a half-German, half-Colombian 26-year-old aspiring development professional. I grew up in a small village in the black forest in Germany and have a passion for socio-environmental challenges, civil society engagement, and Latin America. Next to a Bachelor's in International Relations, I hold a Master's degree in International Development and Management. In addition to the Netherlands and Sweden, where my universities are located, I have had the privilege to have already lived, studied, worked, and volunteered in Colombia, Rwanda, Germany, and Mexico. Today, I am writing to you from Guatemala, where I currently live and where I am completing an internship at the World Food Programme (WFP).

So yes, to some extent you could say that I have already gained quite some experience, considering my young age. And yet, I am only at the beginning of my career. There are still so many things I will have to figure out for myself. Countless questions about my professional and personal future within the development sector remain unanswered to me, and I stumble upon new ones on an almost daily basis. In this sense, I might be just like you: perhaps you are also just entering the professional world of or considering a career within development. Or, if you have already been in this field for several years, you might see in me your younger self: still a fledgling, not knowing what to expect from the sheer endless sea of opportunities out there. Whoever you are that has picked up this book, you probably have an interest in learning more about the dreams, struggles, achievements, and experiences made in the life of a development practitioner (and I can already tell you, there is not just one type of development practitioner); be it to get inspired about the possible paths that lie ahead of you or to reflect on the stories shared by your fellow development professionals.

Dear Development Practitioner is a book about development. It is written by development practitioners, for development practitioners (or those who aspire to be one, like myself). It is full of dilemmas, challenges, success stories, and lessons learned. Some of them are anecdotes you will relate to. Others are scenarios that you can only hardly believe to be true. Some include stories of failure, others of great accomplishment. They speak about global challenges, such as inequality, discrimination, identity, privilege, hunger, gender equality, power, conflicts, and climate change; but also private struggles about one's own place in this sector. For me, what all these letters have in common is the inspiration they share. As a young, aspiring development practitioner it is sometimes hard to find your own way. I am now at a point in my life where I can (and this sometimes feels more like a "have to") decide in which direction I want to proceed: Do I stay with a big UN organisation with many resources or go back to working with civil society organisations where it feels change happens faster? Or perhaps try something completely new, like pursuing a job in the private sector (after all, everybody always talks about the fact that change should be achieved from the inside)? Is my place here, in Latin America, coordinating the implementation of projects; or back in Europe developing methods and tools, or allocating funds? Should I stay in project management or explore my interests in monitoring and evaluation processes? Where exactly are my interests, my passion, my abilities best put to use? And lastly, what fulfils me personally as well as professionally?

While this book does not give me an answer to all my questions, it shows me that a career in development is much more than merely the search for the next higher paying or exciting job. Neither is it "only" the act of assisting in the improvement of other people's (and beings') lives – although that might be a big part of it. What this book has taught me is that development is a constant process of learning. Learning from each other, with each other and from oneself. For me, this is one of the lessons that I would like my future-self to remember; that development itself is not about teaching others how to improve, but an ongoing process of learning together how to live well together and benefit from each other's strengths; that in the many years that lie ahead of me, I should be open to new perspectives, trust in myself, make contacts, immerse myself in the field, ask questions, and learn how to reflect critically.

And with this, dear reader, I hope that you too will find inspiration in this book, the same way I did.

Lorenz Rodrigo Peh, 2022

Acknowledgements

We are deeply grateful to those whose letters are to be found in the pages that follow. Thank you for agreeing to embark on this journey with us and for entrusting us with your contributions. In many cases these contain very personal sentiments – sentiments that many of us are not used to acknowledging, let alone sharing with our peers. As editors, we have sought to comment and edit in a sensitive manner, and we trust that our efforts were received in that vein. We thank you for your honesty, openness, and willingness to share your views and experiences in a way that we hope will prove to be of value to those setting out on similar journeys.

Thank you to Helena Hurd and the team at Routledge for their unwavering enthusiasm and support for this project. Not every publisher would have jumped at something as different as this, but Helena recognised that the unusualness of the proposal was its very value. Thank you again for taking the leap with us. We are also hugely grateful to Lina Abirafeh for her wise counsel in the latter stages of this project.

We would like to make clear that the views expressed are those of the named authors – they do not necessarily represent the views of their employers, those with whom they work or partner, or the other contributors in this collection. Any errors are the responsibility of the authors and the authors alone.

Simon and Lee

Acronyms and abbreviations

ADB	Asian Development Bank
AfDB	African Development Bank
ASEAN	Association of South East Asian Nations
AU	African Union
AusAID	Australian Agency for International Development
CAADP	Comprehensive Africa Agriculture Development Programme
CAR	Central African Republic
CCC	Caribbean Conference of Churches
CEO	Chief Executive Officer
CIHRS	Cairo Institute for Human Rights Studies
CIDA	Canadian International Development Agency
COMESA	Common Market for Eastern and Southern Africa
COP	Conference of Parties
COP26	United Nations Climate Change Conference in Glasgow, UK (2021)
CSO	Civil Society Organisation
DRC	Democratic Republic of the Congo
ECOSOC	Economic and Social Council (of the United Nations)
DAC	Development Assistance Committee
DFI	Development Finance Institution(s)
DfID	Department for International Development (of the United Kingdom
EBRD	European Bank for Reconstruction and Development
EC	European Commission
EOHR	Egyptian Organization for Human Rights
ESG	Environmental, Social, and Governance
EU	European Union
FAO	Food and Agriculture Organization
FDI	Foreign Direct Investment
GDP	Gross Domestic Product
GNI	Gross National Income
GPG	Global Public Goods
GPI	Global Public Investment

GSG	Global Steering Group for Impact Investment
HDI	Human Development Index
HIV	Human Immunodeficiency Virus
HQ	Headquarters
HR	Human Resources
ICT	Information and Communication Technology
ID	International Development
IDA	International Development Association
IDI	International Development Institution(s)
IDP	Internally Displaced Person(s)
ILO	International Labour Organization
IMF	International Monetary Fund
INGO	International Non-Governmental Organisation
IOM	International Organization for Migration
LDCs	Least Development Countries
LGBT	Lesbian, Gay, Bisexual and Trans
LGBTI	Lesbian, Gay, Bisexual and Trans and Intersex
LGBTQ	Lesbian, Gay, Bisexual, Trans and Queer/Questioning
LICs	Low Income Countries
Logframe	Logical Framework
M&E	Monitoring and Evaluation
MDB	Multilateral Development Banks
MDGs	Millennium Development Goals
MICs	Middle Income Countries
MoU	Memorandum of Understanding
n.d.	No date
NGO	Non-Governmental Organisation
NSC	North-South Cooperation
NYHQ	New York Head Quarters
NZAID	New Zealand Agency for International Development
OCHA	Office for the Coordination of Humanitarian Affairs (of the United Nations)
OD	Organisational Development
ODA	Official Development Assistance
OECD	Organisation of Economic Cooperation and Development
ONUCI	L'opération des Nations Unies en Côte d'Ivoire [The United Nations Operation in Côte d'Ivoire]
PGK	Papua New Guinean Kina
PNG	Papua New Guinea
PPP	Public Private Partnership
QC	Queen's Council
REC	Regional Economic Community
SADC	Southern African Development Community
SDC	Swiss Agency for Development and Cooperation
SDGs	Sustainable Development Goals

SSC	South–South Cooperation
ToR	Terms of Reference
UAE	United Arab Emirates
UN	United Nations
UNAIDS	Joint United Nations Programme on HIV and AIDS
UNAVEM III	United Nations Angola Verification Mission III
UNDP	United Nations Development Program
UNESC	United Nations Educational, Scientific and Cultural Organization
UNFPA	United Nations Family Planning Association
UNHCR	United Nations High Commissioner for Refugees
UNICEF	United Nations Children Fund
UNIDO	United Nations Industrial Development Organization
UNSC	United Nations Security Council
UNSW	University of New South Wales
UK	United Kingdom
US	United States of America
USD	United States Dollars
US$	US Dollars
USAID	United States Agency for International Development
UQ	University of Queensland
VSO	Voluntary Service Overseas
WASH	Water, Sanitation and Hygiene
WEF	World Economic Forum
WHO	World Health Organization (of the United Nations)
WB	World Bank
WFP	World Food Program (of the United Nations)

Introduction

Simon Milligan and Lee Wilson

This book, like many ideas, started as a caffeine fuelled conversation in a coffee shop. This one happened to be in Geneva. We, the editors, found ourselves by virtue of our respective spouse's professional journeys resident in the city, which is one of the global centres of humanitarian affairs and development practice. Introduced to each other by a mutual colleague, we came to meet regularly and discuss the issues that had concerned us both for much of our professional careers.

Our conversations revolved for the most part around what seemed right and, above all, what seemed wrong with development policy and practice in the 2010s and 2020s. Coming by very different paths to a view on development practice that was surprisingly convergent, we came to value our different perspectives on the issues that vexed us both in similar ways. The value that we both placed on these conversations led us to consider the degree to which *real* development practice was described and discussed in the confines of trusted social settings, but seldom in academic writing; that the lived experiences of those working in the "development field" were sometimes deeply rewarding but often bruising; that the "art" of diplomacy and development practice was vitally important and typically learned over time, yet often written off as "soft skills"; and, yes, that while we both knew many, many passionate, motivated, and principled people working in the sector, we had also crossed paths with a sizeable number who seemed to lack integrity, who seemed to simply go through the motions, and who failed to model the principles and values espoused in public settings, policies, and protocols. Put bluntly, there sometimes appeared to be a distance – a gaping distance – between the rhetoric and reality of development practice. Many development professionals we know recognised this rift. It troubled them too. So, without wishing to sound too grandiose, we sought to publish a fresh perspective that would bridge the gap between "development as written" and "development as practised" – one that would seek to make sense of the "development world" in the early/mid 2020s through the eyes and lived experiences of practitioners from around the world.

The book was in development for more than three years – not just any three-year period but a period of global turbulence and of associated shocks

DOI: 10.4324/9781003260929-1

and distress to many individuals and households. The coffee shop conversations occurred in late 2019. Just months later the world would be turned upside down by a global pandemic; one that would force hundreds of millions of people into self confinement, and would severely affect many people's physical and mental wellbeing. It was a time that would necessarily lead to sustained periods of contemplation about the global challenges and our roles, as both citizens and "development professionals", in their resolution. This is reflected in our letter writers' contributions.

Superficially, this book sprang from shared concerns about the need for insight and advice about the practice of development, and the value that we had gained from our initial conversations about common challenges we both faced and how we had confronted these issues. It sought to respond to the ever-present need for a mentor, an advisor, a confidant, or critical friend who is able and willing to provide experiential insight into the often-unacknowledged struggles of working in the sector. At a deeper level, however, the book sought to respond to a nagging question that we couldn't escape: shouldn't "we" – those working in the world of development practice and those who shape the institutional frameworks within which we operate – be a little better? Are "we" not able to improve the ways in which we work for the betterment of those whose lives we are seeking to protect or improve? Of course, what "better" means or looks like will likely vary from one person to the next. Afterall, "better" is a very value-laden notion. That said, there must surely be a set of core values or principles that bind the actions of those working in our sector. What might these be? For starters, what about a commitment to act with integrity, to act with empathy, to act with compassion, to be inclusive, to be inquisitive, to seek to be accountable . . .?

These are high bars against which to be judged. We are human, after all. We are all fallible and we will all stumble from time to time. We certainly have and, no, it is not lost on the editors that we are both white, middle-aged, well educated British men and who (now) live in northern Europe. Yet with every experience there is scope to reflect. To learn. To evolve. To revisit assumptions and learned behaviour. To push ourselves that little bit closer to the best version of ourselves.

Who are the contributors?

We do not make this journey alone. A diverse cast of equally inquisitive and reflective contributors have joined us on this voyage. From early 2020, we began contacting a number of people to see if they would be able and willing to share their personal perspectives on the practice of development and to do so as openly as possible. Inspiration came from Fergal Keane's moving letter to his son that was aired on BBC's *From Our Own Correspondent* in 1996. In a similar vein, we asked authors: *with the benefit of wisdom gained from age, what would they tell their younger selves?* Some of the letter writers were personally known to us, some were not. All have made a mark in some way.

The letter writers – drawn from nearly 20 nationalities and a diverse mix of backgrounds – have held a rich mix of jobs across a range of sectors and organisational types. They include those working for funders and recipients of official development assistance; those working in social movements (including a Nobel Peace Prize winner); senior figures in government and international organisations; those working at the frontline in humanitarian aid and civil society organisations; and those who might not have traditionally self-identified as being "development professionals", such as technologists, social entrepreneurs, and changemakers. All write in a personal capacity.

Some of the contributors are known on the national or international stage, many are not. Some have shaped national and international frameworks for development cooperation, while others work at a sub-national level to expand quality health care and combat inequalities. Yet all had valuable insights to share. Many, perhaps liberated by the promise this book offered and fuelled by the deep reflection brought on by a crippling global pandemic, chose to reach far into their inner selves – the inner selves that are often shielded from public view. They share their motivations and aspirations, their successes and failures, and their reflections on the development landscape at a time of increasingly rapid transformation and turmoil.

Why now?

There are at least three answers to this question. Let us start with the big picture. The world is going through a period of unprecedented change. The decade is young but the 2020s are proving to be quite extraordinary. And not in a good way. A protracted global pandemic has reached into every of the corner of the world, claiming the lives of over five million people, disrupting the world economy, and potentially reversing the economic convergence between rich and poor economies that had been under way since the early 1990s (Calleja & Gavas 2021). The central ambition of the UN Climate Change Conference in Glasgow (2021) – namely, to restrict global warming to less than 1.5 degrees Celsius above pre-industrial levels – hangs by a thread. Following 20 years of international military intervention and state-building, the United States' exit from Afghanistan in 2021 prompted the collapse of the government shortly after and a return to Taliban rule. Violence continues to escalate in the country. A *coup d'état* in Myanmar in February 2021 saw the democratically elected members of the country's ruling party ousted by the military and then four democracy activists executed in July 2022 in the country's first known use of capital punishment in over 30 years. In Iran, the government continues to brutally crack down on women-led protests against clerical rule that followed the death in custody of Mahsa Amini in mid-2022 who was detained by morality police for allegedly breaking the stringent rules on the wearing of hijabs. In Europe, Vladimir Putin has once again brought war to the continent. His invasion of Ukraine, driven by a Tsarist vision of Russia and the perceived threat of the ever-growing influence of the North Atlantic Treaty Organization, continues to take a terrible toll on the people of the country. Ukraine has become a battle ground for the struggle between democracy and authoritarianism as America and its allies continue to arm and support the Ukrainian military. The only sure outcome of this conflict is the widespread destruction of Ukraine and the loss of tens of thousands of lives in a war with no apparent end in sight. Yet, in the midst of this challenging outlook – depressing outlook, even – there are people, organisations, and social movements that continue to believe that things can get better and who have dedicated their lives to this belief. The letters that follow are a window on to this committed, diverse cast of actors.

The second reason for this book is that the institutional apparatus that shapes international diplomacy and the practice of development is changing. And quickly. The institutions upon which people, systems, and nation states have depended for much of the last 70 years feel increasingly fragile. As world leaders gathered in New York for the annual United Nations General Assembly in September 2019, The Atlantic asked "whether the multilateral system that's supposed to address [global] challenges (albeit often imperfectly) has itself become a dead man walking".[1] It was a prescient question. Within less than 12 months, the US had formally withdrawn from the 2015 Paris Climate Agreement (a decision that has since been reversed). The US is not alone in creating or deepening fissures in the international system since the mid-2010s. Take for example, the United Kingdom's decision in 2016 to the leave the European Union; South Africa and the Gambia announcing their intent in 2016 to withdraw from the International Criminal Court (both later revoked); and Burundi and the Philippines actual withdrawal from the International Criminal Court in 2017 and 2019 respectively.

Threats to international cooperation and the evident rise of the "national interest-first" narrative have had direct bearing on one long-established form of development cooperation: Official Development Assistance (ODA). In recent years, several Organisation for Economic Co-operation and Development's Development Assistance Committee (OECD DAC) donors have pivoted from explicit development-oriented motives to using ODA to further strategic national interests or, at least, to strike a careful balancing of the two (see Chaturvedi *et al.* 2021, Klingebiel & Gonsior 2020). There may never have been a time when domestic interests were not at the table, so it might be argued that reference to "national interest" and the use of ODA as a lever of soft power is merely a more explicit acknowledgement of something that was ever thus. However, it is evident that global challenges, such as migration and security, have led to and/or are being used by some OECD DAC donors to legitimise or pursue a change in tack from a development-oriented policy position. Standalone ministries and semi-autonomous agencies (e.g., UK Department for International Development) have been folded back into foreign ministries. Even once dependable bastions of a generous ODA footing – Sweden, for example – are looking increasingly fragile.

Yet, there are positive changes too. Five decades on from the launch of ODA by the OECD DAC in 1969, the "development landscape" is more diversified than ever (Calleja & Gavas 2021). Private actors, both for-profit and not-for-profit, are commonplace and influential. The Bill and Melinda Gates Foundation, for example, spends more each year than many mid-sized OECD DAC donors (OECD 2019). "Traditional" ODA in the form of grants, technical assistance, and highly concessional loans is now supplemented by, for instance, measures that seek to mobilise private sector investment (Lonsdale & Tew 2017). Instances of so-called South–South Co-operation and Triangular Co-operation are no longer footnotes. Their establishment as mainstays of development cooperation reflects both the emergence of globally powerful actors such as China and India *and* a desire among one-time "recipients" to be regarded as "partners"; as active participants who demand acknowledgment and respect, who seek to shape the agenda, and who wish to participate in the co-creation of solutions and in the sharing of knowledge, skills, and technology.

The development finance landscape has been reimagined to include the role of business, venture capital, sovereign wealth funds, Islamic finance tools, and non-state resources (e.g., remittances, Mawdsley 2018). The volumes and potential impacts of these other forms of development finance are considerable. For example, the United Nations reports that the private philanthropic donors reporting to the DAC, including the Citi Foundation, the H&M Foundation, and the IKEA Foundation, contributed US$ 6.5 billion for "development purposes" in 2019. The United Nations estimates that 260,000 foundations across 39 countries account for US$ 150 billion of philanthropic expenditure each year and US$ 1.5 trillion in assets (UNESCO 2020). Imagine if private finance could be aligned with the Sustainable Development Goal (SDG) targets. The OECD estimates that moving just 1% of total global financial assets – some US$ 382 trillion – could bridge the financing gap that currently inhibits delivery of the SDGs.[2] Fanciful? Perhaps not. Environmental, social, and governance (ESG) issues are no longer niche; at risk of being a passing fad. The OECD estimates that ESG investing has risen to nearly US$ 18 trillion in assets. Impact investing is also growing, with an estimated market size of more than US$ 500 million.[3]

For some, changes in the development cooperation landscape are occurring quickly, for others, not fast enough. The development cooperation landscape – once the preserve of "donors" in the global North – is now a fusion of old and new actors and old and new modalities. A melting pot of ideas, values, and ideologies. Indeed, the very purpose of ODA is subject to ongoing debate. For years, the purpose of aid was to support development processes *in specific "recipient countries"*. There, it was argued, external support, such as grants and technical assistance, could leverage the highest developmental returns on public money. In recent years, however, a counter-narrative has gained increasing attention; one centred on the notion of Global Public Investment. In place of the narrow focus on poverty within specific countries, public money would address inequality and sustainability *across* countries. All countries would pay in and expect benefit from statutory contributions to measures that tackle shared challenges. Reciprocity instead of "charity"; shared decision making, not imposition (as the advocates would have it, see Calleja & Gavas 2021; Glennie 2020). After all, complex, transnational problems, such as climate change, require international collective action. That means looking beyond "aid" to private finance and the under-utilised potential of domestic resources. And, in turn, that means greater and more effective collaboration across the public sector, the business community, and civil society.

And lastly, there is the personal dimension to the question, "Why now?". Both the editors have crept beyond the mid points in their working lives (though we seek to deny this). It is perhaps natural, therefore, to look back and seek to make sense of the meandering journeys that have taken us to this point in time and the worlds in which we live, work, and teach. Both of us find ourselves at cross-roads. Both of us find ourselves reflecting on our roles and identities in today's "development world". Both of us have had periods when we have wrestled with professional challenges, the personal costs of our chosen careers, and, for both of us at times, how best to navigate the feelings of imposter syndrome that one would have thought might have passed as one enters the third decade of working life. This book is therefore a quest to make sense of the world(s) we – all of us, including the two editors – find ourselves.

For whom is the book intended?

Most obviously this book is aimed at those who are contemplating a career "in development". The new generation of development practitioners, one might say. However, to suggest that the book is *only* of value to the new generation would be to miss the point. Opportunities, career trajectories, the quality of one's working life, and, most importantly, the trajectory of social and economic change, depend, in part, on the established ways of working and social norms that frame what is possible, what is permissible, and what is acceptable. Those in positions of power and influence are therefore duty bound to reflect, learn, and adapt. Therefore, this book is for those people too. Many of the issues raised in the contributions that follow are uncomfortable and challenging. And that is as it should be. Issues of inequality, injustice, and prejudice – be they "out there" among those with whom we work or "within these four walls" of our workplaces and governing systems – must be interrogated, confronted, and addressed by those who, inadvertently or otherwise, sustain the systems and instruments that uphold the status quo.

What this book does (that others do not)?

A common theme in the initial conversations that germinated the idea for this book was the often overlooked importance of *people* in the strategies, plans, and reports that describe the development landscape: that is, the *people* who participate in international cooperation and agenda setting, who craft and implement policy, who mobilise and hold duty-bearers to account, who make investment decisions, who innovate and seek opportunities, and who, above all, enable change. It is *people* who inhabit and shape the work of governments, corporations, civil society organisations, and other entities, and it is *they* who have bearing on what emerges when these organisations seek to collaborate. It is these people – those who work to make a real difference in the lives and wellbeing of others – that are the focus of this book.

This book differs from those that have sought to give voice to those that work in this space; for example, Mosse's edited collection *Adventures in Aidland* (2013), Bergman's collected essays from aid workers in conflict zones (2003), and Alexander's personal memoire from humanitarian contexts (2013; also see Crewe & Harrison 1998, Fechter 2012, Kumi & Kamruzzaman 2021, Roth 2015, Stirrat 2008). *Dear Development Practitioner*, while in a similar vein to this prior body of work, has a different aim in mind. That is, to offer frank and unadulterated advice tempered with the benefit of hindsight to those similarly engaged in development practice: wisdom that is born of experience rather than knowledge derived from academic analysis. This is where we, as editors began this project: trying to understand and make sense of "development" by listening to the formative experiences of those seeking to make a difference from one day to the next.

Our hope is that this book offers a timely contribution to contemporary debates. While discussions about identity and power in development cooperation have been the subject of discussion for some time (e.g., see Crewe & Harrison 1998, McWha 2011, Stirrat 2008, White 2002, Wilson 2012), debates have now moved from the margins to centre stage, spurred in part by the "enticing alternatives" offered by "non-white development actors" such as China (Pailey 2020). Fundamental questions are being asked about the presence and voice of "Southern players" in shaping or framing the agenda, not least as the world seeks to respond to and recover from the COVID-19 pandemic. Such questions fall within broader debates about race and postcolonial politics in development discourse, policies, and practices (e.g., see Goodfellow 2019, Kumi & Kamruzzaman 2021, Rivas 2018). So, yes, while there has been a (partial) departure from outdated language – of "aid", "charity", "donors", "recipients", "beneficiaries" – there is far to travel.

How is the book structured?

We struggled at the outset of this book with the definition of working in "development". The development landscape defined in terms of aid programmes and those who administer and deliver them seemed limiting when we looked at the range of actors who now populate this landscape, and who are actively engaged in attempting to drive positive social change. In this respect, many of our letter writers might not at first glance be seen as development actors in the more traditional sense. They include among their number those who work in human rights, as social entrepreneurs, in impact investment, as advocates, changemakers, and researchers. We chose deliberately to cast our net widely because all their experiences are relevant to the lived practice of "development", and perhaps more significantly, their inclusion reflects the changing nature of the field. Indeed, many of these letter writers are in some way responsible for transformations of the development landscape and the need to destabilise, decolonise, and disrupt the enduring power relations that frame development aid and practice. This having been said, we have taken the liberty of categorising contributors. The book is divided up into five sections: letters from those that have worked in some capacity in civil society or advocacy; those that work in human rights; the policy practitioners; the social entrepreneurs and changemakers; and finally those that have worked to research development practice. These groupings were derived thematically from the letters, and while some of the contributors clearly transcend these categories, their letters speak to experiences corresponding to these themes.

What are our hopes for this book?

The book does not seek to be an exposé. In many respects, it is a celebration of resilience and of people overcoming adversity. It is a testimony to a sense of what is possible. It is therefore a book about hope and reassurance. Yet it is more than that. It is also a book about accountability – a reminder to us all that we are accountable to our colleagues, to ourselves, and to those we seek to support or safeguard. And on a very personal level, it is also about the importance of personal nourishment, of self-care, and of those support networks that catch us when we stumble.

The collection bears testament that there are large numbers of highly committed individuals who are striving to make positive changes to policy and practice. The collection also shows that there is some way to go. Many of the contributors in the following pages speak frankly about the hardships and challenges – both professional and personal – they have endured. Some speak of the inequality, racism, and prejudice they have encountered, and others reflect on the need to overcome the biases, power relations, and relationships of dependency that have shaped policy and practice for decades. Many of the individual contributions also remind us of the personal sacrifices and the threats to wellbeing and safety that many have faced. In all cases, the authors speak from first-hand experience from their direct involvement in projects, programs, policies, and other initiatives.

On one level we hope that readers, be they the next generation of development practitioners or those who have already started their journeys, will find the letters reassuring and insightful. We trust that they provide comfort or guidance as readers seek to make sense of their own experiences and the opportunities or pathways before them. On another level, we hope that readers find them enlightening; that by pulling back the curtains on the practice of development, we – those who shape how development is practised – can think more critically about how issues are framed and by whom; what shapes, enables, or constrains what is possible; and whose voices are valued.

So many of today's challenges are deeply complex in nature. For us to overcome them, we need to forge and sustain strong partnerships, bring new perspectives to the table, and suspend the judgements we often rush to make. We must champion diversity and inclusion, not just in *ends* but in *means* – in the processes we apply and in the voices and perspectives we value. This entails being self-critical, seeking to add value, and being prepared to call out actions that run contrary to the principles and values we espouse. It requires empathy, compassion, humility, and courage. Will we always get it right? No. Should that stop us trying to be a little better tomorrow than we were today? Absolutely not. Hindsight is a wonderful thing. And perhaps this book will go some way to making the hindsight of others available to you, not so that you won't make mistakes but that you too feel compelled to reflect, learn, act, and share with others.

Notes

1 www.theatlantic.com/politics/archive/2019/09/multilateralism-nearly-dead-s-terrible-news/598615/
2 www.oecd.org/development/private-finance-for-sustainable-development-conference-paris-january-2020.html
3 www.oecd.org/development/private-finance-for-sustainable-development-conference-paris-january-2020.html

References

Alexander, Jessica. 2013. *Chasing chaos: my decade in and out of humanitarian aid.* New York: Crown.

Bergman, Carol. 2003. *Another day in paradise: international humanitarian workers tell their stories.* New York: Orbis.

Calleja, Rachael and Mikaele Gavas. 2021. Development agencies and the "new normal". *Center for Global Development*, 01 December 2021. Retrieved 10 January 2022, from www.cgdev.org/blog/development-agencies-and-new-normal

Chaturvedi, Sachin, Heiner Jones, Stephan Klingebiel, Li Xiaoyun, André de Mello e Souza, Elizabeth Sidiropoulos and Dorothea Wehrmann. 2021. Development cooperation in the context of contested global governance. In: Chaturvedi *et al.* 2021, *The Palgrave handbook of development cooperation for achieving the 2030 Agenda.* London: Palgrave.

Crewe, Emma and Elizabeth Harrison. 1998. *Whose development? An ethnography of aid.* London: Zed.

Fechter, Anne-Meike. 2012. The personal and the professional: aid workers' relationships and values in the development process. *Third World Quarterly*, 33 (8), 1387–1404.

Glennie, Jonathan. 2020. *The future of aid: global public investment.* London: Routledge.

Goodfellow, Maya. 2019. *Race and processes of racialisation in British international development discourse, 1997–2017*. PhD thesis. SOAS University of London. https://doi.org/10.25501/SOAS.00032235

Klingebiel, Stephan and Victoria Gonsior. 2020. Development policy from a systemic perspective: changes, trends and its future role within a broader framework for transnational co-operation. *Revisita Brasileira de Politica Internacional*, 63 (2). https://doi.org/10.1590/0034-7329202000209

Kumi, Emmanuel and Palash Kamruzzaman. 2021. Understanding the motivations and roles of national development experts in Ghana: "We do all the donkey work and they take the glory". *Third World Quarterly*, 42 (6), 1157–1175. https://doi.org/10.1080/01436597.2021.1877127

Lonsdale, Cordelia and Rob Tew. 2017. *An introduction to ODA modernisation: demystifying the process of ODA modernisation for the development community*. Development Initiatives Background Paper. 25 September 2017. Bristol: Development Initiatives. Retrieved 10 January 2022, from https://devinit.org/resources/oda-modernisation-background-paper-changing-rules-aid/

Mawdsley, Emma. 2018. "From billions to trillions": financing the SDGs in a world "beyond aid". *Dialogues in Human Geography*, 8, 191–195. https://doi.org/10.1177%2F2043820618780789

McWha Ishbel. 2011. The roles of, and relationships between, expatriates, volunteers, and local development workers. *Development in Practice*, 21 (1), 29–40. https://doi.org/10.1080/09614524.2011.530225

Mosse, David (ed.). 2013. *Adventures in Aidland: the anthropology of professionals in international development*. Oxford: Berghahn.

OECD. 2019. *Development co-operation report 2019: a fairer, greener, safer tomorrow*. Paris: OECD. https://doi.org/10.1787/9a58c83f-en

Pailey, Robtel Neajai. 2020. De-centring the "white gaze" of development. *Development and Change*, 51, 729–745. https://doi.org/10.1111/dech.12550

Rivas, Althea-Maria. 2018. The everyday practices of development. In: Rutazibuwa, Olivia U. and Shilliam, Robbie (eds.). *Routledge handbook of postcolonial politics*. London: Routledge.

Roth, Silke. 2015. *The paradoxes of aid work: passionate professionals*. London: Routledge.

Stirrat, Roderick. 2008. Mercenaries, missionaries and misfits: representations of development personnel. *Critique of Anthropology*, 28 (4), 406–425. https://doi.org/10.1177%2F0308275X08098259

UNESCO. 2020. Trends and progress in international development cooperation: report of the Secretary General (E/2020/10). Retrieved 07 January 2022, from: www.un.org/development/desa/financing/sites/www.un.org.development.desa.financing/files/2020-04/English_36.pdf

White, Susan. 2002. Thinking race, thinking development. *Third World Quarterly*, 23 (3), 407–419. https://doi.org/10.1080/01436590220138358

Wilson, Kalpana. 2012. *Race, racism and development: interrogating history, discourse and practice*. London: Zed Books.

Section I

Civil society and advocacy

1

Different is good

Anna Bwana

Hi Young Anna,

You are just about to step into your first job, just over ten years ago now. You are young, smart, driven. A bit naïve, to be honest. You love your country and want to "make a difference", so you have decided to work in the development sector. It will allow you, you believe, to invest your skills and abilities into making your country better, into tackling the poverty and disadvantage that you constantly see around you.

You are privileged. You know it. So, you want to "give back".

Over the first ten or so years of your career, you will have six different jobs, in four different international organisations. You will grow, learn, and establish yourself as a professional. That growth will take you from being an intern with a campaigns team, to being the Country Director of an international media development organisation. You remain faithful to your original aim – you've never left your country.

Some of your naïvety wears off, but you refuse to replace it with the cynicism that you see so many flounder under. Of course, you will learn that the world of development is messier, uglier, less altruistic than anything you had imagined, but you will learn how to navigate that and to (sometimes) make your peace with it. At other times you will get angry, you will get loud, and you will cast your eyes at alternatives – at politics, academia, the public sector. Yet, you realise that you are still in the right place. Sometimes . . .

Many people you work with genuinely want to do good as well (and many of these people are women, to be honest). They are intelligent, passionate, and committed, and they see injustice in their privileges, just like you. Make sure you make good use of these people! These are people who can help challenge the institutional blockages and who can use their privileges to confront injustice with humility and empathy. They do not forget about the people – the real people with emotions and feelings – who sometimes get lost in the logframes of this development machine. So, you make peace with the knowledge that it is "the system" rather than the individuals who sometimes make it difficult for you to feel at home in this sector.

DOI: 10.4324/9781003260929-3

But some realities are just harder to deal with. You don't know it now, but I must tell you something: you will never be managed by a Tanzanian. In the ten years ahead of you, will never have a black manager. You will never know what it is to be managed by a fellow "local".

Should that be a problem? You will ask yourself that on the first day in your job as a Country Director. At first it will be just a reflection on the fact that you had never worked in an organisation that was being led by a person of colour, let alone by a Tanzanian. It will then hit home that you had never even been managed by a Tanzanian. So, hooray – you will be breaking ceilings, charting new paths . . . but with no role model.

Being a "local hire" in this industry is not easy. Being a local hire at levels of seniority is even harder, I think. Its not (just) about the differences in benefits and privileges that your nationality bestows on you. You will realise that the hardest part is the fact that you start to believe in those differences. At some level, you will start to believe that only "expats" are fit to be senior managers and country directors, that there is something intrinsically better about them that you can't possibly replicate. You will feel like an imposter.

So, when you break the latest ceiling, and find yourself sitting in the Country Director seat, it makes you uncomfortable. How do you provide leadership as a Tanzanian in an international organisation? How do you build a rapport with Head Office when you don't always understand the jokes they make? How do you break into that tight expat bubble so that you can also socialise and network with potential donors?

You have never seen someone else do it. You won't have years of being exposed to successful local managers and directors. You won't have had the privilege of learning incrementally. There are scenarios and circumstances that you know feel different to you because you understand deep down what the driving factor was behind a certain behaviour from staff, or a lack of buy-in from local partners and communities. But you've never seen anyone use this innate knowledge to make decisions, so you don't know what to do with it.

You will question whether you deserve to be in that position.

You will find that you are strong enough to allow yourself the room to grow, and you will know that everything you have been through has led you to this point. You hope that those experiences will allow you to – hopefully – provide a different kind of leadership, and that "different" can be good.

Different IS good.

Working in development as someone from the Global South can be painful. Conceptualising, implementing, evaluating development projects is more than just an intellectual exercise. Field trips or meeting with beneficiaries is not an "interesting" experience: it's too close to home to be "interesting". Those women talking about their experiences with violence, with their babies strapped to their backs, are not photo ops – they are your family. You know too well what they are going through, what uncertainties they face, what fears they carry. This isn't just one posting of many that you will hop to; this is your reality and your home.

That tension will constantly chip away at you, and at your conscience. It will make you uncomfortable. And uncomfortable is good. Never get comfortable with calling painful experiences "interesting", don't be complacent with absorbing someone else's interpretation of your world as more legitimate (just because it can be worded in impartial terminology). It will take ten years of constant navigation and challenging yourself and others – but that's what you are good at.

And that is the leadership that you will find yourself looking to provide. Yes, it is harder because you're never quite sure if you are doing it right (and to be honest you still think there is a magic code that they didn't give to you when they hired you), but that uncertainty can also make you more genuine, more honest, and hopefully show others that it's not unrealistic.

And even when you lack enough young, Tanzanian women in this sector to be your role models, remember, there are so many amazing women leaders and mentors that you have had over the years. These women will inspire you, allow you to stumble and pick yourself up, and generally just show you that there are so many ways to be a woman and a leader. And that your journey is just starting.

Anna is Country Director of BBC Media Action. She has worked for both non-governmental agencies and donor agencies, typically in the field of governance and service delivery. She and her family live in Dar es Salaam, Tanzania.

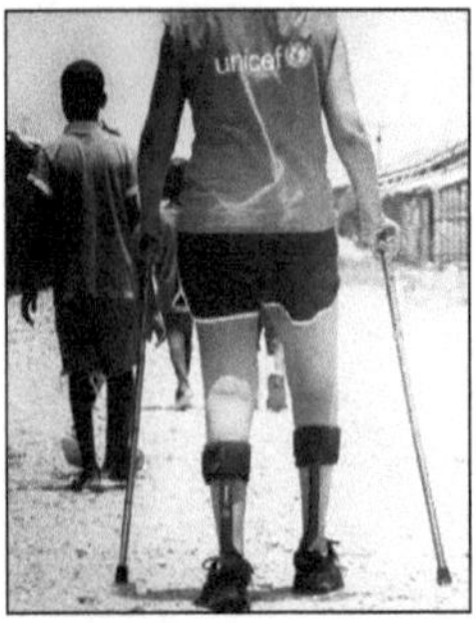

2

Don't go. There is a place where you belong

Cara Yar Khan

Hello Princess,

My, how you have changed over the past 20 years. You've done some proper growing up, following your dream since you walked around at Halloween with an orange UNICEF Trick-or-Treat box collecting money for children in faraway countries. However, you have yet to get your finance sorted; but hey, you are only human and perfectly imperfect. In your heart, 20 years on, you are still the peripatetic expat humanitarian who's most comfortable in emergency settings, regretting only never having fulfilled your dream of serving in a conflict zone such as Syria or the Congo. And now, no longer in the field, with its adventurous lifestyle, what you miss the most is the sense of belonging – to both your compatriots and those being served – a bond that cannot be matched outside of mission life. Working in an environment where you heard languages from every continent, collaborating with some of the most brilliant experts in their fields, you were challenged by lessons learned from their past missions and inspired by their world travels, a tremendous journey that no text or course on International Development could have taught you.

Your first day on the job with WFP Ecuador in 2001, 24 years old, you wept when you arrived at the UN field mission and saw the pale blue flag. It had been such a struggle to get to this first assignment. After five years of undergraduate studies, while working part-time so you wouldn't have any debt when you graduate, anyone can understand that it's a little demoralising to be waitressing to make ends meet. Why do students have this disillusionment that finding a job, especially in your desired field will be quick or easy? Living in the makeshift back room (basically a converted broom closet) off of your best friend's kitchen, sleeping on a mattress on the floor, working 12-hour night shifts to make ends meet, and spending hours in the back of a convenience store where you paid by the hour for access to a computer was a good hustle that I like to think built you more character and made the offer all that more sweet. What's ironic is that the application to the United Nations Association of Canada was the first of 57 international internships you would apply to. In all honesty, it was the only

DOI: 10.4324/9781003260929-4

one you wanted but desperate as you were, you would have taken anything that took you to the field.

You felt such immense pride to see your name next to the UN logo on your first business card that you mailed it to your father. This was your dream come true, one that you had strived for since middle school. As a young intern, although you were intimidated by your colleagues, with your gung-ho attitude, not only were you going to contribute, you were going to change things! Luckily for you, this sentiment was shared by your Country Director, who gave you special treatment with more responsibilities than most interns would be granted, while still holding you to the highest expectations.

The myriad procedures and obligatory signatures made for a frustrating bureaucracy that you always thought would be better served if the organisation were run like a private company. You were a little too outspoken and bold for your age, reminded on numerous occasions in your first decade that you were still junior staff. One adored leader told you, early on, "with time will come a softening of your ways". That was true but your conviction was nonetheless steady. You felt a responsibility to "protect" the brand and image, which was rightfully and wrongfully criticised and you were not ashamed to push back at HR or supervisors who you did not agree with. Might a little more humility have served you better in the long run?

Soon you will be thrown a curveball, which will not only change the trajectory of your entire life but define your eventual role in the organisation, and later, in the message you want to send out to the world. I hate to be the bearer of what will appear as bad news now, but you are soon going to be faced with one of the most terrifying and extraordinary life transformations anyone can experience. You will undertake this journey, at least the first decade of it, in the field. The nomadic explorer that you are will venture from Quito to Panama, Shanghai, Luanda, Beijing, Antananarivo, Bologna, Bangkok, Maputo, Antananarivo (again), and then to Port-au-Prince, before making the heart-breaking decision to move to Atlanta. You are probably confused right now. For you, the idea of living in the United States could not be more antithetical to your multicultural, multi-ethnic identity and socialist values that make you so intrinsically Canadian. What could be so tectonic, you wonder?

In your mid–late twenties, in the early 2000s, while living in Quito, and then Panama, you will begin to experience a series of inexplicable falls. You might have just been walking on uneven pavement, dancing salsa, or even moving around your home. In 2006, before your thirtieth birthday, you will be diagnosed with a recessive muscle wasting disease, a genetic condition that affects all your 650 skeletal muscles, from head to toe. Within 10–15 years of its onset, you will become severely incapacitated. Hereditary Inclusion Body Myopathy, or HIBM, has no approved treatment or cure.

I commend you on your response to this frightening news. You charge forward, taking on a new UNICEF assignment in Luanda, which after 27 years of brutal civil war, UNICEF declared the worst place in the world for a child to be born. I don't blame you for not telling everyone about the diagnosis, for fear of losing your job. In 2006 UNICEF did not have a policy that protected the rights of staff members with disabilities. Living in countries where polio had been common made for the perfect cover up when a colleague assumed your limp was from having survived polio as a child. Your physical condition will deteriorate progressively. To get around, you will require a cane, then two, followed by leg braces, then a walker, and eventually you will be confined to a wheelchair. But none of these impediments will deter you from your mission.

UNICEF offices across the world have a long way to become universally inclusive and accessible. Accommodations (like the allocation of a barrier free shipping container, one that had no stairs) and accessibility, inclusion, and representation of people with disabilities were concepts limited to National Strategic Frameworks and Country Program Documents, and even then to certain programmatic pillars. It was only on 4 October 2011 that UNICEF Executive Director Mr Anthony Lake issued a statement outlining UNICEF support for the active promotion of hiring of persons with disabilities and dedication to their accommodation in the workplace.

Almost everyone is going to discourage you from going to Haiti after the 2010 earthquake and Cholera outbreak, even though you are arriving a year and a half since the island shook, leaving mass destruction, displacement and death in its wake. "How will you manage in a country recovering from such an enormous natural disaster where there is not even the most basic infrastructure for Haitians with disabilities?", you will be asked. Ignore them! You will hear scepticism from those who came here during the Emergency surge or were repeating a media-fed vision of what it might be like here. Despite the programmatic response for people with disabilities, specifically the ~4,000 new earthquake-injured amputees, that does not necessarily mean that organisations will embrace hiring staff with disabilities. There is a disconnect in how most humanitarian organisations serve beneficiaries and how they employ staff.

When you receive notification that you are the preferred candidate, you will be afraid to broach the subject of assistance for people with disabilities. Yes, a policy now exists but you are not yet convinced it indeed protects you from being discriminated against. However, you believe in the valuable contribution you can make, which fosters the courage you need to ask if there are any restrictions to someone with a physical impairment to serve in an Emergency Operations. "I don't know but I'll find out" is the honest and hopeful answer your immediate supervisor offers. Lucky for you, UNICEF Haiti Representative, Francoise Gruloos-Ackermans is in your corner, "Of course she must come to Haiti", she exclaims. You could not be more delighted to later learn that within moments Francoise will be on the phone with Rosangela Berman-Bieler, UNICEF's Senior Advisor on children with disabilities in NYHQ. Fast forward to Indiana Gonzalez, the Chief of Operations, who will make the necessary accessibility adjustments and arrangements for your safety and comfort. You will be sent a list of potential accommodations for your shipping container office on the UN MINUSTAH base and identifying which of the 36 drivers will be comfortable assisting you.

You will be chosen as the "Disability Focal Point" and it will be your responsibility to work diligently and effectively to break down the stigmas and stereotypes that surround this community. This is all the more difficult in a country such as Haiti, where the discrimination and dread of people with disabilities is deeply embedded in the psyche and culture of the people. In your time there, several atrocities will be carried out against children and women with disabilities. Sadly, many of these cases were uninvestigated.

Changing the value system and culture of an entire society takes generations. It will be your responsibility to help shift the mindset. Luckily you have gracious colleagues in the Child Protection Unit who have experience working with this beneficiary group. They will guide you and help you thrive. You will also have a brilliant ally at the political level in Haitian Secretary of State for the Inclusion of People with Disabilities, Mr Gerald Oriol. You'll have the honour of accompanying him to UNICEF HQ in New York, to speak about the situation of children with disabilities in Haiti. Secretary Oriol will become a good friend who will graciously teach you volumes.

There will also be moments in this exciting new role where you will be reminded that a lot of people are paying attention so you need to learn fast and catch up. Your time in the field teaches you that implementing partners on the ground sometimes know more than UNICEF. While speaking at the Shafallah Forum on Disaster and Disability in Qatar a program officer from an international NGO, also working in Haiti, is going to humiliate you in front of the entire auditorium after you present a high-level speech on UNICEF's global efforts to mainstream children with disabilities. The criticism was aimed at UNICEF but you will take the brunt of it, as it's representative that day. While your ego is bruised and morale mortified, it will be an excellent reminder that you have a moral and professional responsibility to be top of your game if you are going to do this work, and especially if you are going to be in the spotlight.

The experience will also lead you to be unapologetically outspoken about UNICEF, the agency you love but are not willing to always make look like the saviour. This honesty will also earn your criticism, albeit less harsh, from fundraising colleagues in National Committees who don't want their donors or Board members in any way disillusioned.

But it's not all pins and needles. In fact, you get to ride the massive wave of programmatic focus and progress, helped enormously when UNICEF's flagship publication in 2013, State of the World's Children, focused on children with disabilities. It was a great start to a global effort.

It will be your duty to help shift the mindset of local staff, who may have never engaged with someone with a disability in the workplace, nor believe that people with disabilities can make valuable contributions to society. Programmatic Communications colleagues teach you that knowledge is the first step to changing attitudes and in turn behaviour. Your main effort will be giving your colleagues first-hand knowledge and experience working with you and when the opportunities arise, meeting some of the kids with disabilities at partner organisations like Mon Petit Frère et Souer, a residential care centre and rehabilitation programme in Tabarre.

You might even aspire to see a local Haitian staff member with a disability hired to fill your post. Without a dedicated focal point, the work will get siloed into whichever programmatic section has the greatest buy-in, if any at all. This representation is necessary to highlight the local experience but also shatter stigma they will face among government counterparts and partner organisations.

My advice to you for the future is to continue in the field, using your unique talents, regardless of your physical limitations, to continue the good fight. It's where you belong, where you feel most alive and can have the most profound impact. In the field you can better promote opportunities for staff with disabilities, a group of people rarely seen working in the field within the humanitarian agencies of the United Nations. I want you to know that I am proud of you. Your resilience has served you well and blossomed into an art. You've been through tremendous challenges. In giving purpose to your struggle, facing your fears, and finding the courage to push beyond them, your life will be extraordinary.

Onward!

Cara is a South Asian, bi-racial international speaker and disability inclusion professional who is also producing a documentary film about her work and life, called "Her Inescapable Brave Mission". Her TED talk, "The beautiful balance between courage and fear", has been viewed 2.5 million times and has been translated into 25 languages. Raised by Indian, English, and Chinese parents, Cara brings a unique lens to all she does, prioritising diversity, equitable inclusion, and equal access. Most of the first two decades of her career Cara has worked with the humanitarian agencies of the United Nations. Presently, Cara lives in the USA.

3

Education, education, education

Harpinder Collacott

Dear Harpinder,

I am writing to you from your future. I wanted to share with you some important lessons you have learnt as you have grown and developed. I can see you now, sitting in your favourite reading place – the wardrobe – reading this letter. Being 14 and growing up juxtaposed between two cultures is not easy. Teenage years are tough for everyone. This is particularly acute when you have one culture and education system showing you what is possible, while another imposes strong gender-limiting parameters on your ambitions.

The times ahead of you will not be easy, growing up in a multi-generational family sandwiched between two high-achieving brothers and brought up by your grandmother as your parents spend their days working long hours in Birmingham factories on the minimum wage. You have a lot of high expectations placed on you; indeed, different expectations to those placed on your brothers. As a girl, you are expected to cook, to clean, and to have the skills that will make you a good wife and mother. You, however, have different ideas.

You are fascinated by strong women. Leaders like Margaret Thatcher and Indira Gandhi. You watch them on the nightly news, translating for your grandmother. They motivate you to dream of politics instead of domestic life. These are women who are leading their countries and trying to change the world. They inspire you and show you that there are different roles and spaces out there in the world for women to those that you see in your everyday life, defined by strict gender norms. They give you hope. They allow you to dream of different futures to that of being a wife or a mother.

Well, do not worry, you are right. There are six lessons I can offer you as you embark on your life and chase these dreams:

Lesson 1: Education will be your passport out of poverty

Be patient with your grandmother. She is a tough lady who left her home in India to come to England late in her life to bring up her grandchildren.

DOI: 10.4324/9781003260929-5

Leaving behind everything she knew and loved, she now finds herself in an alien society where she cannot communicate. As an illiterate woman the spoken word is essential to her, yet now she finds herself mute. As a result, she holds onto her Indian culture tightly and imposes that on you as she fears you will grow to be more "English" than Indian. Your family are caught in-between two cultures as they try and position their children within them both. You will need to develop patience for them as they prevent you doing things which seem so normal for your friends.

Despite the patriarchal structure in which you grow up, your family offer you something so many others do not allow their girls to access – education! Take it and run with it. This is your golden ticket to your future. Soon you will find yourself lost and bewildered on the streets of Cambridge, but full of curiosity, optimism, and energy for the opportunity life has offered you because of access to universal education in the UK and your family's value for education.

Lesson 2: Tolerance and appreciation of others

Throughout this period, you will learn the importance of diversity and tolerance through your own deep desire to understand the perspective of others. At no time in your life will you feel so different than when you arrive in Cambridge – an alien world in every respect. You will relish your world opening out and filling you with greater diversity than inner-city Birmingham offered you. It will teach you that you can belong anywhere. Here you will study alongside royalty from the Middle East, play an organising role in the Universities Black and Asian Caucus meeting with the children of barristers and doctors, and become familiar with the lives of people who have grown up in rural England in boarding schools. You will learn that we are all shaped by our upbringing and early life experiences, and it is these that can dictate how we see the world and others in it. We are creatures of our environment. You will grow and learn from it, fascinated by the experiences of others. At the same time, you will be troubled that the future leaders of our country are sheltered from what you consider to be "the real world" – that in which you, your family, and friends from Birmingham live and the different struggles less privileged people face. Exchanges in the debating society seem to lack balance in your opinion because of the inability of those debating to see the whole picture.

This will motivate you to add your voice to the mix and stand up for those who are not represented and who do not have a voice in society. You will speak for those from the inner cities too. You will throw your energy into supporting applicants from inner cities to Cambridge to bring more people like you into this environment. The pull towards politics will become stronger as you become more politically engaged and motivated. Your values of equality, fairness, and, inclusion will become solidified as you define your voice into young adulthood.

Lesson 3: Awareness and knowledge of different cultures are an asset

Now you are frustrated as you must spend your weekends at the temple or participating in cultural events with your family and community while your friends are off to the movies, ice skating, or hanging out. You cannot do what other kids are doing, but be patient, you will have your freedom. In the meantime, you will gain invaluable skills of cultural awareness and sensitivity, and come to understand Hinduism, Sikhism, and Islam better than most growing up among members of these communities. In the future, you will be able to seamlessly move between cultures and integrate with ease. You will develop a profound sense of respect and inquisitiveness of other religions and cultures, and this will set you in good stead to navigate the world of politics and stand as a candidate for the UK parliamentary elections at the age of 25. Although you will not succeed in your first attempt at being elected, you will secure over 12,000 votes – a tremendous success for your first foray into national politics.

With your UK Parliamentary dream on hold for a while, you will go off and explore new opportunities to broaden your experiences while making a difference in another way – working through the UN systems, exploring life in think tanks and NGOs, and seeing the world from different perspectives. The US, Afghanistan, Pakistan, India, and eventually Sierra Leone and Liberia beckon.

Lesson 4: Seek out mentors and role models. They will shape your life and guide you, giving you opportunities beyond your dreams

Working with Americans in Washington DC will always be an incredibly important and powerful experience for you. Here, you will find an immensely inspiring mentor in Ambassador Dennis Kux (a retired US Ambassador) and his incredibly talented wife, Maria Kux. Shadowing and supporting them, you will learn a great deal about the foreign policy and see it in action. You will travel with them to war-torn locations to explore the challenges of peacekeeping and development in highly fragile contexts. You will come to understand how with good connections, passion, and a lot of hard work, you can raise significant money for girls' education in places where society makes it impossible for girls to go to school.

Mentors will play an important part in your life from there on in. Following Dennis Kux will be the inspiring and charismatic Sir Desmond de Silva QC from whom you will learn how to navigate the trickiest political issues without losing your sense of fun and humour. And then Tony German and Judith Randel, who will believe in you, your vision and abilities, despite your lack of experience in development economics and statistics. You will become their successor, taking on the leadership of their company, Development Initiatives. From them you will learn how to be bold with your ideas even when they may seem completely out of place with everyone around you, to think big, think different, and never be afraid to speak up. You will spend years working on this quality – how to articulate your voice in a room full of "more experienced, more suitable" and often white males and being comfortable putting out ideas and a voice which contrasts to others. From them you will also learn you are a visionary – you believe deeply in every individual's ability to make a difference and are committed to pushing forward big ideas to make big change possible. You will not be satisfied with small incremental change.

Lesson 5: Perseverance, grit and a down-to-earth style go a long way in helping to achieve success

You will learn early on in life the importance of hard work. Nothing in life comes easily to anyone, although some make it look easier than others. The key to success will be perseverance and grit, which you have in abundance, alongside the importance of education, which opens doors that are otherwise closed. You are not scared; you know you have to keep going despite the ups and downs you will encounter. You will quickly learn not to give up and to walk away when things look and feel difficult. Through your travels around the world, starting with your trips to India in your youth, you will encounter the hardships that life throws at people. You will see poverty at its most extreme, including little children no older than five working for a little food or a few rupees. Experiences in Afghanistan immediately after the invasion will motivate you to work more closely with people in fragile contexts, people who are facing abject poverty, whose lives are destroyed by conflict, and whom the rest of the world seem to have forgotten.

You will work hard in a very tough environment in Sierra Leone immediately after the war, taking on the role as political advisor to the Chief Prosecutor of the hybrid war crimes tribunal, the Special Court for Sierra Leone. This will be one of the most important and memorable points in your career. Your perseverance and grit will serve you well as you labour behind the scenes for months and years with the Chief Prosecutor to obtain the trust and confidence of world leaders. This will eventually lead to the arrest of the former President of Liberia, Charles Taylor, who will have been indicted of war crimes but who will have escaped to Nigeria where he will be granted asylum. The victims of his atrocities will be able to finally rest, knowing the man responsible was finally facing justice.

Lesson 6: An open and positive mindset will serve you well as you travel the world and learn about yourself and others at every step of the way

Throughout your career you will meet people who will sacrifice their own lives and families to stand up for human rights, right to freedom of expression, and for their civil and political liberties. Their courage, passion, and commitment to do what is right will inspire you. You will also be the happiest when you are campaigning and fighting for the rights of people who are under-represented, who are marginalised, and are often disempowered. Your flexibility and ability to think that all barriers can be overcome and that change can happen, will mean you are able to obtain success throughout your career in the campaigns you lead.

At Development Initiatives, an organisation where you will venture into the field of pure economic development for the first time. You will miss the hard-nosed aspect of campaigning for human rights and advocating for the rights of the most marginalised people. Yet you will learn many new skills and be able to apply what you have learnt in your life to the issues of poverty and inequality. Your own personal experiences of growing up in a tough working-class environment will now become relevant, including the trips as a child and young person to India, where you witnessed extreme poverty, life in rural villages living without working toilets in your home, and coming face to face with the challenges of the caste system. Life in Sierra Leone and Afghanistan, two of the poorest countries in the world, will become more relevant now for you in this role. The plight of these people will inform your thinking around development and poverty eradication.

What will surprise you most about the development discussions are that people around the table are always middle-class representatives speaking on behalf of the poor people who live in far-off countries. They seem to be incredibly academic in their approach and somewhat removed from the realities of people's lives. They are well-meaning but people who have the least experience of poverty, marginalisation, and exclusion. They also seem the most certain of what works to end poverty.

You already know at the age of 14 that poverty is so much more than income. Poverty destroys motivation, it squashes ambitions, and it robs people of their dreams. Education, grit, luck, and a lot of sacrifice by your family got you and your siblings out of the cycle of poverty that they could have fallen into as immigrants. But this is not the case for most people who struggle with it, day in, day out. Routes to prosperity are difficult and the path narrow, scattered with obstacles that for many are insurmountable.

You will do well to remember communities can remain marginalised and lacking in aspirations and progress even when they exist just above the poverty line. Never forget the importance of education, the cornerstone of all development and progress. It needs to be supported with spaces for civic engagement, access to information on healthy nutrition, to healthcare and all health services, and good community services that meet the needs of the community and ensure their inclusion, development, and prosperity. Good jobs and opportunities for social progress are essential. Social inclusion is as important in tackling poverty as economic inclusion.

And so, your leadership and voice at Development Initiatives will be important because of your personal experiences. You will offer a diverse view, bring some reality to an often-theoretical field, and challenge the views of "experts" in economic development who know much about, but have never experienced, poverty. You will be honoured to lead an organisation that undertakes analysis to tackle issues of poverty and social exclusion; an organisation that is committed to ending poverty, giving a voice to people who are excluded, and building resilience of the world's most vulnerable communities.

I am proud of the journey you will undertake, your desire to challenge boundaries and seek transformation, and of the battles you will fight for others – especially young girls like you, who have so much talent but little encouragement and opportunity. Keep going. Keep fighting and keep giving. Do not give up.

The future is yours for the taking.

At the time of writing, Harpinder was the Chief Executive of Development Initiatives, a global organisation that works to ensure data-driven evidence is used to combat poverty, reduce inequality, and increase resilience. She is now the Executive Director for Mercy Corps Europe. A graduate of Cambridge and LSE, Harpinder has held many roles and worked in the public, private, and charitable sectors across the world. For instance, Harpinder worked for the UN Special Court for Sierra Leone as the Chief Prosecutor's Political Advisor, working closely with the Chief Prosecutor to secure the arrest of Liberian President Charles Taylor in March 2006. She is married with two lovely children and lives in Bristol, UK.

4

Learning to be the platform, not the app

Ingrid Srinath

Dear Ingrid,

Standing at the threshold of your new job as Secretary General of CIVICUS – World Alliance for Citizen Participation, in April 2008, you find yourself confronted with the hardest decision of your life. In transit in Dubai, from São Paulo, Brazil where you represented your new organisation at an international conference for the first time, you turned on your phone to learn the news that your brother had just died, shattering the hearts and lives of many, most particularly his four-year-old daughter, his young wife, and your mother, herself widowed only a few years previously. There are protocols to negotiate and ceremonies to plan immediately, but when they are done, you will have to answer the question: should you leave your grieving, heartbroken family to embark on a new job in "international development" based a continent away in Johannesburg, South Africa?

Looking back over a decade later, the answer is still not cut and dried, but one with which many women (and men, but women in particular) grapple. For you, the choice will be made easier by the unequivocal support and encouragement your family provides, now, as they have each time you have deviated from the narrow path laid down for women in your deeply patriarchal society. As friends will remind you in years to come, you may be married to the only Indian man who is OK with the idea that his wife lives on a different continent from him, meeting occasionally in exotic locales, leaving him to shoulder the responsibilities of caring for ageing parents single-handedly while simultaneously leading a major corporation. It will help that Zanzibar, mid-way between Mumbai and Joburg flying-time-wise, is a convenient location for the occasional assignation.

More than your MBA or the decade you've spent in the private sector, followed by another in the non-profit world in India, it is those rare privileges and freedoms, gifted to you and nurtured by progressive parents, tolerant teachers and nuns at your Catholic convent school in Mumbai, cheerleading in-laws, as well as forbearing bosses and colleagues through your career, that enable you to give yourself the permission to leap into the entirely unfamiliar

DOI: 10.4324/9781003260929-6

world of global institutions, geopolitics, and the myriad complex issues that civil society contends with across national borders.

CIVICUS, as you will come to realise, is unique in the "global development" community. Headquartered in Johannesburg, far, in every sense, from the power hubs of New York, Geneva, Washington DC, Brussels, London, Berlin or Paris, it is tiny when measured by annual budget, staff strength, or storied past. It does not command the clout that comes from access to funding or influence from governments or billionaires. Its strength is the credibility it commands by virtue of its members – civil society organisations, large and small – and the legitimacy of their claims to represent the voices of citizens across the globe. It is also among the very few global organisations that span the gamut of issues – from climate justice to human rights, and ODA to democratic freedoms – as it pursues its mission to strengthen and protect civil society and citizen action around the world. In the intensely competitive arena of global NGO brands and emerging Southern voices, the fact that CIVICUS does not compete for the same resources means that it can be a trusted broker and convenor.

Leading CIVICUS will entail a steep learning curve across the range of issues and contexts, the politics of international development, and the labyrinthine corridors of international institutions from the IMF, World Bank, OECD, and numerous UN agencies and fora, to the rarefied Alpine air of the World Economic Forum at Davos. Overnight, it seems, you will have to not only grasp the nuances of policy discourse but be prepared to convene and lead global alliances, networks, and gatherings, and negotiate complex agreements and stances that reflect the diversity of international civil society groups. Deciphering and mastering the acronym forest and jargon jungle of international development should itself merit a badge of honour. All this, while spending almost 50% of your time in various stages of jet lag in airports, planes, and a beige blur of hotel rooms. Your Indian passport that requires a visa to travel to most countries will pose challenges that would defeat Phileas Fogg.

Fortunately, you will be surrounded by colleagues and peers who are more than generous with their hospitality, advice, and camaraderie. People you meet for the first time in remote corners of the world will extend warm welcomes and invaluable guidance, trusting you with their stories and challenges. South Africans, in particular, will make you feel at home in their remarkable nation, where, despite overwhelming odds, democracy and social justice are still tangible goals every citizen believes in. The music, the humour, and the incredible food at these encounters all over the planet are unforgettable. I'll leave you to decide whether you prefer the deep-fried spiders in that peppery dipping sauce to the buttery crocodile. And whether a mezze feast outdoes a poutine.

You will need to be prepared to accept that the pace of progress in every aspect of your work will be glacial. Every comma in each bracket of any global agreement will require endless, nerve-racking negotiation. But sharing both the joys of hard-won victories and the despair of every battle lost, with indomitable women and men waging struggles from Flint to Phnom Penh, Maputo to Moscow, Beirut to Budapest, and Caracas to Kathmandu will keep your spirits from flagging and strengthen your resolve. Finding that balance, making the time for joyfulness and contemplation, especially in dark times, will be critical to your health and sanity. As the suffragette anthem reminds us: yes, it is bread we fight for. But we fight for roses, too.

As the world's economies begin to implode in August 2008, baring the brazen inner workings of global finance and stealing the futures of hundreds of millions of citizens, the role of civil society will be both more critical and more threatened than ever. With the international community focused on domestic crises, dictators from Belarus to Zimbabwe will try to seize greater power, intimidating and incarcerating activists and quashing dissent by any means possible. Mobilising support – from governments, media, and international organisations – to respond to each community under threat will stretch your CIVICUS team and resources to their utmost limits. Yet what can match the satisfaction of seeing an activist reunited with her family? Or wresting one more commitment to protect our planet in the teeth of ferocious resistance from big business? Or helping to get another draconian law deferred? Or seeing civil society space become a core issue for thousands of organisations around the world? Or marching down a rain-drenched Glasgow street chanting "Hum sab ek hain! (We are all one!)" with The Elders' Ela Bhatt and Mary Robinson? Or a hug from Archbishop Desmond Tutu?

In early 2011, revolution will ripple across the Arab world, whose citizens will capture the imagination of the world as they mobilise to shake off the shackles of decades of oppressive authoritarian rule. They will be joined over the next few months by students in Chile and the UK and by protestors in Zuccotti Park near Wall Street and other public squares around the world, who will launch Occupy, a movement to try and prevent a return to business as usual in the financial capitals of the world. They will be ignored or tear-gassed even as most of us in "international development" quibble over whether and how we can ally with them. Most uprisings will be ruthlessly squashed, with young activists and women in particular bearing the brunt of the reprisals. Nine years later, too many still languish in prisons around the world. But the spirit that inspired these movements refuses to die.

What might we in "international development" have done differently? Could we not have done more to protect and amplify these movements? Follow your instincts, Ingrid, when they suggest that CIVICUS and you need to focus on the voices of women and young people across the Arab world and beyond. No one has more to gain or lose. Ensure their voices are heard loud and clear and that they are not relegated to the peripheries of the political negotiations that follow their successful uprisings. Failing to do so will only transfer power from one set of patriarchal autocrats to others. As Mona Eltahawy will teach you, the Mubaraks in the bedroom and on the street are as much of a threat as the Mubarak in the palace. Without women's active participation, all the promise of these revolutions will be compromised by converging military, religious, and economic fundamentalisms. Back the courageous women of WOZA – Women of Zimbabwe Arise. The consequences of their being side-lined will be catastrophic. Pay heed too, to the nagging inner voice that suggests that reform of the global financial system may not be as inevitable as it evidently seems. Resist the temptation to defer to the "experts" who insist that these issues are best left to bankers and economists. Trust instead the jargon-free voices of students standing their ground in streets from Santiago to London in the face of violent police action.

Could we have bent the arc of history sooner or more sharply? Have we even now learned the lessons of those struggles, from our failure to ensure women were adequately represented, to permitting our governments to put business interests and arms sales ahead of citizens' rights and freedoms? Could we have seen the consequences of those failures as clearly as we do now in the present surge of majoritarian populism, polarised societies, pervasive surveillance capitalism, planetary tipping points, and a rampaging pandemic? What, in particular, might we have done to accelerate reform of the institutions of global governance whose effectiveness we so desperately lack now? Will we finally stop believing that change can happen through back-room diplomacy with the powers that be, rather than with the full involvement, and leadership, of those most affected by the decisions being made? In the "international development" community, we bear, in the words of Fernando Pessoa, the wounds of every battle we avoided.

One lesson will resonate strongly. Hans Zomer, then at Dóchas, the Irish association of development NGOs, said it best: "Be the platform, not the app". It will become your mantra for leadership within your own team, for your organisation's role in the ecosystem and for 21st century leadership more generally. Others would express it as "distributing the capacity to solve, rather than distributing solutions". Jeremy Heimans and Henry Timms would write the book *New Power* expanding on the concept. Movements like BlackLivesMatter will express it most succinctly as: "Pass the mic".

Today we are seeing young people all over the world – Fridays For Future, for instance – whole-heartedly adopt that model with ever increasing success. Looking back, I feel that we were, perhaps, too complacent, assuming change would be inevitable once the glaring inequities had been exposed, too diffident in challenging those in power as well as our peers, too willing to play by their rules rather than working to determine who sets the rules, seeking to fit in rather than to stand out, too willing to err on the side of pragmatism rather than idealism, more suited to fire-fighting than to imagining new, shared ways of being.

Those lessons will certainly be a huge help when you return to India bringing all the knowledge, experiences, and relationships you gained, to help create South Asia's first academic centre on philanthropy and civil society at a time of concerted assault on civil society space and democratic freedoms back home. You will bring too your profound respect for the sheer courage of those defending the frontlines of our societies, young people and women in particular, often at great personal cost. You will carry your trust in the lived experience and wisdom of communities especially those who have lived with structural discrimination and exploitation over generations. You will always cherish the value of solidarity, and of difficult women, and the solidarity of difficult women. You will know how to connect the dots linking poverty, unemployment, inequality, refugee crises, racism, sexism, majoritarianism, the climate crisis, and an array of fundamentalisms to the predatory economic model underlying them all. You will have learned that justice, dignity, and love always trump efficiency, productivity, and the pursuit of unfettered growth. Critically, you will know that the revolutions we seek need great music and laughter more than they need superhuman leaders. And, perhaps most importantly, you will know that, unlike Winnie the Pooh, you're not as brave as you believe, not as strong as you seem, and not as smart as you think, but that you can count on your optimism, resilience, sense of humour, and the unwavering love of your family and friends to prevail over anything life throws at you.

With love, hugs, and best wishes,

Ingrid

Ingrid has been a passionate advocate for human rights, social justice, and civil society in India and around the world for over 20 years. From 2008 to 2012, she served as Secretary General of CIVICUS: World Alliance for Citizen Participation, an influential global network dedicated to defending and strengthening civil society throughout the world. She served as Executive Director of CHILDLINE India Foundation, India's emergency helpline for children in distress, from 2013 to 2014 and was subsequently Chief Executive Officer of Hivos India Advisory Services, a for-profit venture from the Dutch INGO Hivos. Ingrid joined the Centre for Social Impact and Philanthropy at Ashoka University as its Founder Director in 2016. She is based in Mumbai, India.

5 Fly forward to new horizons!

Lysa John

My dear eight-year-old self,

As I write this, we are in the midst of an unusual global emergency. A pandemic has forced restrictions on movement and activity that would have been unthinkable a year ago. As the head of a global alliance of citizens and civic organisations, I'm working in South Africa to amplify the demand that governments release human rights defenders who have been unfairly arrested and detained. All of this may seem inconceivable to you as you play hopscotch by yourself in a dusty playground behind the girls' dormitory. And yet this is just one stop in an incredible journey that will take you further than you could ever have imagined!

At eight, you have already been at a boarding school for five years and this has meant growing up doing most things by and for yourself. You know that your family is far less affluent than those of most of your schoolmates. What you haven't grasped yet is that choosing an education they could barely afford is the most valuable investment your parents have made in you. It will give you the gift of choice; the ability to live your life on your own terms. You will also be surprised to learn that your angst towards your headstrong mother – who seems to have very little in common with the mothers of your friends and cousins – will give way to deep admiration. You will rally against her "unusualness" for a good two decades and then finally become her: inheriting her tenacious ability to aspire for a better self and a better future.

When you return to Mumbai after completing school, you will feel more out of sorts than ever before. Learning how to get around in this enormous city will take up much of your time and energy; especially since your parents enrol you in a college that takes a good two hours and three different forms of transport to get to each day! You will, however, love the time you spend navigating the city on that incomparable mode of mass transit – the Mumbai local train. You will be astounded at the sheer volume and diversity of people you come across in a single day and will learn an incredibly valuable life lesson: how to hold your space in the midst of unmitigated chaos!

A major turning point will come about when you enrol for a bachelor's degree in Social Work. You opt for Social Work only because you cannot

DOI: 10.4324/9781003260929-7

bear the idea of being confined to a boring classroom, which is what all other courses seem to entail. Joining this programme literally changes your life! It not only provides you with values and perspectives that definitively shape your purpose and identity, it also gives you – for the very first time – a sense that you have something unique to contribute to the world. Embrace this time; treasure each moment, each and every day! In addition to finding your professional foundations, you will also make remarkable friends who remain your trusted confidants for life.

You will take up your first job with a non-profit, working for human rights and social justice in Mumbai and feel incredibly fortunate to join this organisation. It is one of the few that connects local and global streams of activism with equal ease. Your insights into the potential for local communities to collectively shape national and global outcomes will be fostered in this period. Years later, it will inspire you to contribute to a campaign that results in 300,000 children petitioning the Prime Minister of India to increase expenditure on health and education – an effort that draws significant national and global attention, and one that contributes to subsequent budgetary increases. It will also set the groundwork for your efforts to support a mammoth initiative of locally led public hearings across 260+ parliamentary constituencies ahead of India's national elections.

As you start your professional journey, you have no inkling that a decade later you will have the exciting opportunity to lead a civil society delegation to UN Secretary General Ban Ki-Moon. Or that you will subsequently go on to serve as Head of Outreach for the UN High Level Panel that produces the blueprint for what is one of the most important global agreements of this century: the UN Sustainable Development Goals. Instead, in your first year at work you will apply yourself wholeheartedly to learning from new experiences – and to making more friends. That, happily enough, remains a constant! While "being alone" remains a key theme through your childhood, having remarkable friends is the one thing you can count on in your future years.

When you represent the first organisation you have worked with at a global conference, it will be the first time you travel outside your home country. You are nervous and excited to be undertaking this long journey all by yourself. When you finally reach Sydney, Australia that evening you are too afraid to go down to the restaurant at the hotel so choose to sleep on an empty stomach instead. I wish I could tell you that this would be the last time you would be overwhelmed in a new context. The experience of being an outsider, as someone who does not quite fit in, will, however, be a constant theme.

You will, for instance, work in a large, global organisation many years later and be surprised at how few people from the Global South are present in leadership roles. You will spend two years ignoring your discomfort, finding ways to work around it. Then, in the third year, your distress will force you to think deeply about your identity and contribution as an activist. In another instance, being out of work and surviving a seemingly endless stream of failed interviews will challenge you to define and value yourself beyond your employment. It will be a desperately difficult time as it coincides with other experiences of personal loss. The bleakest periods of your life, however, will also hone your internal defences, making you stronger and more resilient as your grow older. Choosing agency over disempowerment, dignity over desperation, purpose over compromise – particularly when the consequences seem daunting – these choices will make you proudest of yourself!

My advice, little one, is to hold on to the little things that bring you joy and inspiration. Never let them get away. Don't give up on the simple delights that are fundamental to your sense of "being". The long walks, the quirky music, your alone time with books: don't give that up because you no longer have time for yourself as you manage a job and raise a family. And if you do lose sight of life's little wonders, don't despair. Inspiration to connect with your inner self again will come from unexpected quarters: your daughter. She will face many of the same dilemmas you did and will use the insights you have gained to consider her options. Her spirited enthusiasm will create fresh momentum for change, especially when you think you're too old or too tired for new adventures. Soar up and fly forward brave girl – never stop looking for new horizons!

Lysa has championed human rights and international mobilisation for two decades. She started her career working for grassroots organisations fighting to end urban poverty in India, and subsequently spearheaded trans-national campaigns calling for government accountability to the Millennium Development Goals. Before joining CIVICUS, she worked as Global Campaigns Director at Save the Children, and as Head of Outreach for the UN panel that drafted the blueprint for the Sustainable Development Goals. These roles have shaped a deep interest in and understanding of grassroots-to-global activism, which continues to drive and inform her work. Lysa currently lives in South Africa and can be reached through her Twitter handle: @lysajohnSA.

6

Whose reality counts?

Finding the North Star and learning to make decisions the right way

Mark Goldring

The only thing I knew for sure in my final year studying law was that I didn't want to be a lawyer. What I *did* want was something that felt different to the conventional jobs that my peers were busy interviewing for. The careers officer listened patiently to my incoherent ramblings about wanting a sense of purpose and suggested I apply for the Hong Kong police force. Instead, I tried for the Foreign Office and VSO's international volunteer programme. VSO involved fewer exams and came through first. And so, via two years teaching in Borneo, I began what gradually became a career in international development.

If there's a moral to this part of the story it's to have the confidence to follow your instinct. After all, it's closer to your heart than your brain, and probably less aligned with your peers' desires to own BMWs or your parents' exhortations to get a "proper job".

I've moved through a range of programme and headquarter-based roles since those early days in the 1980s, always choosing the next step based on what stimulated and stretched me, rather than following any career plan. The excitement of opening a completely new programme in the closed Kingdom of Bhutan contrasted with the professional stimulus of working at scale in what felt like a centre for innovation in neighbouring Bangladesh. I later moved on from one of the world's biggest developing countries to the very particular challenges of the tiny island states of the South Pacific.

Like so many others in this field of international development – though I'm not sure quite how many would actually admit to it – I've come to live with always being rather less sure about what really works than I could ever let on. What makes a genuine improvement in people's lives, as opposed to what sounds like a good project that impresses donors, colleagues, and head office? I've lived with this uncertainty right from those early days of teaching an English medium curriculum to children for whom English was usually a third or fourth language, through grandiose UN capacity-building projects to earnest efforts to "empower" village women in many countries. There have been so many times where I have seen disadvantaged people enjoy the benefits of our good intent and their endeavour with new and real opportunities.

DOI: 10.4324/9781003260929-8

I've seen people stand tall, growing with their increased skills and power, with the ability to feed their family or educate their children. And, perhaps just as often, I've watched – sometimes without realising it until much later – as "partner" governments, communities, families, or women's groups have gone through the motions of engaging with the aid agency as a way of getting the computer, the building, the loan, or the meal they want. The price they had to pay all too often included listening to and eventually learning "development speak", waiting interminably for the "important" visitor to eventually arrive and speak to them in a foreign language and trying to guess what answers the prospective donor wanted to hear.

What I have gradually learnt is that the more senior you get, the more temptation there is to believe your own rhetoric and that of your employer and colleagues. You have to fight to remember the limits of your own knowledge of the reality of others' lives and try and listen to what those you really work for are actually saying. The bureaucratic procedures that we apply to try and ensure impact and effectiveness all too often actually distort and even hinder those very same ambitions. Listening makes things complicated, even messy, so it can be easier to only hear what we want to.

Never was this more evident to me than in a brief spell in UNDP 30 years ago. I've seen wonderful work by UNDP in many countries, but at that time and in that place the need for headquarters approval, the necessity for grand plans, and the imperative to spend money was what really mattered. It was the lens through which success was viewed. And if you couldn't spend quickly enough then you needed to spend even more time revising your budget (rather than engaging with the intended partners and beneficiaries) so you weren't seen to be failing. In such a context it's easy for otherwise well-intentioned individuals to slip into such ways. I certainly fell into the trap, lived in a bubble of peers and colleagues and became, I'm sure, insufferably self-important in dealing with those less powerful. But I also knew deep down that something felt wrong, and I got out when I could.

A few years later, working for the UK Department for International Development at the height of the popularity of the "log frame", I've got what are now painful memories of organisations placing rigid application of the tool over and above the voices of the people they sought to help. One memory that gives me goosebumps to this day is of making a roomful of bored playwrights, actors, and dancers spend what felt like days in interminable workshops explaining and charting just how their inspiring and powerful dramas were going to fill the boxes on my chart and demonstrably and measurably lead to increased girls' education or reduced domestic violence. They wanted to act, inspire, and change the world. I needed to plan, justify, and report. I held the purse strings; it was my rules that counted.

This distance from the real world of those we exist to serve isn't just the preserve of big bilateral and multilateral agencies. Many of my colleagues in Oxfam and other NGOs would have similar experiences. For many of us, it's seeing the impact on specific individuals that really tells us what works. Forty years on, I remember the names, faces, and jokes of children whose progress at school helped them into further studies and to secure a job that has supported their extended family ever since. I remember individual farmers whose improved yields directly resulted in a better diet and their children staying in school. I can see the face of the young woman in Yemen whose food ration kept her and her orphaned siblings from near starvation. These stories, and we all have them, inspire us all in our work.

It's seeing the link between the grand ambitions, efforts at systemic change, and benefits to individuals that has kept me working in development for most of the last 40 years. I've always been influenced and energised by feeling the impact on people who I have met. But we can't all see all of the people all of the time. We have to think and imagine. I hope I have always done this, but in recent years I have felt and acted on it in a way that is more explicit. One individual has supported and guided me, helping me lead, make choices and decisions – big and small.

Caro is a young Congolese woman, aged about 15 when she first arrived, about ten years ago, in a camp for displaced people supported by Oxfam. She'd been through hell and back; abducted, enslaved, raped, pregnant, and, having fled a militia, arriving at the camp with nothing. Still living in the most rudimentary conditions a couple of years later, she had called her child Happiness, as that's what her daughter brought her.

Caro combines powerlessness with dignity and determination. Her image stuck with me as I continued my work leading Oxfam in the UK. More than a memory or "case study", she seemed always to be there as I weighed up the daily decisions that are part and parcel of leading a big, overstretched, and often controversial development agency. In approaching tough choices, I kept thinking what would make the biggest difference to people like Caro? In the words of one of my colleagues, "what would make Caro proud?".

Do you campaign against a company that's got something wrong, or enter into a partnership with it as it tries to get it right, all the while never being quite sure of what's real and what's a public relations exercise? Do you work on a short-term solution that will bring immediate benefit, or struggle and possibly fail to tackle the underlying power and policy issues that perpetuate the underlying problem? When cuts are required, do you choose this activity or that one, this team or that? You certainly require all the data and analysis, but you also require a moral compass, a North Star. Caro, and others like her, became mine. It doesn't mean the decisions will always be right, but it does mean you will make them for the right reason.

In 2018, Oxfam was all over the world's media for weeks; attacked by governments, the press, and many activists for the horrific behaviour of some of its staff in Haiti in 2011 and the organisation's subsequent response. While I wasn't in Oxfam in 2011, I certainly was in 2018. Leading the organisation as the media attacked and politicians called for blood was no small challenge. Donors pulled out, programmes had to close overnight, and peers kept their heads down. Once the immediate storm eased the unpleasant work of downsizing had to begin. It included having to lose many of those who were not in any way implicated in the failings and may well have been part of the solution. Colleagues, family, and friends were hugely supportive, but right through the terrible period and as we concentrated first on surviving, then on renewing efforts to put right the shortcomings, it was the picture of Caro that kept me going through long days and sleepless nights. What would do right by her? What would make Caro proud?

We all have our own Caros. We must think of the most powerless people we know. The ones who can't fight for their own rights alone, who can't make us listen, who so often get left out, and who are so often women and girls. These are the very people who our organisations exist to serve. And if we respect and honour them in the way we work, then we will have a career we can be proud of, regardless of our seniority. I didn't need to meet Caro 40 years earlier as I set out on my career; my almost accidental career. But I'd have done a better job if I'd always thought more consciously and deliberately of people like her as I drove the ubiquitous white land cruiser or walked the corridors of power.

Mark was Chief Executive of Oxfam GB between 2013 and 2018. Prior to that he led VSO, the international volunteer organisation, and Mencap, the UK's largest disability charity. He began his career as a VSO volunteer in Sarawak, East Malaysia in 1980. Later, living and working across Asia, the Caribbean, and the Pacific, he managed country programmes for VSO, UNDP, and Oxfam and worked as a regional advisor for DFID. Mark studied law at Oxford and has a Masters in Social Policy and Planning in Developing Countries from the London School of Economics. He now combines leading Asylum Welcome, a small charity supporting refugees and asylum seekers around Oxford, England, where he lives, with a mentoring role helping less experienced charity leaders avoid making the same mistakes that he has.

7
Challenging power and discrimination

Salmah Eva-Lina Lawrence

Kabul, 2010

Hermetically sealed in an armoured 4x4, the Tajik driver is transporting me to my residence at the Green Village. The almost four-tonnes of armour is an unmissable and unmistakeable barrier against would-be suicide bombers. This reassures me little. Instead, it makes me more anxious that I am now a differentiated and, therefore, visible target in this tank-like transport emblazoned with the UN logo.

It is also a reminder of privilege. Apparently, as a foreigner employed by the UN, my life is worth more than that of my Afghan driver who must return the armoured vehicle at the end of each day and make his way home, unprotected. The privilege makes me cringe each time he is body searched entering the compound to pick me up and drop me off. The conspicuous subtext is that Westerners must be protected from these Others and the savagery of their religion and customs. In this context, I am a Westerner and the threat of violence is the justification for the apartheid that separates Afghans and foreigners. It is also a reminder of the privilege that continues to separate whites from Papuan New Guineans in Port Moresby from where I have come for this mission.

An Afghan colleague is with me in the vehicle. She knows nothing about Papua New Guinea except for UN statistics on gender-based violence. What it is that causes Papua New Guinean men to be so aggressive, she wonders aloud to me. At least we can blame Islam, she adds. I am struck by her question. Six years later I am writing a doctoral thesis triggered by that conversation. My interest is in the politics of international development which cannot be understood without also considering race.

Isn't it strange, younger self, that international development never comes up as a possible profession for me in my youth? Despite the fact that, as it was pointed out to me by an acquaintance in France many, many years later, I come from a family of those who provided service – missionaries, diplomats, public servants, international civil service professionals. And despite the fact of having been born in Papua New Guinea (PNG) and passing my adolescence in the Marcos-era Philippines, the latter a place of stark contrasts of

DOI: 10.4324/9781003260929-9

wealth and poverty. Perhaps it was that the PNG of my very early youth was a place of promise and prosperity. Not the prosperity of possessing things. Rather, the prosperity of the well-fed, the well-nourished, who had no needs, only wants. There was no discernible poverty in PNG in this era, no people sleeping on the streets, no street urchins unfed and uneducated. And this was not because my first decade of life was spent as a colonial subject in an ordered and orderly town that became the city of Port Moresby. Or perhaps it was – since colonial laws controlled the movement of people away from their home districts. One of the effects was that the Port Moresby in which I grew up was peopled primarily by the indigenous people of the Central Province and people indigenous to an area in PNG did not, in general, find themselves homeless, since customary laws over land rights prevailed. I think that absence of poverty in my homeland was a factor in deciding which path to pursue. That is, I did not feel a sense of obligation to do something in "development". That came later.

I still recall the giddy euphoria of finishing school and of wanting, actually, to be an artist – to paint, to write, to craft things. But art as a profession was not in the DNA of my parents who directed me to get serious and be practical. So, I found myself doing an accounting degree which I loathed so much I dropped out. Indeed, who goes from art to accounting and survives with psyche intact? Let me reassure you, younger self, it was the right decision. A few years later, I'd head to London from PNG for a month-long holiday and I would remain for a decade, putting myself through university – political economy this time – following which the City of London beckoned. And I found myself working for an accounting firm. Was it written in my fate to be an accountant? Thankfully, it was not. But the skills and experience gained from that period of my life have served me in very good stead. So that was a good decision, younger self. It was, in fact, that experience of living in London, then New York, working with global corporates, managing change programs, technology projects, transformation strategies, and advising on how to manage the risk around these in order to enhance corporate profits that left me feeling singularly unfulfilled and dissatisfied: a sense of disenchantment that led to contemplating a profession of service in international development. It wasn't clear to me what shape that might take – it just seemed to be more worthy than what I was doing. But it would take half a decade after my global corporate years before it happened.

Along the way, I worked in community development in PNG on projects funded by, *inter alia*, bilateral donors and aid organisations. And I found I was wary of international development. In PNG, as in other places, one of its most visible aspects was the ubiquitous white 4x4 which transported mainly white people many of whom, it seemed to me, were filled with their own self-importance.

One day, a young Japanese woman who worked for a UN agency and whom I'd met at a diplomatic cocktail party, rang and offered me a project management role on a project in Port Moresby funded by her agency. She was very eager for me to start, insisting I go to her office later that day. I, in turn, insisted on knowing the rate at which the role was being remunerated before proceeding.

PGK200.

Equivalent then to USD50.

Per day.

This was in 2007. To put this in context, my charge out rate in my global corporate life had been USD400 per hour. Yes, *per hour*. Of course, I didn't expect that in international development but nor did I expect that it would be my nationality that would determine what I was to be paid by this UN agency. Never mind my education at a prestigious British university, never mind my experience in project management with global corporates. The only thing that appeared to matter in this context was that I was Papua New Guinean – that much was made clear. The young Japanese woman was completely oblivious to the fact that she was practising discrimination. When I later complained to expatriate friends who worked in international development, their response was "that is the way it works, it cannot be changed". Discrimination was/is thus a norm in international development.

I refused the role. It's ironic that, although I experienced racism in my global corporate career, it was my ability to run a profitable business that counted the most, and these skills and expertise were the basis on which I was rewarded and remunerated.

I would later hear from other Papua New Guinean women – women with masters' degrees and PhDs – that frequently they would be the ones asked by their white counterparts – often also women – to make the coffee or do the photocopying. I also heard egregious stories from qualified, educated, and experienced Papua New Guineans of their experiences of being passed over in preference for a foreign "expert" who would be remunerated many multiples more.

The field of international development is saturated with power dynamics and hierarchies that, even in this era of equality and inclusion, remain for the most part unchallenged. "Experts" come from the "developed" world. It is those from the "developed" world who "develop" those from the "developing" world. Implicit in this vocabulary is the infantilisation of the vast majority of people on this planet who are not white – we are apparently in need of "development", supposedly lacking expertise of our own. It would be more accurate to talk about this development as economic development for we are enmeshed in a global economic order not of our making. To bring even more precision into the language one should replace "developed/developing" with high income/low income which serves to make explicit the inequitable financial flows of the global economy. Implicit also in the language and practice of international development is cultural discrimination, since interventions are often designed from within a Western cultural framework with little substantive regard for the ethics and epistemologies of local communities.

We from the majority world are caught up in a world order not of our making – we remain disadvantaged because the values – such as individualism – that underpin this order, are often at odds with the values in our own cultures. The focus on the rights of the individual and the rights of capital have fractured many societies across the majority world – I use "majority world" to designate societies whose ethical and epistemic roots are not Anglo European; we are the demographic majority on this planet. It is not that we of this majority world do not have individual rights in our societies – many of us do. What we also have are responsibilities. In my matrilineal society it is nonsense to speak only of rights – every individual, woman, man, girl, boy, has rights that are embedded in responsibilities, to each other, to the land, to the community, and to self. Individuals exist within communities – that is why one cannot speak of rights without also invoking responsibilities. Nonetheless, despite being caught up in this global political and economic order created by former colonial powers to ensure most of the benefits continue to flow to them, we of the majority world remain resilient even when we recognise, as pointed out by Maori scholar Linda Tuhiwai Smith, "we are still being colonized (and know it)" (2012:34).1

How is one to find the strength to keep going under these circumstances? Well, just as our ancestors fought and resisted Anglo European imperialism and colonialism, so there are many in the contemporary world who assert and fight for our right to be free of this continued discrimination. So, this is part of my approach, younger self, to keep me sane – to draw strength from these elders past and present. Were I to buy into the narrative that as a Papua New Guinean, as a member of the "developing" world, I lack, I am undeveloped, then who knows what it would do to my psyche. Indeed what does it do to the psyches of millions, perhaps billions, to be constantly communicated the message that they lack, that they are not enough? I have had to make an explicit turn away from anger and disillusionment in order not to be consumed by cynicism. Part of my approach to doing work in the international development space surrounded by people who see only violence and lack when Papua New Guinea is mentioned, is to invest in ways to maintain mental and emotional balance and this is where the yoga and meditation practice introduced to me at age nine by my mother's sister has been invaluable and has led me to become a Vipassana practitioner. The other aspect of my approach is to ground myself in my culture and the values of my matrilineal society and this gives me enormous psychological stability. In other words, I refuse to accept the narrative that there is only one aspect to Papua New Guinea and that is violence. My culture teaches me that a single narrative is nonsensical. So, besides the rights/responsibilities balance, I also balance the narrative by providing equal attention to the strengths inherent in the communities in which I work. In work on gender equality, we tend to focus so much on oppression that we don't ask "in what ways do women already have autonomy and what can we do to enhance that?" Finally, part of my approach is to ask how others across the majority world are addressing similar issues. It makes more sense to draw inspiration from others in the Global South who have similar trajectories to Papua New Guinea by way of colonisation, but also because our value systems are often more compatible with each other than with Anglo-European value systems. For instance, we have a much broader and inclusive definition of family than the nuclear model of white societies.

So, what can one conclude, younger self? The trajectory has by no means been a straight line, but has it been a worthwhile one? I'd like to think so. In my work in PNG and around the Pacific, whether in gender-related projects, whether in governance, I'd like to think that I make a positive contribution to the communities impacted by these interventions. In fact, I know so, because I am so often approached by my countrywomen and men who tell me they are grateful and appreciative that it is a fellow Papua New Guinean sharing with them. It makes a difference to them to see themselves reflected back from a position of authority. I'd like also to think that I have been able to challenge the power relations and assumptions – conscious or otherwise – of those who work in this field called international development. And I ask myself with each new engagement:

- In what ways is this intervention weakening local communities, systems, knowledge, and ways of being?
- In what ways is this intervention strengthening local communities, systems, knowledge, and ways of being?

It is the latter to which I strive, preferably without the discriminatory and destructive aspects of the former.

Salmah works across the private sector and the field of international development. She is also a decolonial researcher meaning she is grounded in and draws strength from the ethics and epistemologies of her own Papua New Guinean and matrilineal culture within a broader Oceanic/Pasifika culture. She works to decolonise international development through her roles in executive management, governance, and gender equality. She is currently Director Systemic Change & Partnerships at the International Women's Development Agency. She is also a non-executive director of WaterAid Australia and an Adjunct Fellow at Macquarie University. She lives in Sydney, Australia.

Note

1 Smith, Linda Tuhiwai. 2012. *Decolonizing methodologies: research and indigenous peoples*. London: Zed Books.

Section II

Human rights

8
The challenge of being true to oneself

Bahey eldin Hassan

Dear younger Bahey,

Do you remember being passionate about politics since you were an eight-year-old boy, even though our humble family had nothing to do with politics? You aspired to study political science after finishing high school, but you will not be able to do so. You will, however, end up in the field of political science through your work in journalism and human rights.

During your undergraduate studies you will major in geology. Yet starting your first year there, you will know that this is not where you belong. You will expect to fail in geology and hope to study literature instead. The notion of studying law will not occur to you because you think it does not require any intellectual creativity and that it is based on the ability to memorise legal codes. But that is wrong.

Years later you will passionately study the social history of law and then learn law through years of voluntary human rights work. In fact, you will reach a point where many will assume that you majored in law and that you are a practising lawyer, perhaps compounded by the strong relationships you will hold with prominent judges and lawyers. Curious then, that you won't fail in geology but instead graduate in the subject. While you will never fall in love with geology, your undergraduate years will enable you to meet others like you; people who love culture, politics, literature, and art. The miserable educational system will place them, like you, in science. Yet, the years of study will provide a good opportunity to better understand our world, and some of those you will meet will influence you to become the person that I am today.

After graduation you will be forced to take up jobs that you will neither love nor have interest in. But your passion for politics will lead you to work as a journalist at a newspaper's International Affairs department. Two years later you will publish your first "political" book which will focus on the elections in Egypt. Amina Shafiq, one of the most prominent figures in the history of the journalists' syndicate, will tell you that you should focus on academia instead of journalism. Ironically, two years later, you and Shafiq will split the first prize by the syndicate for your respective work on two separate projects.

DOI: 10.4324/9781003260929-11

You will go on to publish political articles in Egyptian opposition and independent newspapers, including one published on the front page; and from there, articles in the *Washington Post* and the *New York Times*. You will make contributions to academic volumes on the political and human rights situation in the Arab region, and participate in public debates with politicians and political science experts. A remarkable journey for a geologist!

At times you will wish you had followed your heart from the beginning. You will think that you wasted precious years because you did not take this road earlier. Don't despair. Those beliefs will shape you in ways you are yet to realise. Those nagging feelings lead you to follow hunches later in your life; experience will teach you to do so. However, that does not mean that you will always be right. You will come to learn that what matters more than mistakes is learning from them. Treat them like opportunities, not the end of the world. Mistakes can be seen as an opportunity to explore your dispositions and to better understand your own psychology. But this is not enough; as you will grow to understand, investing time and energy in understanding and being honest with yourself are crucial. My worst mistakes are a result of me not talking to you on time . . .

Disagreements

Your passion for politics will never transform into a wish to be a political leader or a government official. In fact, you will decline to take up a governmental position after the January 2011 uprising in Egypt. However, you will be the only Egyptian human rights defender to have bilateral meetings with the Egyptian Prime Minister and the Ministers of the Interior, Foreign Affairs, and Justice. You will also meet Arab presidents and ministers. You will have the opportunity to meet different US secretaries of state over a period of 16 years, as well as advisors to European and American heads of states, from George Bush to Donald Trump. You might be surprised to know that I am still as shy today as you are now.

Perhaps it's your spirit of equality in dealing with Egyptian and foreign officials that will allow you to establish good working relationships with many of them, but that spirit will also be a huge obstacle with others, especially senior military and Islamist figures. This is likely because both Islamists and generals think they hold an "absolute truth". But things are different with non-Egyptian Islamist leaders. You will meet Rachid al-Ghannouchi, the intellectual and historical leader of Tunisia's Islamist Ennahda movement, and the current speaker of the Tunisian Parliament. Your first meeting with him, which takes place 25 years before I write you this letter, will be at a seminar in London where you will severely criticise his writings and positions on human rights issues. However, to his credit, this didn't stop your relationship with him from developing. You will invite him to a seminar in Alexandria but regrettably he will not be able to attend due to concerns over his security in relation to the Egyptian government. After the Tunisian revolution in 2010 and his return from exile, he will host you at his office and invite you to his home in Tunisia.

That visit to Tunisia will be your first in 17 years – an enforced period of absence due to you being barred from entry because of your constant efforts to defend the rights of Tunisians. One of those you will defend is Moncef al-Marzouki, who will later become the elected president. You and he will have critical differences, but he will invite you to meet him. That meeting will be your first with an Arab president at the presidential palace. The only time you will visit an Egyptian presidential palace will be upon the invitation of Marzouki, who will be staying there during his visit to Egypt. How strange that as a human rights defender you will be kept at arm's length from your own head of state but yet you will visit the Elysée palace and the White House countless times. When you meet President Obama in February 2010, he will jokingly scold you for criticising him while in the White House. During your talks with Obama, you will criticise the gap between the promises he makes during his historic speech at Cairo University in 2009, and his actual policies on the Arab region. The first time you criticise Obama's speech will be during a meeting with Hilary Clinton, then Secretary of State, where you will criticise his apologetic discourse for democracy in the Middle East. Your disagreement with Clinton will dominate a meeting that was supposed to celebrate Obama's speech, which he had concluded a few minutes before the meeting. By the end of the meeting, you will get to know the Assistant Secretary of State for Near East Affairs, Jeffery Feltman. Your working relationship will strengthen as he assumes the position of the United Nation's Undersecretary General for Political Affairs. In February 2014, you will submit to him a detailed memo on the importance and means of restructuring the UN's daily interactions with the Arab region, given the rise of counter-revolutionary forces and the proliferation of armed conflicts and proxy wars across the region. While Feltman will take interest in the memo and share it for internal discussions inside the UN, the Egyptian government and other actors will abort the initiative. I believe that the death threat you will receive in June 2014, three weeks after President Ab-delfatah al-Sisi formally assumed power, was triggered by that memo.

Danger and optimism along the way

Why do I share these personal and political reflections with you? It's a call for you to be courageous; to stick to your principles and to do what is right after weighing your options and listening carefully to your inner voice. This won't always be easy, but you will understand more as you go along. You will receive the death threat in June 2014 calmly; by that time danger will be nothing new to you. For over 25 years, danger will be an inescapable feeling that comes along with your exposure to tens of thousands of complaints, reports, letters, and studies on the daily brutal practices committed in Egypt and the rest of the region. You will never fear prison or death, even if you always think of them. This will be particularly acute when you oversee the first documented report on torture in Egypt in January 1990. And you will feel danger again when you work on the first comprehensive report submitted by an Egyptian organisation to the UN in which criticisms are publicly levelled at the Egyptian government's laws, practices, and constitution from a human rights perspective. Later on, you will realise that you were the first Egyptian to be trained at the UN in Geneva on its advocacy mechanisms ahead of drafting this report. But more than 20 years later, after the Egyptian security establishment's pushback against the 2011 revolution, you will start feeling that danger is coming closer. Accordingly, you will register the Cairo Institute for Human Rights Studies (CIHRS), the NGO you will serve as its director, in Tunisia. After the death threat and the crackdown on civil society, Tunisia will become CIHRS' regional headquarters.

Even in your early years, you will come to the conclusion that if fear ever got to you, then you should leave human rights work to those who are better able to face it. This outlook will remain with you to the current day. And it will serve you well. Human rights defenders effectively commit suicide the moment they start thinking of themselves as victims; then they can neither help the victims of human rights crimes nor themselves. You will get to know those defenders who have an incredible psychological and mental resilience that has allowed them to face persistent dangers from security forces while also facing the embattling pressures of regressive societal, cultural, political, and religious norms.

But you will also get to know another type of defenders that did not have the mental and psychological resilience to do so. I can no longer recognise them. Some of them are running in circles; they make it look as if they are going somewhere whereas they aren't taking a single step in any direction. Others think about giving up on political rights and focusing instead on social and economic rights. They think this will buy them temporary reprieve, even though they know that the government's crackdown on platforms such as political parties, free press, and syndicates would render their work futile, leaving them running in circles. Other human rights defenders will turn into marginalised human beings after the military coup in 2013. Inexplicably, they will focus their efforts on undermining other rights organisations and defenders, while trying to find avenues to whitewash the practices of the brutal dictatorship. Women's rights will erode, with Egypt's current president being the first to publicly defend "virginity checks" for female detainees. To your shock, you will see some human rights defenders audaciously celebrating his rhetoric on the rights of women.

The first death threat you will receive will not be from the government, but from a lawyer affiliated to an armed Islamist movement. This Islamist movement was the subject of a heated contention within the Egyptian Organization for Human Rights (EOHR), Egypt's first human rights NGO. Back then, the EOHR was a fairly independent organisation, but unfortunately within two decades it will become co-opted by the government. The contention within the organisation revolved around a key question: are the members of armed Islamist movements entitled to their human rights, specifically when imprisoned? Your answer will be yes; everyone, no matter the circumstances, is entitled to their rights. However, you will regard members of that Islamist movement as violent terrorists who infringe on the rights of Muslim and non-Muslim citizens – and therefore do not qualify to be labelled as prisoners of conscience or freedom fighters. But those Islamists expected to be seen as people serving a superior cause according to their understanding of Islam. Two years later this movement will assassinate Farag Fouda, a leading secular intellectual and your colleague at the board of the EOHR. After leaving the EOHR, and a month before his assassination, he wrote and presented an unprecedentedly bold paper on the persecution of religious minorities in Egypt, upon your invitation at a conference you were organising. During the conference, you and Fouda will be verbally attacked by non-violent Islamists for the content of your speeches.

In all the challenges that lay ahead, Bahey, maintain the right mindset. Being optimistic in such challenging contexts may seem like wishful thinking. As if "Waiting for Godot". Yet wishful thinking means you just wait for things to go your way, whereas optimism leads you to embrace both negative developments and risks as potential opportunities to extract any gains upon which you can build. You will come to understand that such an outlook is indispensable for human rights defenders, especially in a region that suffers chronic failures, centuries-long multidimensional setbacks, and one that kills any development that might give some hope. You may recall that the first seminar you moderated over 40 years ago, had the title "what should be changed after the setback?". Yet since then, other historical setbacks have taken place in Egypt; the title is still very relevant today.

Revisions

Despite the leftist intellectual formation you will develop, economic, social, and developmental rights will not be your primary motivation to enter the field of human rights: civil and political ones will take precedence. One of the things that will have a huge impact on you is the Solidarity workers uprising in Poland in the 1970s; an uprising against a regime that presented itself as the "dictatorship of the proletariat". The uprising will force you to revise and rethink many ideas you previously took for granted.

The following years will prove to you that, unlike in the Global North, where democratic systems are predominant, in the Arab region it is hard to achieve any meaningful change in economic and social rights without a minimum degree of civil and political rights. Freedom of expression and journalism, and the freedom to form political parties, syndicates, and civil society platforms are all essential building blocks for the pursuit of economic and social rights. This is why you will become part of the initial deliberations on forming the first Egyptian human rights organisation in 1985 and, three years later, be elected as its Secretary General.

Winning minds before hearts

The path that will define the second half of your life will be heavily influenced by two actors: the first, a person, and the other, a book.

You will always refuse the notion that the exceptional nature of Arab societies means abandoning the universalism of human rights in favour of the region's cultural specifics. Therefore, you will never find a contradiction between defending the human rights of all people, including violent Islamists who attacked religious minorities, while also defending freedom of religion, including the right to not believe in any religion. This will put you at the crossfires of opposing fronts, including the government, its religious institutions, and political Islamists. Meeting Mohamed El Sayed Said will have a qualitative impact on you in this regard.

Said was an exceptionally bright political science academic in Egypt. You will manage to convince him to volunteer some of his time to work at the Board of the EOHR when you are elected to be its Secretary General. This will be the beginning of a wonderful intellectual partnership between both of you and will last until his passing 20 years later. Through your shared human rights experience, Said will be able to crystalise a long-term intellectual strategy that addresses the cultural shortcomings and flaws of the Arab region, such as the predominant view on women's rights. Those views were employed by governments, conservative intellectuals, politicians, and religious preachers to justify some human rights violations and/or challenge its universality. This meant establishing a fundamentally different type of organisation, one with a predominantly intellectual inclination, unhindered by the typical short-term concerns of other organisations; an institution with the mission of planting the cultural seeds of long-term progress. Such progress, which is achieved through intellectually combating reactionary views, requires the mobilisation of political scientists, sociologists, historians, novelists, poets, film artists, and enlightened religious preachers. In the context of such struggle, international human rights conventions are not conceived as final products ought to be religiously preached but should rather organically take root in the indigenous culture. When you and Said consulted Arab experts, they will advise that the activities of the new organisation shouldn't be limited to Egypt and should extend to the Arab region, seeing that the region shares similar cultural challenges and flaws, and that no Arab organisation addressed the issue similarly. Those ideas will come to shape your understanding of human rights and how to meaningfully advance it in your region. They will put you on a path that you will pursue for many decades to come. Through this perspective, CIHRS will be ultimately born in 1994, and Said will remain its academic advisor and the editor-in-chief of its academic journal, *Rowaq Arabi*, until he passes away in 2009.

The second actor that will influence your path will be *States of Denial*, a book by Stanley Cohen, the prominent Israeli academic and human rights defender. The book was first published in 2001 and was reprinted at least 22 times afterwards. However, you will first come across its contents in 1995, when it was still in the form of a draft report that a friend at an American foundation will share with you. Over the course of Cohen's work, he documented the brutal torture practices directed at Palestinians. His concern, which he sought to answer in the book, was why, despite all the documented reports circulated by his organisation and others (such as Amnesty International), the predominantly Western and liberal Israeli public never gave enough attention to the torture of Palestinians. Even though it focused on a different political culture and context, Cohen's work highlighted different dimensions of the same issue CIHRS sought to address. As the fight for human rights is essentially a fight over people's hearts and minds, Cohen's book will motivate you to contemplate how best to frame human rights messaging. Over time, you will realise that the culture of the target audience matters, as does their political psychology.

A job or a calling?

Many actors believe that the only major obstacle hindering the human rights cause is the repressive regimes that have been ruling the Arab region for a long time. They consider international organisations and treaties, United Nations mechanisms, capacity building trainings, and generous donations to be sufficient to advance human rights. I am sure you understand what I mean – you used to share their perspective during the early days of your human rights work. But later you will realise that this is a naïve outlook. According to this outlook, the effectiveness of this formula depends on the existence of brave national human rights defenders equipped with effective means of communication. During your early days, there still wasn't any communication by cell phones and email. It was the "heroic" fax machine! Do you still remember it? Such a mechanistic approach incorrectly believes that national human rights defenders are robots; that when programmed correctly by those international actors they will achieve their mission. It assumes that "the people" will automatically stand behind those seeking to enable them. As you will later realise, the reality is different for two reasons.

Firstly, for international human rights organisations, the target audience and constituency are somewhat limited to Western governments and international mechanisms, which explains why the discourse of these organisations is overwhelmingly legal and technical. On the other hand, while national human rights organisations also target the same international audience, their primary goal is to influence the national public opinion. Accordingly, national organisations need to account for specific cultural, political, and societal factors when formulating their discourse. Accounting for those factors is increasingly complicated in societies that are deeply polarised on political, social, value, and religious levels. It is even more complicated in societies where governments and even parts of the opposition have resorted to violence to solve their differences. These political considerations have a substantial impact on shaping the day-to-day human rights discourse, actions, and messages, but not the universal values. National human rights defenders should therefore maintain an in-depth understanding of the variables in their societies, in addition to their grasp of international human rights standards and mechanisms. This does not mean that national human rights defenders are political, cultural, and/or societal actors in the traditional sense, but rather have what might be called a specific "political responsibility" towards their societies. While steering clear from political parties and agendas, and actively defending their independence from the government and the opposition, advancing human rights should be your only concern.

The second reason is that some of the inherited components of the predominant political, social, and religious cultures play a negative role in strengthening the resistance of some Arab rulers and political opposition to human rights, and sometimes facilitate oppressing human rights defenders. I guess you still remember why in a public debate in 1993 you will argue against the idealistic notion of transforming Egypt's first human rights organisation into an open-membership popular organisation. Such transformation would have entailed abandoning some universal human rights standards (such as women's rights and freedom of conscience) given their "unpopularity". Such transformation would have also meant politicising the organisation through turning it into a platform for conflict between competing partisan groups. In the years after the debate, you will be pleasantly surprised, as dozens of human rights organisations were established in Egypt, and none of them adopted the open-membership popular structure, including the organisations established by those who previously advocated for such a structure. Ultimately, Arab organisations that adopted the open-membership popular structure were co-opted by political parties (be they governing or in opposition) or turned into a battlefield for competing political opposition groups. The latter case shaped the early collapse of the Egyptian section of Amnesty International. This does not mean that you will be in principle against open-membership structure of human rights organisations, but that you will correctly identify that the current political and cultural context in the Arab region does not accommodate it.

The view that national human rights defenders are mere robots is often reflected in the policies of some donor agencies. Those donors look at national organisations through a lens of a technical checklist tailored to specific social, political, and cultural settings. Factors such as the numbers of reports produced, the extent of media coverage, and the number of political prisoners released are prime examples of such criteria. In the aftermath of the Arab Spring, this misguided approach further flourished. Some donor agencies pursued non-existent similarities between the Arab uprisings and the orange revolutions that swept across Eastern and Central Europe decades earlier. Accordingly, irrelevant criteria were put into place and funds were allocated merely because the projects were tailored to match these meaningless criteria. As you encounter this culture of readymade checklists, fight it and speak out against it; the events that will unfold before you across the region will show you and them that they couldn't have been more wrong.

Reform as a radical recipe

Bahey, you may still be confused about your journey. How did a geologist who was supposed to be mining beneath the earth turn out to be a human rights defender? Your name appears on the front pages of newspapers, sometimes celebrated as a renowned human rights defender, and other times, you are portrayed as a traitor who got sentenced by a court for 15 years in prison while being in exile. How did your radical transformation into a reformist take place? Well, you may agree with me that the whole journey remained committed to pursuing the same values, rather than being one of switching ideologies and political beliefs. Critical thinking is the magic key for this journey, even in dealing with the human rights' concept. For you, it is not another holy text like the Bible or the Quran; it is a concept that should have its relevance examined every day and everywhere. It is a concept that should be permanently open for further development by peoples' experiences and reflections across different contexts.

But you may slightly misinterpret your journey. In adopting the concept of the universality of human rights, you seem to be adopting a radical outlook. However, your approach of implementation, which you developed with Said, is a reformist one. This may explain the irony of being considered one of the most radical human rights voices in Egypt, while also meeting with many high-level Egyptian officials. While you are keen to expose serious human rights violations and hold their perpetrators accountable, you are also fully aware that behind those perpetrators are ailing state institutions, deeply rooted traditional and religious cultures, and a society polarised over its identity and values. It is a long road ahead.

In the context of this struggle for values, and how it may last for decades, Arab human rights organisations and their national and international allies may have to learn how to strictly adhere to the universalism of human rights – which some think are too radical, while being conscious that the implementation of those values will not happen radically overnight, or even by revolution. They will rather be implemented incrementally and over the long term. Therefore, it is vital to identify reformists within state institutions and work with them.

Perhaps you noticed in my letter to you the meandering course that marked my path, from the moment I was you until the moment you became me. Throughout this ongoing journey I did my best to stay true to myself.

Bahey is the Director of the Cairo Institute for Human Rights Studies (CIHRS). CIHRS is an independent regional non-governmental organisation, founded in 1993 to promote respect for the principles of human rights and democracy in the Arab region. CIHRS produces analysis on the difficulties of applying international human rights law and disseminating human rights culture in the Arab region, conducts advocacy in national, regional, and international human rights mechanisms, and contributes to the capacity development of Arab human rights-focused NGOs. Bahey is also a member of the Board of the EuroMed Human Rights Foundation, a member of the Advisory Board of Middle East Watch at Human Rights Watch, and is a lecturer on human rights and democracy in the Arab region. He is the editor of several books. Due to his human rights work, he was sentenced in absentia to 15 years in prison. He lives in France.

9

Keep an eye on the ball

Morten Kjærum

Congratulations Morten, you have just been appointed director of the Danish Center for Human Rights. It is a good choice to move into human rights after seven years in the humanitarian field working with refugee protection. It's a nice continuation in that by strengthening the protection of human rights you will get a chance to contribute to preventing conflicts that make it necessary for people to flee. Since the collapse of the Berlin wall and the end of the cold war one year ago there will be a particular window of opportunity in the coming years to root human rights and democracy across all continents. The profundity of the current changes can only be compared to the aftermath of the second world war in the 1940s and 1950s, and the COVID-19 crisis that emerged in 2020. With the new position you will be given a unique platform to contribute to change, not by naming and shaming but by supporting those duty bearers who are eager to build the future of their society on human rights and democratic values. Please carry that responsibility with devotion and attentiveness.

No one has yet travelled the journey that you are embarking upon, so the road map is rudimentary at best. In your daily work you will be persistently confronted with the choice to remain loyal to the old well-tested methodologies and routes that you and the institution feel familiar with, or to dive into the new challenges with an open mind. Many inside and outside the Center will advise you to decline when the institution is invited to assist in addressing some of the new problems that emerge from these profound changes. From a logical perspective, they will try to convince you by saying: we do not have the expertise and knowledge in the institution, so we should not embark upon this task.

Yet with challenge, comes opportunity. Let's say that the newly elected minister of justice in South Africa calls you in 1994 to ask that the Center helps to reshape the apartheid legal system, turning it into a democratic human rights-based justice system. Do you say yes or no? Or when important companies approach you to get your assistance in creating a human rights agenda, do you turn them down? Or when the mayor of a city wants to

DOI: 10.4324/9781003260929-12

integrate human rights into the city's strategies? For sure, the Center does not at the moment possess expertise in these new fields, so you could refuse. However, before you do so you could, as a first step, look around and see if other organisations or institutions are better equipped than your Center. If so, you could refer the minister, the CEO, and the mayor to these organisations. If they do not exist because these tasks are all new, the next question to ask is whether the task is important from a human rights perspective and relevant for where you want your institute to be? If the answer is yes, then the creative process starts by identifying how best to address the specific task and creating a team that combines people with different skill sets.

Many of the people that you engage will not be human rights experts, so you have to make sure that they share a human rights-based approach to their role. You will meet a lot of interesting people on that journey, from corporate strategists and architects to economists and social workers. Each of them will bring human rights back to their professional environments. The notion of co-creation is key when finding ways to transform human rights standards to the realities on the ground and you have to make it clear from the beginning that this is new territory and that nobody in the group has the answer. At times, co-creation can be difficult to comprehend, particularly for lawyers who are brought up in an environment in which a legal text provides the answers to the questions in an authoritative way. Yet, when co-creation works it is inspiring and has the potential to bring about new methodologies and approaches that can be used by others.

You will be entering into a very politicised area since human rights is about limiting or directing the use of power by those that hold it. They rarely like that and often have profound explanations of why the steps they take are justified despite the fact that their actions constitute clear human rights violations. When you choose to work with duty bearers there will always be limits to what you can do and say. Some will say that simply by being there you will have sold your human rights soul, while others, realising the importance of entering that complex space, will back you. The potential impact you can have navigating that territory is considerable. However, the fundamental challenge is to make your actions understood by and remain credible to those people in a vulnerable situation to whom human rights protection means the most.

From my experience working in the European Union (EU), where one runs the risk of being totally petrified by the very many different interests in play, I developed a methodology that you may find useful. I have called it the Ernesto test. Ernesto is my grandchild. When confronted with profound moral, ethical, and political dilemmas you need a tool to clarify the issues that confront you in order for you to move on and do what you consider to be right. I developed the test when illiberal and anti-human rights changes gathered pace in Hungary. Working on human rights in the EU at the time it was difficult to sit still and do nothing. However, the EU mandate on these issues was weak so many officials warned me not to prepare special reports on these developments. Their main argument was that the institution did not have a clear mandate to do so; at best, it sat at the very edge of our mandate. With the Ernesto test in mind I projected myself into 2028 and saw Ernesto as a big boy asking me what I did when illiberal developments in Europe took root and at a time when I was in a high human rights position in the EU. Should I tell him that I didn't do anything, due to all sorts of complicated EU legislation and bureaucratic barriers? Posing that cross-generational question the Ernesto test helped me make the (right) decision to produce the reports - reports that, in the end, made a contribution to enhancing the attention in the EU system to rule of law issues in EU member states. There is still a long way to go and a lot for you to do later on in your career.

These highly complex and political situations are unavoidable, and they will come to you in many shapes and colours. Once a friend from the humanitarian world consulted me when she came back from a conflict zone. Local dairy production had collapsed and she was asked to identify whether and how her organisation could assist. She came back from the mission with the message that the local dairy factory needed a spare part to get the production up and running again. That was a disappointing message to return home with since the spare part could be bought for €200, whereas providing milk powder to the area for years to come would generate a lot of funding for the organisation. She insisted the organisation provide the spare part and ultimately got her way. My advice to you, Morten, is to create for yourself a system or model that can keep you loyal to your core values since it is easy to be diverted into considering first what is good for the organisation prior to the beneficiaries of your services. Ask people you trust to regularly test your moral compass to ensure that it is still orientated to where you would like it to be.

Creating a strong organisation requires that people can speak their mind in an open and safe manner. In the think-tank in which you will work, the organisation's main resource is people's minds, so treat them well and create a conducive work environment for all – it's a win for the Center and win for the staff. Develop a culture and language where it becomes natural and legitimate to address difficult questions as well as those of a more personal nature. You will see the importance of this during the COVID-19 crisis during which time the organisation must spend considerable energy creating and safeguarding a culture in which staff can address private issues that take on important workplace dimensions, such as social isolation, attending to children while working from home, or, for some, the unhappiness of being stuck 24 hours with one's spouse.

While creating language for difficult and sensitive issues you need to be meticulous. Language can conceal important factors and twist interventions. This is why you always need to look beyond the surface of the mental models that language creates. For very good reasons, humanitarian assistance is often provided after so-called "natural disasters". As long as it is *nature* to be blamed for the disaster there is very little we can do and no one expects *nature* to be held accountable. However, most often it only becomes a disaster due to human failures, neglect, corruption or the like. For instance, disaster ensues when funding disappears in the pockets of corrupt or fraudulent officials and politicians; when buildings are not made earthquake ready; or when officials for years do not react to tsunami risk warnings and leave big settlements with no protection or emergency preparedness in place. As long as we remain with the language of "natural disasters" we are less inclined to hold people responsible. The language of natural disasters is often a veil of protection for the corrupt or negligent officials. So, be conscious about your perceptions and the language used.

My last piece of advice to you, Morten, is to always remember that the essence of human rights and humanitarian work is about the individual human being and the protection of their dignity. Everybody will claim that this is the focus of their work. Too often though this focus will become blurred or obfuscated by other priorities. What human rights can bring to both the humanitarian field and development work is a powerful analytical tool to identify those persons who are most at risk. Far too often in humanitarian emergencies people with disabilities and the elderly are left behind and women are not sufficiently protected against rape and other sorts of violence. A human rights framework works to strengthen the focus on the needs of those in the most vulnerable situation. Making these needs more visible will often require that you speak to people who are in need of help and personally involve them in the work. The more you can engage people in finding solutions to their own challenges, the more you are bound to have success in your work. You can be sure that they know the issues they face better than you and by working creatively with them your support will have a longer and deeper impact. It sounds banal, but it is not. In the world that you are stepping into, as well as the world that you are leaving, there is a strong tendency to do things for others rather than letting them take the lead.

One thing I have regretted that I did not do early on in my career, where you are now, was to explore and better understand the nature of biases, in particular those that are unconscious. Like anyone else, we as human rights or humanitarian actors from the Global North are conducting our work with a mental luggage of biases that play into our work in many different ways. However, the understanding and awareness of this is often minimal. Or it is simply just denied. Fortunately, things are changing, but you can be at the forefront if you start early, and there is no doubt that your work will only gain from that since your ability to listen and learn from the people you meet will be dramatically improved when you are ready to challenge your own biases.

Working with biases, perceptions and language is the key to moving ahead with a deeper global dialogue on human rights and humanitarian issues. The UN Sustainable Development Goals that we have today offer a powerful international framework for this dialogue. Morten, I hope you will always keep a firm eye on your core values, engaging those that you work with in an open, non-biased dialogue, and do not shy away from stepping into new territories. I wish you lots of success in your work, it is very much needed and will be for many years.

Morten has been Director of the Raoul Wallenberg Institute of Human Rights and Humanitarian Law in Sweden since 2015. He started his career in the non-governmental sector, at the Danish Refugee Council. Morten was the first Director of the European Union Agency for Fundamental Rights in Vienna, Austria and was Director of the Danish Institute for Human Rights from 1991 to 2008. Appointed by the UN Secretary-General, he is Chairperson of the UN Voluntary Fund for Technical Cooperation in the Field of Human Rights and of the Universal Periodic Review Trust Fund for Financial and Technical Assistance. He is currently Chair of the Board of the European Council on Refugees and Exiles. He holds an honorary professorship at the University of Aalborg and lives in Copenhagen, Denmark.

10

In your footsteps, my brave little girl

Tawakkol Karman

Dear Tawakkol,

Almost 25 years have passed since the commotion you caused as a high school sophomore. Back then, you led your classmates in what looked like a small demonstration towards the principal's office to protest against the change of a classroom teacher.

The principal did not reverse their decision, but it was a chance for you to prove yourself and to do so whatever the consequences. You found out that the failure of your plan to reinstate the teacher was not the end of the world. Quite the reverse: you realised that, above all else, you are strong and courageous. These qualities have served you well over the years.

With great reverence and amazement, I still remember those moments well. I still admire the courage you had to lead a protest inside an administratively strict school, and without fear for the potential implications. Now, after all these years, it may be appropriate for me to reveal a secret. Once, having entered the public sphere, and later having decided to call for demonstrations and protests, you became my role model. At that time, I used to tell myself: "I will not let the little Tawakkol down". I made up my mind to be faithful to your courage and I made a promise to myself that I would never hesitate to express what I believe freely and without fear.

My little Tawakkol

Let me remind you of an important conversation that will cast a shadow over our lives to this day. You disclosed to our father, Abdul Salam Karman, who was a politician, lawman, and a Yemeni minister at one time, that your dream was to be the President of the Republic. His response? "You will have made yourself smaller if the Republic of Yemen is all you look for. Your dream should be directed to something bigger." That conversation taught me a lesson about a principle that has accompanied me up to the present time – that the whole world is what we should belong to and be concerned about.

So, when former United Nations Secretary-General Ban Ki-moon named me among 27 members of the high-level panel of eminent persons on the

DOI: 10.4324/9781003260929-13

post-2015 development agenda, I took this appointment so seriously. Once the panel's first meeting convened, I was well briefed on UN literature concerning sustainable development, the Millennium Declaration, the Rio climate summits, the global summits on financing of development agendas, and various UN resolutions. Frankly, this was equivalent to an intensive reading course for me, and pretty much enabled me to develop a coherent vision.

I decided to attend the meeting in person. I did so despite my many reservations and criticisms, including the wide gap between the rich and comprehensive content of the United Nations literature, decisions and declarations on the one hand, and operational realities on the other, marked as they were by great failure and deficit. This gap exists because the UN mechanisms allow declarations and agreements but, at the same time, provide the member states with the option of voluntary implementation, without any legally binding oversight or accountability. I had always wondered, what is the point of all those global plans, agreements, and declarations?

Nevertheless, I was determined to continue and to be a person of positive spirit. Like the young Tawakkol, I was determined that the right outcome be achieved. I was conscious that some of my fellow panel members held senior positions at home or abroad, and I felt that an opportunity to participate in such a serious and responsible discussion may not present itself again. Everything was clear to us: poverty was deeply entrenched in societies; globalisation was widening the socio-economic gap; many countries were suffering from widespread corruption and the lack of good governance; religious and political tyranny were resulting in significant challenges, most notably in failing states, the escalation of conflicts, the spread of extremism and the terrorist groups; high rates of organised crime were of growing concern; and, the climate had deteriorated to alarming levels.

We discussed everything. We defined the post-2015 sustainable development agenda and goals, coming up with 19 objectives as solutions to these problems. In theory, this was a really great achievement, especially since the General Assembly approved the plan at its global summit. Anything else, not least implementation, was up to countries and governments. As is always the case, practice makes perfect – the gaps between written commitments and meaningful action remain.

Dear little Tawakkol

Upon receiving the Nobel Peace Prize 2011, I stated in different words that the award was a global recognition of the peaceful struggle by young people of the Arab Spring in Yemen and elsewhere. In fact, the prize was a tribute to revolutionaries and freedom fighters, as far as it was a heavy blow to the Arab dictatorships that spared no effort to fabricate all kinds of charges against me. Their non-stop smear campaigns to bring me to my knees went unheeded. My determination and willpower undiminished, I am still optimistic about the bright future awaiting our great Arab homeland.

At an early age, I decided to stand up to injustice and political corruption, whatever the cost. Since you, little Tawakkol, were with me throughout, you remember the confusing decision I made not to hold public office. I had worked in the Ministry of Local Administration for three months before I left to devote myself to human rights activism. Corruption and failure were everywhere, sponsored by the regime at the highest levels. This was enough for me not to stay in the public service, as I was aware that independence and freedom are crucial to standing up to corruption. Instead, I founded the "Women Journalists Without Chains", an NGO that sought to defend rights and freedoms, and fight against public corruption. I endured great hardship in order to obtain a licence, as the authority had begun to realise that I was serious about fighting its corruption. It resorted to various tricks to prevent me from having the licence. But, in the end, I decided to work without waiting for anyone's permission. I developed innovative ways to proceed with my human rights activities, unconcerned with any threats or consequences. Later, I got the licence, and began calling for an end to the censorship of newspapers and the media. It was met with obstinacy by the authorities concerned.

Dear little Tawakkol

I guess you won't disagree with me that Ali Abdullah Saleh's regime must leave for us to make real reforms. In 2006, when Saleh and his regime were at their greatest power, I wrote an article in the left-wing Al-Thawri newspaper calling on him to leave power. The word "leave!" was not familiar in Yemen's prevailing political discourse. In 2011, only five years after this article, millions of Yemenis took to the streets, repeating this word in its various forms. The dictator's problem was no longer our article, but rather the people. He never recovered from the shock. He died at the hands of a militia from the regime's former allies, the Huthi rebel movement, in the Yemeni Spring of December 2017.

These were extraordinary times. Events were triggered when I invited student leaders of Sana'a University and a number of human rights activists to convene a meeting in my house, immediately upon the announcement of the fall of Tunisian President Zine El Abidine Ben Ali in January 2011. It was a solemn moment marked by the first manifesto of the revolution, in which we called for the overthrow of Ali Abdullah Saleh's regime but through peaceful demonstrations. We set the next day – 16 January 2011 – as the first demonstration that would demand the regime's departure, and we would do so in front of Sana'a University. At the beginning of the demonstrations – in fact, on 23 January 2011 while returning home at night – I was arrested by the regime's security services for instigating and participating in the protests. This further fuelled the revolution. The numbers of demonstrators swelled from thousands to tens of thousands. They took to the streets in several cities in protest against my arrest and chanted our slogans. They forced the regime to release me only two days later. I realised that from that point it would be up to the revolution to have the final say, and this was enough for me to be certain that things would change.

It is true that the revolution was subjected to a brutal machine of repression. It was also let down by the political parties, including those who showed support for the revolutionaries. However, the will of the people proved to be stronger than expected. On 11 May 2011 and alongside a group of revolutionaries, I decided to march towards the government's headquarters and the parliament. It was a step the revolution-affiliated parties refused to take under the excuse that it was a provocation to the regime. "The revolution in its nature is provocative to the core", we replied. On that day, we were met with a brutal repression and a number of young activists were martyred and wounded. What's more, the revolution-affiliated parties actually launched a campaign against us, accusing us of treason. Nevertheless, all that did not detract from our resolve.

Dear little Tawakkol

When leaving for New York in October 2011, I was met with a warm welcome from the Secretary-General of the United Nations and all the delegates to the UN Security Council. I was there to ask for a UNSC resolution that obliged Ali Abdullah Saleh to respond to his people's demands for change. Barely a few days later, a decision was issued. It provided for the establishment of a commission of inquiry into the crimes and violations against the demonstrators. As is customary, the delegates, including the relevant state member's delegate, had to comment on the decision in a press conference. The problem was that the Yemeni delegate still owed allegiance to Ali Saleh, and therefore would not have welcomed the decision. So I had no choice but to attend the conference instead of him and to comment on the decision on behalf of Yemen. He had no way to stop me since the revolution was supported by everyone in the corridors of the United Nations, the Security Council, and even among the United Nations staff and media.

Today, Yemen is facing great challenges because of regional plots and international complicity. While Saudi Arabia, the UAE, and Iran adopt hostile policies and provide financial support for armed groups with fascist tendencies to subvert the revolution's image and the political process, I along with most Yemenis are fighting for a democratic state that ensures freedom of expression and respect for human rights. It is true that we face great threats, but our faith in our state and our mission in this world is greater. As with the removal of the classroom teacher all those years ago, I continue to fight for what is right.

Dear little Tawakkol

My story is one of courage, determination, and commitment. The pursuit of being on the right side of history is never easy. It will also take forms you can never imagine at your young, tender age. Let me give you an example. In 2020, I was appointed to the oversight board for Facebook and Instagram content. It outraged some dictatorial regimes to such an extent that they funded intensive media campaigns against me as they sought to pressure the Facebook administration to undo the step. Moral and physical assassinations against opponents are the most preferred practice of our region's tyrannical regimes. For me, the determination to go ahead with the fight for human rights and the struggle against tyranny in all its forms has been my usual response to campaigns of hatred. Admittedly, tyranny and terrorism are two sides of the same coin. Personally, I have always been subject to politicised religious fatwas threatening my life. Yet my will has never weakened.

Of course, my involvement in one organisation in particular stands above all else: the Tawakkol Karman Foundation, one that is now active in various charitable fields. It is the source of immense personal pride. While seeing how the Foundation grows step by step, I recall that day when you told our family members that, one day, you would have a large organisation that would work to favour the poor. That dream – that commitment – has been fulfilled. Upon its foundation on 20 December 2016, I made sure that it focused on people's needs and served as a platform for spreading democratic ideas, as tyranny is the root of all evil.

When you first thought of this ambition you had big dreams and goals. Some have proven possible, others not. No individual has the ability to replace the state and its institutions, even under a humanitarian banner. Likewise, no one has the ability to access all the needy. There is a difference between dreams and reality, but it's important for us to do our best and spare no effort when seeking to achieve our goals. In a short time, it has been able to achieve many significant things.

The Bidaya project, for example, trains and supports qualification of young people; the Sharaka project supports small enterprises and entrepreneurship among both young women and men; and the Work-For-Food project supports the poor and vulnerable to secure basic means. The Foundation's aid and scholarship project has benefitted thousands of students, while a range of democracy and peace-building activities provide young people and others with the capacity and opportunity to continue the struggle against tyranny, war merchants, and human rights violators. Much remains to be done but I feel proud that we have lit a candle in this darkness.

Dear little Tawakkol

Some good habits need to take root from an early age, and here I have to be thankful to you. Your love of reading and music, alongside caring for public affairs, has had a great impact on my personality. Indeed, this helped shape my thoughts and outlook on life, my different ideas and beliefs. These would not have formed in the ways that they have had I not learned from you to rebel and stand by the truth no matter the consequences. And, yes, my thirst for reading has expanded and developed, even if my present preoccupations are, to some extent, an obstacle to such a good habit. Still, the passion for knowledge is still alive and vital, and I promise it will remain so.

You no doubt remember that one of my dreams was to have a platform to address the world. Today I feel that I can do it, and not only that, but I can convert words to deeds. I know that the difficulties are many, but I pledge to all of you that I will remain as always, Tawakkol who never compromises on justice nor on rights.

Tawakkol was awarded the Nobel Peace Prize in 2011, in recognition for her non-violent struggle for democracy and her advocacy for women's rights in Yemen. Karman has been imprisoned on a number of occasions for her pro-democracy, pro-human rights protests. Amongst Yemen's Youth movement, she is known as "mother of the revolution", "the iron woman", and the Lady of the Arab Spring. She is a human rights activist, journalist, politician, the Founder of Peaceful Youth Revolution Council, and the Founder of Tawakkol Karman International Foundation. TIME Magazine described her as a "Torchbearer of the Arab Spring" and named her both one of the 100 most influential women defining the last century and one of the Most Rebellious Women in History. She was a member of the High-Level Panel of eminent persons on the Post-2015 Development Agenda. She is now a board member of the Facebook oversight board, and Nobel Women initiative.

Section III

Public service

11 And it breaks my heart

Admiral Ncube

Years ago, I joined the cause for it looked so noble
It looked so noble, as it professed values so high
Never did I think, never had I seen such at all
That behind the veil, an evil drowned it all
Nobility had died, and it so broke my heart!

People are at the heart, they said from the start
But my heart bled, when I saw them depart
To focus on money, and those who gave it
To reduce people to projects, no one heeded it
Humanity had died, and it so broke my heart!

So hard I worked, so hopeful I remained
Hoping that one day, favour I'd have gained
To sit with them, whose voices direct the work
To speak for those, whose lives create the work
But inclusion never lived, it broke my heart!

Little did I know, not all of us are equal
Where you come from, determines it all
How your skin looks, makes or breaks it all
Privilege reigns, forget about being equal
Transparency had died, and it broke my heart!

Proposals I wrote, money came but for who?
Somewhere in some city, overheads went
Raised for the poor, to whom little was sent
Accountability they preached, but to who?
Accountability never existed, and it broke my heart!

What could I do, when that which appears noble rots
When experts reduce people's lives to a logframe

DOI: 10.4324/9781003260929-15

When desperation is marketed to bring a profit
When policies are made by those few privileged
When the life of the poor is reduced to a pilot
When race dominates who leads in the office
When a saviour mentality is showcased as compassion
When technical expertise masks white privilege
When all that matters is power and money
An industry was dead, it broke my heart!

Admiral is a Zimbabwean national currently working in Botswana as a development professional. Holding a doctoral degree in development studies, his area of interest has been resource mobilization, partnerships, and project management in both development and humanitarian settings. Admiral brings over 16 years of experience from various contexts such as Asia, Africa, and the Middle East, working with different INGOs and UN agencies. It is this experience that has exposed him to some of the contradictions and shortfalls in the sector. Admiral is married to Margret and has three boys (Christian, Myles and Kai).

12 In search of a blueprint

Adrian Schlaepfer

Dear Adrian,

Welcome home and happy twenty-third birthday! I'm glad to hear that your internship with a shrimp export company in Colombia went well and that you have come back to Switzerland with new ideas on what you want to do in life. I reckon that you have finally overcome that initial culture shock which you wrote about in an earlier letter and which almost had you take a flight home. As you say, the same daily sight of the misery of Cartagena's shantytowns that you found so repulsive in the beginning, gave way to your growing awareness and curiosity about the world's poverty and inequality. So, your mind seems set on a professional career in the field of development, a far cry from your earlier ambition to become a banker and quickly make your first million. As you say, after your Colombian exposure to poverty, your vision is now that of helping to make the world a better place for all.

Do I think this is a good idea? Absolutely! Is a degree in economics a useful starting point for a career in International Development (ID)? Definitely, albeit not exclusively. Can I give you some clues on what to expect and how to proceed? Sure, that is the purpose of this letter.

Commitment first – but be realistic!

International Development is not a career like any other. It is a philanthropic cause that takes special personal dedication. The French call it *feu sacré*. Whatever your academic background, what counts first and foremost is your personal commitment to a world where all people are treated as equals and share the global wealth. It is about transformation, justice, equal opportunity, power. You meet the challenges of change in an environment that may not always be conducive and withstand forces that may undermine your efforts. You need an almost religious vision of what your ideal world should look like, and an almost missionary attitude in the pursuit of your contribution to that vision. But don't get carried away, don't be naïve! Your part will most likely always remain a drop in the ocean, and real success stories in ID are elusive. Don't despair. Set yourself realistic goals, accept uncomfortable

DOI: 10.4324/9781003260929-16

realities, and know that your commitment will be tested over and over again. The gap between an overwhelming personal commitment, and the lack of tangible results is probably the reason why ID professionals are particularly prone to "burnouts".

A career in International Development?

If you read my professional biography, you will notice a curvy string of turning points. My ID career did not follow a straight line from A to B and it owed a lot to opportunities and circumstances. At your age, could I have imagined that I would one day end up being the Swiss ambassador in Tanzania? Was that planned? Was it even plannable? Not really, but in retrospect I realise that the nature and sequence of the numerous functions I held during my professional career made rather good sense, both in terms of accumulating ID know-how, and of my personal job satisfaction. Hence, I would recommend that you consider a number of my following principles in your own ID career path.

Field exposure

Maybe more than other careers, working in ID is an everlasting learning process. In terms of that process, arguably my most valuable experience was an assignment as chief technical advisor with an integrated rural development project in Honduras, early in my ID career. There I learnt – mostly by trial and error in an unfamiliar cultural context – how to build the social dynamics that lead to sustainable change, and how to plan and implement concrete projects within such dynamics. In all my subsequent functions, this early exposure to the multi-sectoral realities on the ground, and of working as a member of a team of local professionals, proved to be an extremely robust and durable practical guidance. Even towards the end of my career some 30 years later, the lessons learnt during my Honduran field exposure remained an essential reference for my more policy-oriented ID work.

Bilateral vs. multilateral aid

Whatever they may say, to effectively meet the world's big development challenges, aid is not the only – or even primary – trigger. Hence, to reach the necessary critical mass of influence (finance, know-how, policy) and to secure the momentum for sustained change, it is crucial that efforts be well coordinated between all ID actors, both public and private, both country to country and through multilateral channels. Where bilateral cooperation, including charities and NGOs, may be best at the grassroots work, multilateral actors, such as the specialised UN agencies and international finance institutions, may have an edge in coordinating policy interactions and in dealing with global public goods. My own experience in the multilateral world as a

Junior Professional Officer with the UN Development Programme (UNDP) helped me understand the respective comparative advantages and appreciate the positive effects of this informal division of labour, but also sharpened my awareness for overlaps and the waste and clumsiness of an increasingly overblown aid bureaucracy.

Operational work vs. advocacy

Your strongest drive at this stage may well be to go out to the "field" and to work on concrete development projects: to build bridges, eradicate malaria, train teachers, combat hunger, increase yields, promote gender equality, etc. But the success of your operational work hinges on there being a supportive policy and governance environment. As your experience in operational development work grows, you will become increasingly aware of the importance of non-operational aspects. To achieve systemic change – which is the goal that justifies the costly ID investment – you will quickly realise that building "islands of perfection" (i.e., stand-alone development projects) in the midst of an otherwise unchanged environment is not the solution. I am sure your attention will soon enough shift to the necessity of concomitant "policy dialogue" and advocacy. In recipient countries, advocacy is needed to create and sustain a political and governance framework that is conducive to the implementation of systemic ID interventions. In the donor countries themselves, ID advocacy is equally important, as a tool to convince taxpayers and voters, members of parliament, and public opinion of the usefulness and effectiveness of aid.

Development vs. humanitarian aid

Having been a developmental professional throughout my ID career, it was only after retirement that I got the opportunity to work in humanitarian aid, when I spent four months as acting resident director for the Swiss humanitarian programme in the Middle East. From that glimpse into this other branch of ID, could I imagine dedicating my professional life to humanitarian aid? Frankly speaking, I'm not sure. Here's what's at stake and what you should consider for your ID career. Humanitarian aid is about life, survival, safety, relief – an extremely noble and humanely rewarding commitment. Challenges are urgent; reactions must be immediate. Considerations of cost and efficiency may not always be first on your mind. And, yes, it can be frustrating to spend your energy trying to mend the misery perpetrated by man-made catastrophes, without having the tools to address the root causes of such catastrophes. In contrast, development is a long-term endeavour, aimed at systemic change with sustainability, scalability, and efficiency, often without immediately discernible results and needing corrective action along the way. Two quite different tasks in ID – up to you to choose which suits you better.

Drivers and barriers of International Development

Over my 35 years as an ID hand in the most diverse functions, a series of thematic and methodological understandings and perceptions evolved to become cornerstones of my professional capacity. Those are among the things that I might have wished to know at your age, in order to be more focused and effective. That said, ID is not a precise science. It is subject to the constant whims of change. As such, in my view there has never been a single "exact" way to work on the challenges of development. While the purpose of writing this letter is to hand down some of my own relevant learnings for your inspiration, your most important source of knowledge will always be the lessons you and your colleagues will learn on the job. Thus, whatever you may want to keep and use from my input, this is not a blueprint!

An unequal partnership

"Partnership" is one of the most frequently used – and abused – terms in ID. It implies shared values and the willingness to join forces in pursuing common objectives. In the context of ID, such objectives target the transfer of knowledge and the management of socio-economic change. For us donors, the pillars of a good partnership are equality, reliability, transparency, and mutual accountability. But in the reality of development cooperation, is partnership truly a relationship between equals? Do my partners in Africa or Asia really share my understanding of what constitutes a good partnership? Do I understand what partnership means to them? Is there a hidden agenda? Are there implicit assumptions that may be cultural, and that we are not even aware of? Or – behold! – is it the money and power I embody as a donor that make local development actors seek my "partnership"? Don't forget, whether we like it or not, we representatives of wealthy donors are usually perceived as immensely rich and powerful. Maybe as a consequence, but quite unintentionally and even unconsciously, on the ground we often find ourselves working and socialising in the company of the local rich and mighty who may not share our interest in empowering the powerless.

Lost in translation

You may wonder why I emphasise these points, but during my ID career there was hardly one more tenacious obstacle to real partnership and sustainable development than the difference in culture and the resulting misunderstandings. Is a "yes" actually a "no"? Is a "tomorrow" a "never"? Is an "I don't know" actually an "I don't want you to know"? Is a "friend" also a "partner"? This may sound trivial, but you would not believe how many of my own misjudgements were due to such basic ambiguities. Hence, I cannot stress enough the need for you to constantly make sure that you understand and that you are understood. If possible, make an effort to learn the local language. Don't be rushed by overambitious logical frameworks, unrealistic critical paths, and the urge to spend approved budgets. Take your time and seek assistance to ensure that nothing is lost in translation . . .

Truth vs. might

ID and Aid are not "exact sciences". Again, this sounds trivial, but again, when choosing this career, you should be comfortable with this and be prepared to face endless discussions about the "right way". ID depends a lot on empirical knowledge. It is a lifelong learning exercise. Probably as a consequence, ID programmes are often strongly influenced by the particular likings – agendas – of stakeholders. What's more, in countries whose institutional frameworks are weak, and the principle of checks and balances is flawed, to depend on the preference of any particular group of stakeholders can easily lead to the distortion of ID objectives. Those in power may steer aid in accordance not with what's proven right, but pursuing their own interests to grab the benefits. As an ID professional you should be aware of this dichotomy between truth and might, and develop mechanisms that allow you to observe and correct any usurpation of development projects by the mighty. After all, the *raison d'être* of ID is to empower those in need, not to enhance the power of those already holding it.

The catwalk of paradigms

Is it a consequence of what I say above about the "exact science"? Or is it because ID professionals tend to be a particularly creative lot? Looking back on the 35 years I spent in ID, the amount of development fads and paradigms that came and went is simply staggering. Here's a selection – no claim for comprehensiveness: UN Development Decade, Whole of Government Approach, Millennium Development Goals, Sector Wide Approach, The Washington Consensus, Trade not Aid, The Limits of Growth, Public–Private Partnership, Basic Needs Approach, Integrated Rural Development, Structural Adjustment Programme, Highly Indebted Poor Countries Initiative, Global Compact, Paris Agenda, Trickle Down Effect, General Budget Support, The Quick Winners, The Bottom Billion, Leave No One Behind, Failed States, Sustainable Development Goals, Planetary Boundaries, Aid Architecture, Aid Harmonisation, Aid Conditionality, South–South Cooperation, Holistic Development – you name it! And the process is ongoing, alas not necessarily in the direction of more clarity and easier manageability. An example: the UN's erstwhile eight Millennium Goals provided an easily manageable, albeit somewhat simplistic thematic guidance for the global ID community from 2000 to 2015. They served as a useful reference for prioritising ID resources on the most urgent needs, without however addressing the challenges of governance and the framework conditions. The subsequent

Sustainable Development Goals (SDGs), which were defined by the UN following a lengthy process, pretend to be much more holistic. Indeed, there is hardly an aspect of development that you won't find included among its 17 goals and 169 targets, from eradicating extreme poverty to halving food waste. Looking at their complexity and sheer number, I fear that the SDGs will be tricky to implement and monitor, and will not be easily used for awareness building and advocacy.

The best job in the world?

Dear Adrian, this has become a much longer letter than I intended, and I could easily carry on. There is so much to be said about ID – take the length of the letter as a token for the continued enthusiasm I feel for it. I also realise that, instead of praising the ID cause and highlighting the success stories of cooperation, I may have put too much emphasis on obstacles and caveats. Don't be discouraged. Build your ID career with dedication, an open spirit, and a pinch of humility. Knowing you, the challenges I line up will enhance your motivation rather than stifle it. As for me, when I look back, I'm grateful for that decisive and enlightening experience in Colombia 50 years ago, and to have chosen a career in ID – it turned out to be the most fascinating job I could imagine.

Sincerely yours, your older self

Adrian was formerly the Swiss Ambassador to Tanzania and Assistant Director General of the Swiss Agency for Development and Cooperation (SDC). While with the SDC, he was also Head of the Bilateral Development Cooperation Department, Resident Country Director, Division Head, Project Manager, and Project Officer at various points. Beyond the Swiss Government, he also worked as a Junior Professional Officer for the United Nations Development Program and as a consultant for a research project for the World Bank. Adrian obtained his Master's Degree in Economics from Zurich University and proceeded with his postgraduate studies on development policy at the Federal Institute of Technology in Zurich. He is retired and lives in Bern, Switzerland.

13

Be true to yourself – take risks

Brian Atwood

Dear Brian,

How many times on this journey have you half jokingly told others: "I don't really know what I want to be when I grow up!" As the years moved on there was increasing irony in that statement. Yet there was also an important lesson: you never know what fate will bring you.

It takes courage to be oneself. Your sense of self may have emanated from the myths your mother led you to believe – that despite your very ordinary middle class background, you were a descendent of Myles Standish of *Mayflower* fame, and of an aristocratic family that escaped from revolutionary France. There was scant evidence of this, but out of myths grow self-belief. And, as you know, that self-belief was fragile in your formative years. And, as you also know, that idealistic boy was to overcome his insecurities and use them as motivation to reach beyond a humble beginning, fueled by the teachings of his parents and his religion that the highest calling was social justice and public service.

An introduction to the world

It can be hard to pinpoint why things are as they are. However, an early turning point was your selection at the age of 16 to be an American Field Service exchange student to Luxembourg. You had lived a relatively sheltered life before you met your AFS "brother", Alex Lutgen. He gave you a lesson that persists to this day. You were bragging about your home country when one day Alex became exasperated: "You Americans are the same as the Soviets." You were distraught. "How could you say that about America? We are a democracy!" His reply has remained with you: "But you both want to dominate us." That comment contained a lesson: that citizens of smaller countries – of all countries – are proud of their history. Luxembourgers had seen enough of those who wanted to dominate them.

You may not have known in 1959 what you wanted to be, but from those formative experiences in Luxembourg you knew that it would be a life in

DOI: 10.4324/9781003260929-17

the international arena. You were fortunate in later years to represent your country, which is a privilege afforded to so few. You quickly realised what Alex might attest: that the United States' relationship with most countries is of the love–hate variety. You were also to learn early on that respect for those of other societies accentuated the positive.

Your first posting in the US Foreign Service was in Africa. Based in Abidjan, Côte D'Ivoire, you had an opportunity to witness first-hand the effects of colonialism and poverty. While there, you also witnessed something else: the importance and potential impact of effective development assistance. A friend, who was working with the US Agency of International Development (USAID), was tasked with immunising Ivorians against the smallpox virus: a deadly infectious disease that was claiming the lives of many Ivorians but which had not broken out at home since the late 1940s, thanks to the success of vaccination. The necessity was both pressing and, in some ways, personally felt. You received that inoculation as a child and recall your parents describing the horrible disease it would guard against. Your friend and the agency with which he worked was saving the lives of the less fortunate – a worthy vocation. Little did you know then that one day you would often cite the eradication of smallpox as a major triumph of the government agency you ran. In fact, that same agency: USAID.

Protecting USAID

In the best of times, leading a large foreign aid agency is a test. The early 1990s, at the end of the Cold War when fiscal conservatives expected a peace dividend, were not the best of times. How do I know this? I was confirmed by the Senate as Administrator of USAID in May 1993.

In the last year of his administration, President George H. W. Bush appointed a bipartisan commission headed by his friend, George Ferris. The Ferris report was highly critical of USAID management and recommended that the Agency be merged into the State Department. That contradicted a transition study by career State officers, but it was now out there and you felt it had to be refuted.

The first step was to create a team of presidential appointees and senior executives who knew development, the Department of State, and Capitol Hill. Many had been congressional staffers. Most had worked at State and all had expertise respected by the career professionals.

As you brought your experienced team together, the next task was to make political and strategic sense out of the many things the Agency did. One report said that USAID had 33 strategic goals. That made no sense politically, and it wasn't very strategic either. You asked your policy team to produce a "white paper" that would limit the Agency's strategic objectives to five broad categories. You also created an Office of Transition Initiatives, the purpose of which was to encourage reconciliation to diffuse an increasing number of post-conflict situations.

A year later, the structural and policy reforms were mostly in place and you invited the Ferris Commission in for a briefing. Later that day George Ferris issued a statement declaring the reforms "the most dramatic transformation of a government agency he had seen". He also rescinded his recommendation that the Agency be merged with the State Department. That, and an award from Vice President Gore's "Reinventing Government" initiative, gave the Agency a strong defence when an effort was made just a year later by the new Chair of the Senate Foreign Relations Committee, Jesse Helms, to merge USAID into State.

The merger battle that ensued would come to define your government career. The heads of the other two agencies to be merged within State, the US Information Agency and the Arms Control and Disarmament Agency, agreed to try to make it work. You believed that moving USAID into State would be bad for both entities. In the end the Vice President made the decision to leave USAID where it was – as an independent agency. Of course, these pressures and competing worldviews are not unique to the United States, as the recent merger of the UK Department of International Development into the Foreign and Commonwealth Office would confirm.

The reform efforts, and your stubborn persistence, saved the Agency. It wasn't a walk in the park as you faced opposition from colleagues at the State Department and at one point had to manage a reduction in workforce. Those who understood the importance of development cooperation appreciated your efforts, but you had acquired a reputation that was very unlike your real persona. The outside world may have seen you as obstinate and unyielding, but you were uncomfortable in this posture. If a compromise were available, you would have considered it. However, as you saw it, the battle was over preserving a vital humanitarian mission – development cooperation – not just a bureaucracy.

Leading USAID

Of your many visits to USAID missions, one two-week trip gained more attention than any other. After first meeting with the Israeli Prime Minister Yitzhak Rabin and Foreign Minister Shimon Peres, you travelled to Gaza to meet with Yasir Arafat two weeks after his return from Tunisia. Returning to Tel Aviv that evening, you met with the Israeli press. They noted that a monument to a housing complex USAID had donated to the Palestinian authority used the word "president" to refer to Chairman Arafat. You called it a "poor translation"; that seemed to deflate the controversy.

That evening CNN led with a new story out of Rwanda. An exodus of Hutu refugees was pouring into Goma in Eastern Zaire. The White House asked you to get to Goma as quickly as possible to observe the impending disaster. Two days later you were in Nairobi, Kenya arranging to fly to Goma on a World Food Program plane. As you approached the small Goma airport you could see hundreds of refugees on the tarmac. The plane did a flyover to scatter the crowd so it could land.

When finally on the ground the effects of the genocide in Rwanda could be seen in the faces of the two million people who had escaped. Intermingled with the innocents were the Hutu military and the dreaded Interahamwe, the perpetrators of the genocide. The most indelible of impressions were in the faces of the dispossessed children, their parents killed, their eyes deadened by the pain they had experienced. You spent hours viewing the disaster in a Red Cross vehicle and visiting the thoroughly inadequate facilities set up to provide relief. On your way back to the airport you ran into Lionel Rosenblatt, President of Refugees International. He underscored the seriousness of the situation and urged you to call for a humanitarian intervention by the US military.

Returning to Nairobi, the White House asked you to respond to requests for television interviews. You spent hours in a studio as your press person lined up interview after interview. You described in vivid terms what these people were facing: impending disease and starvation. You knew that it would be controversial, but you said you would recommend to the President that the US military be deployed. That created quite a stir in Washington as the Defense Department wasn't enamored with the idea, in part because of the legacy of the US military's operation in Mogadishu, Somalia in 1993.

In the last interview of the day, late night host Ted Koppell told you that the Pentagon was quite upset and asked you to comment. You said that you had been sent as a presidential emissary to make recommendations and that is what was needed. Koppell cut that out of the interview as a favor, but you weren't sure what you would face when you got home. When you returned, you were ushered into the Oval Office to brief the President. You didn't know it at the time, but the decision had already been made to send the military to Goma. You walked out with the President and he made the announcement. Thousands of lives would be saved.

Why did you do it? There seemed no other choice and Rosenblatt's comment had given you courage. Those poor children with the dead eyes were haunting. Anyone with a heart would have to respond to that. There seemed to be no time for a bureaucratic decision process.

Moving on

The six years with USAID passed quickly. In December 1998, President Clinton nominated you to be the US Ambassador to Brazil. Yet politics is a complicated arena and people have long memories. Chairman Helms, still perturbed that you opposed merging USAID into State, refused to give you a hearing. While one change was blocked, others were under way. In anticipation of your move to South America, a new Administrator had been named as your replacement. Helms' resistance meant that you were forced to ask the President to withdraw your nomination for Brazil. You remained in place at USAID and became the humanitarian coordinator for the Kosovo crisis, visiting refugee camps in Macedonia and Albania.

You ended up resigning from the administration that July. It wasn't the end you had hoped for, but some things are worth the sacrifice. Diplomacy requires resources, but investments in long-term development eventually would have been lost had you capitulated to Helms. Abandoning the Agency and its development partners was for you not an option; it was not the legacy you wanted.

In reflection, the most satisfying part of the job was the "development diplomacy" you conducted with other donors and USAID's partners. Encouraged by the success of honing USAID's strategic goals several years earlier, you urged your colleagues at a 1994 High Level meeting of the OECD Development Assistance Committee (DAC) to consider issuing a political statement on the goals of the donor community.

Two years later, in 1996, the report was released. Called "Shaping the 21st Century: The Contribution of Development Cooperation", the goals in that report would be adopted as the UN Millennium Development Goals in 2001. The MDGs evolved in 2015 into the universal Sustainable Development Goals. Having tangible goals meant that governments could set targets and measure results.

It is possible that the inherent logic of creating global goals would have seen them emerge over time. However, your efforts to take your USAID goals exercise forward on the global level most likely advanced the timetable. Many were engaged in this enterprise, but you certainly didn't object when one publication referred to you as "the father of the MDGs".

Of course, the politics and technical realities of "development" are tightly intertwined. Your time as President of the National Democratic Institute and, later, Under Secretary of State for Management had allowed you to further develop your relationships on Capitol Hill, while providing invaluable opportunities to pursue democracy-related dividends in Eastern Europe, the Philippines, and Chile, and, from an administrative perspective, to gain the skills and understanding of internal management systems. These insights and experiences mattered. Had you not had the opportunity of working in the political arena, you might not have approached your USAID experience the same way. Development work is complex. It is broken down into sectors and each has a language intelligible to its practitioners but not always to the outside world. Setting goals that were politically salient produced the desired effect. In the decade following the UN's acceptance of the MDGs, Official Development Assistance increased by 50%. Equally important, results measurement became a vital accountability indicator. The recipients of development were the real winners.

Reflections

Might Alex be proud – be reassured, perhaps – by what the young Brian has become? I hope so but one can never be 100% sure. Self-promotion is awkward, after all. But what if I were to offer advice to others, as Alex guided me all those years ago? Well, be generous of your time and of your spirit, and be courageous. In all humility, you have been honest and open with others to a fault, willing to take risks, persistent when you thought you were right, open to criticism, political in the positive sense of the word, and very lucky. These qualities (plus the luck) are valuable and should be both remembered and nurtured.

Of course, you never did it alone. You were raised with a strong ethical foundation and had a loving and supportive family. You chose your colleagues well, and your superiors were excellent role models. Your network was global and you made tangible use of each of your experiences. You retained your optimism despite the setbacks. You quite surprisingly were able to influence issues on a global scale and enhance the lives of less fortunate human beings. The broader message to convey here is "If I could do that, so can you". There is more to be done, so keep applying these lessons!

Brian is a Senior Fellow for Public and International Affairs at Brown University's Thomas Watson Institute for International and Public Affairs, and Professor Emeritus at the University of Minnesota's Hubert H Humphrey School of Public Affairs. He served for six years as Administrator of the US Agency for International Development (USAID) during the Administration of President William Clinton. In the Clinton Administration, Brian led the transition team at the State Department and was Under Secretary of State for Management prior to his appointment as head of USAID. From 2010 to 2012, he was the member-elected Chair of the Development Assistance Committee of the Organization of Economic Cooperation and Development (OECD). He lives in the USA.

14

Insist and persist

Fekitamoeloa Katoa 'Utoikamanu

Dear Fekita,

Here you are. You sure look older – your daughter is now the age you are when your exciting, challenging, and just so enriching journey started. Has anything really changed other than the colour of your hair?

The little much-loved girl you were when you grew up on an island in the vast Pacific region last century – one without mobile phones, without a World Wide Web, without microwaves and all that – never imagined all the blessings in her life. She certainly never imagined that one day she would be working for the United Nations and then become her country's first ever female Minister of Foreign Affairs. As they say, it's all in the journey and how we travel the journey by staying true to ourselves.

Know that you will be the first to do much that you do and that you will have to overcome many setbacks. Do not be afraid. Your path will require determination, courage, resilience, insistence, and persistence.

You are lucky to have parents who know how important education is, regardless of gender or social class. They know that their three daughters, of whom you're the eldest, should be self-sufficient. They want you to find your own path. And that will mean taking risks, insisting, and truly finding your own paths. You know how systems too often assign you a role in life before you've even had a chance to begin a journey. You want your own journey.

There you are growing up in the only remaining kingdom in the Pacific. Society is governed by strong cultural and social practices. Being part of a community prevails over being an individual. Education will be your ticket to breakthrough. This, and the love, encouragement, and support of your parents, extended family, and friends.

You will apply for a scholarship to study for a Bachelor of Commerce in Economics – the first time for a woman in your country to do so in an area dominated by men. Instead of encouraging you, the scholarship panel will tell you to level down and apply for a diploma in accounting. Once again, our parents will encourage you to believe in yourself, as they do by making efforts to pay for your studies.

DOI: 10.4324/9781003260929-18

You will shatter a ceiling when you graduate with your first degree, showing that a woman can indeed successfully study economics! It will lead to your scholarship for your postgraduate studies. The time will then come to give back to your country, Tonga.

Do you remember how in that last century (as it was then), so many professionals in your first job were women?! No, they will not work in education or social services. They, like you, will be with the Central Planning Department. You will work with macro-economic projections and do so across all sectors. You will coordinate aid programs and act as the Secretariat to the Cabinet subcommittee on Development Coordination.

You will not just work together. You will be a team of women – a team of young professionals, support staff, and cleaners, and you all want to make a difference for people. You will you forge lasting friendships. Look out for the young German woman who will join you. There is every reason why you and she will remain strangers. Yet you will not. You will find that you are both idealistic, that you want to make a difference, that your differences will make the exchange richer, and that almost four decades later your friendship will remain alive.

The two of you will work on something so new it will raise eyebrows. That was the first integrated regional development plan for the Vavau region. The plan will be formulated by listening to the people from the region. The approach will work well, and you will become the Secretary for the Vavau Regional Development Committee. This approach will take hold and the integrated regional development approach will be replicated in each of the other regional groups. Yet another ceiling shattered.

This experience will teach you to engage with people, with all sectors and development partners. Intuitively you knew that it was the only way to ensure results, sustainability, and efficient aid coordination. You will become a member of the aid negotiation teams, leading negotiations with bilateral and multilateral partners and establishing many national, regional, and even international networks.

Remember to observe, listen, and keep learning. You will learn from experienced diplomats and leaders. Watch how they engage at national, bilateral, and multilateral levels. The journey will be enriching, and you will become a member of Tonga's delegation to regional leaders' meetings. You will attend multilateral meetings, including the negotiation by the ACP Group of countries of the Lomé III, Lomé IV, and Cotonou Agreements with the EU. You will actively participate in such meetings because you love your country and its people. You will want to contribute. You will take the lead in consultations with civil society and other stakeholders and the private sector.

Participation, mainstreaming, and sustainability were not theoretical concepts to you in your early career and that will never change. It is all in doing, and doing all the while with the support and encouragement of your family and, in time, your own family. Ego and unbridled career desires will not come into it. It was and it remains about beliefs.

In time, you will experience another first. You will become the first woman to take the post of Permanent Representative to the United Nations, with concurrent accreditation as Ambassador to the United States, Cuba, and Venezuela, and High Commissioner to Canada. Later, you will uproot your family and write a truly new chapter once again, assuming the Chair of the Pacific Small Island States. There you will lead the work to bring the topic of climate change and its security implications to the Security Council.

In your first meetings you will be welcomed somewhat sceptically. A number of states will ask you, "why do you want to take this to the Security Council? Do you want the peacekeepers to stop the water from going onto the islands?". Once more, this will strengthen your resolve. As a group, as a team, the islanders will come together and reaffirm that this issue is critical – a matter certainly of livelihood, if not life.

The feeling of this being a "life or death issue" will make you determined. However, a spoiler alert: you will not be fully successful in your efforts to get this issue to the attention of the Security Council. Nonetheless, you will negotiate and submit a resolution on "Climate Change and its possible security implication" and this will be adopted A/Res/63/281 by the General Assembly in 2009.

Your country, Tonga, will be the first country from the Pacific region to submit a report and undergo the Universal Periodic Review process with the Human Rights Council in Geneva. You will lead the technical team and field all the questions during the discussions on Tonga's report. The Tonga session will become a model for preparing other Pacific countries for their sessions.

And then it will be time to move once again. You will take up the post of Deputy Director General and Director of Education, Training and Human Development of the Pacific Community. The Community is comprised of all 22 Pacific islands countries, trusts, and territories, and the four metropolitan members: New Zealand, Australia, the United States, and France. During this time, you will also serve as Deputy Pro Chancellor and Deputy Chair of Council and, for 11 months, the Acting Pro Chancellor of the University of the South Pacific.

This may look like a busy life. It is. Yet people and their hopes, dreams, disappointments, and struggles will remain the guiding line of your life. Never forget that it is a privilege to champion gender equality, human rights, culture, and youth in the Pacific region. And through it all you will remain committed to walk the talk, turning words about reform into lived reality. You will come to understand how difficult it is to change behaviours. You will learn many lessons.

One day, after all the observing, the setbacks, the listening, the learning, and the experiences, something will happen that you have never planned for: you will become the High Representative and Under-Secretary-General for the Least Developed Countries: Landlocked Developing Countries and Small Island States. You, a woman from a small state; you, the first-ever woman from the Pacific islands will take on the next challenge. You will draw strength from your foundations: the road you have travelled to that point and the unwavering support from family and friends. You will become a champion – an advocate – for the 46 Least Developed Countries (LDCs), 32 Landlocked Developing Countries (LLDCs), and 38 Small Island Developing States (SIDS). Though people across those 116 countries face their own unique sets of challenges as they walk their hopeful path to sustainable development, all are bound by the same need: for the internationally agreed goals to be realised. You will also become an international gender champion. A National Adaptation Plans champion. And a Paris 21 champion for statistical development.

Now, you are here: the Minister of Foreign Affairs for your country and again, the first woman ever in this position. Suddenly, though, it seems all the roads travelled make sense. They have prepared you for the biggest responsibility and challenge yet.

Yes, you have met Heads of State and Heads of Governments; Ministers; CEOs; representatives of academic institutions; civil society; private sector leaders; and development partners. You have engaged with your colleagues from other UN agencies and international and regional organisations. Yet, there is a constant. It is about observing, listening, bringing people together, helping find direction and solutions, helping to move forward, and believing in what you do. It is about *insisting* and *persisting* for people and their futures.

By now, you know you no longer have abundant time ahead of you as was once the case, but you are grateful for the love, friendships, luck, and meaning the road travelled has given you. Yes, the hair changed colour, but the heart and mind remain as young as ever full of hope now for the young and the desire to do the best you can for them and your country.

Fekitamoeloa Katoa 'Utoikamanu is a Tongan civil servant, diplomat, and Cabinet Minister currently serving as Tonga's Minister of Foreign Affairs. From 2005 to 2009 she was Tonga's permanent ambassador to the United Nations, and from 2017 to 2021 she was United Nations High Representative for the Least Developed Countries, Landlocked Developing Countries, and Small Island Developing States. She lives in Nuku'alofa, Tonga.

15

Who should be allowed to work in international development?

Fernando Damazio dos Santos

Dear future Fernando,

My head went to familiar and unvisited places and different points in time as I try to reach you. As I hope this letter reaches you, I will just give up guessing what our future will be like. I thought long and hard about what I might share with my older self. So, without the benefit of hindsight that is available when writing to one's younger self, I will humbly try to offer you something from the past – a kind reminder of your ideals and position as of now. You may change. You are more than allowed to change. Actually, you are *encouraged* to change. As I am trying to become you, I should not idealise you, just as I don't need to follow my own or anyone's expectations from the past. If that had happened, I should have stayed in the little beach town in southern Brazil. That need to challenge both myself and the status quo raises one question: who should be able to bring positive change to the world? Who can be an international development practitioner? I sincerely hope you can view this letter as a tender intersection in time with me, your younger self.

I am so curious about what is about to come! And that makes imparting advice and wisdom to someone in the future difficult. I can hardly resist asking about your – our – future. Are you still often moving to different countries? What moves you now? Have you found your purpose? Is it to help people or to understand yourself? Maybe it can and should be both. Is your purpose one that makes you proud? Does it give you peace of mind when you go to bed with that cheerful smile? Or can we finally agree that "purpose" is not necessarily a thing to be overly concerned about?

What kind of work do you do now? What is the future of international development practice where/when you are now? And climate change and the environment? How do you look back on your time in Malmö and Lund? Don't tell me you finally learned how to deal with cold, dark, Swedish winters. I think I can assume you still cherish your time and friends from Jo'burg, despite surviving an inexplicable and frightening COVID-19 Delta variant

DOI: 10.4324/9781003260929-19

infection. Where are you right now? Just give me a tip – are you saluting people with "läget", "howzit", or "tudo bem"? Or maybe another expression? There are so many questions I would love to ask you, and yet too many decisions to make here and now.

As I write this letter, I am preparing to move to my next post in Angola. Do you have any advice for me? Unfortunately, the wisdom of hindsight is not available to me yet. However, I/we need to move on, game on, but if I do anything that isn't ideal, please remember all the pressure I am under right now. And most of it comes from within. I need to develop my career, publish academic articles, pursue additional courses and licences. I must present myself assertively. I must be prepared, thoughtful, strategic. I must possess many skills that will require decades to hone; however, I need to be ready and perform now. Oh, and I must also relax, have a healthy life, enjoy friends, nurture romances, and establish a family (did we?). With this simple recipe you will have a brilliant career, they say.

Hmmm . . . what's a brilliant career? And is there a feasible brilliant career as an international development practitioner for a gay cisgender man from Brazil? And one who comes from a family that has no academic degrees? Isn't it too much to expect of yourself? You were the first one in your family to attend a university and yet, you earned an MSc degree from one of the most traditional universities in Sweden, one of the top 100 in the world. Isn't it enough for you? Maybe you should stop this international dream and go back to your roots and what others expect of you . . .

Wait, go back to where? So, on that part, I think I may have some answers – answers that offer the motivation to keep moving on. You have tried. You have *tried* to stay and live to your expected reality and even improve it. You have *tried* to fit in but you could not, because of the ones you love and the unapologetical way of being you – a proud gay man, "viado". *Do not forget this*!

Now, let's face it, you were not willing to pay the price of giving up on yourself to fit in on what was initially available to you. In your hometown of Imbituba, you would be expected to pretend to be straight so you could access better jobs or be proudly gay and face social stigma and economic discrimination. I am glad that I did not fit in, and that I can now contribute to dismantling this kind of oppression in other contexts for sexual and gender diverse people. And let's be honest, I am and you were a curious and brave – almost crazy – person, and perhaps too much so to stay in that small beach town . . . even though we did not know where we were heading.

Now the question is, Future Fernando, have you fitted into the international development sector? Did the sector allow you to fit in? What strategies have worked for you? Please tell me! I'm not sure if you are as accomplished and well connected as some of your colleagues you admire. Yet, what I hope for you is that you are focused on things that make you sleep well and with a slight smile on your face after a well-worked day. That when you go to bed, you sleep tired but satisfied with what you're doing. Whatever it is, wherever you find it.

I hope I'm on that pathway. With my stubborn determination to realize myself as both a person and a professional, I have moved closer to amazing people and opportunities. I have just finished my Masters in Sweden and lived in Johannesburg where I did an amazing internship. This led to joining a diversity-affirming team, spending some quality time in the Caribbean with a good old friend and finally reaching our hometown in southern Brazil after two and a half years away (on top of a pandemic).

I know how privileged I am to have such opportunities. I will do my best to not forget all the people who have helped me so far and who will do so in the future. Future Fernando, I hope you are generous in helping others. Not only to the ones you work for and with, but the newcomers, the young, the anxious and smart new development practitioners, and whoever else wants to make positive change. Be generous to me, to us, and to many more like us. You know how many times strangers and now friends helped you more than you could have asked for. Yeah, yeah, you must be busy, with more urgent things happening, unspent money to implement in the next few months and all, but your time and experience in the future are invaluable to people like me when needed the most.

Of course, generosity to yourself goes beyond eating healthy food and buying expensive gadgets. I know Fernando is an enthusiast of things working well and as planned, but life and work do not go as planned. And that is ok. As you know, Mom died when we were 11 years old and at a time when you were starting to realize your sexual orientation and the social implications of it. That was certainly a tragedy and a hard time. There have been (and I'm sure there will be) many other difficult moments in your life, including now. We survived, and I trust that you – we – will survive so many more. But hey, all of it also pushed us to be aware of our emotions and to work on how to communicate them to people, friends, work colleagues, and "beneficiaries". And they all have emotions, feelings, and histories too. Embrace it, do not forget this. If you have become a high-level expert staff or a freelance consultant meeting new people every few months, I hope you are mindful of your emotions and how to communicate them. I have experienced how often people in international development try to convince themselves they are objective, non-emotional productive robots during work time or they simply throw their emotions violently at work colleagues, unaware of doing so. Future Fernando, please, work for a more empathetic workplace with your team; keep normalizing and incentivising therapy to your colleagues. You will work under pressure with people who have even more urgent needs, I can only imagine the stress that is coming, the mistakes we are going to make. Own them and learn from them. Try to not be so harsh to yourself or others. They are also doing their best and you don't know their current burden and history. Everybody is human just as you are, just try to understand them on their own terms.

And by identifying everybody as humans, Fernando, do not forget to behold the diversity in being human. And obviously in our case, we must shout

out loud to people in international development that the sector should be more inclusive of LGBTI people! People everywhere can be sexual and/or gender diverse: international development practitioners (staff, consultants, interns . . .), "beneficiaries", "target groups", partners, donors, members of consortia . . . I am not sure whether you will be working in the sector in the future and I hope the need for inclusivity decreases, but if you are, please be open to people in all their diversity and proveniences. Continue to be brave enough to strategically advocate for a more inclusive sector. So, yes Fernando, maybe try to understand results-based management, agile methods and all the new fancy approaches and buzzwords to come. But, above all, I trust that you will remember that the most important thing is the people: their priorities, feelings, needs, and humanity. Maybe you should focus on this idealistic perspective when bored by the manuals and bureaucracies ahead . . .

Sorry, time is up. I need to go back to making decisions now, so you can make your own decisions in the future and try to have those better sleep nights. I hope this letter reminds you of your doubts and ideals; the good and bad memories; and, more importantly, makes you go forward and realize yourself. In fact, ourselves. You and me. We are happening now, via this letter. We can have the certainty of being alive, being able and deserving to be happy. So many decisions in the future, so much future to come, within or outside "international development". No matter what scale, please, always try to bring positive change for all!

Fernando is an international development practitioner and researcher with a special interest in advocating for the rights and inclusion of marginalized people and communities. He thrives in multi-stakeholder initiatives that aim to bring change at national, regional, and international levels. His experience includes working with LGBTIQ+ people in Sub-Saharan Africa, LGBTIQ+ asylum seekers and refugees in Europe, and refugees and youth in South America, while engaged by international organizations, non-governmental organizations, and government agencies. He has an MSc in International Development and Management from Lund University, Sweden, where he was a Swedish Institute Global Professional scholar. He has received scholarships and fellowships from Global Affairs Canada, DAAD, and French Delegation for Regional Cooperation in Southern Cone and Brazil. He is currently based in Luanda, Angola.

16 Charting a course for change

Hannah Birdsey

Dear Younger Me,

I see you there, younger me, no real plan to speak of, wondering how to put an extended education in political science to some sort of remunerated use. You don't yet know that you are going to be lucky. Lucky to find an entry point to a career so rich in diversity that 20 years later you will struggle to find the common themes, the useful guideposts, the meaningful lessons. Any lesson you capture is likely to have its counterpoints, and in a few years, be regarded as obsolete, having failed to take into account this factor or that contextual shift.

So maybe that is a good place to start. International development is the business of change – incentivising change, accelerating change, shaping change – so it is perhaps unsurprising that the theory, the practice, the drivers themselves also continue to change and evolve. It appeals to people who are comfortable with change, who embrace it as an opportunity to learn, to improve, to wonder. I think that is you, so let's talk about that for a moment.

International development is an environment where knowledge and practice are evolving and contested. Against this backdrop, some people respond by seeking out and espousing immutable rules that "should" work (even, sometimes, in the face of several years' evidence to the contrary), while others wallow in well-intentioned chaos and take a "something is better than nothing" approach to implementation. You will encounter both, but these are extremes and of course you will also see a wide range in-between.

Let me give you an example. In the course of a development relationship spanning decades, donor partners will, at times, channel more funds through the host government's systems. The donors will be motivated by the voices calling for systemic change, the research showing that weak states can be undermined by development efforts that are poorly coordinated or not "owned" by government, and the need to demonstrate "good practice". At other times, the cycle will swing back in favour of shorter-term and quantifiable results, delivered by the most direct, flexible, and innovative means possible. Non-government partners will come to the fore and success will be measured, in part, by the number of private sector or community partners

DOI: 10.4324/9781003260929-20

delivering "on-the-ground" programs. Nothing specific or identifiable in the context, in the country itself, will trigger these cyclical changes or suggest that one approach is always going to deliver inherently better development outcomes than the other, but the pendulum will swing back and forth, struggling to land between these competing truths.

For you, seeking to make some small but effective contribution, the swing will at times induce nausea, particularly in contexts where change is slow and results are hard won, and the temptation to question your own judgement (or the challenge of responding to entirely legitimate questioning from others) is real. Perhaps all you can do is respond to each line of questioning in a genuine spirit of enquiry, and avoid defensiveness. In so doing, you will best navigate a particular context, or a specific set of objectives and partners. You will constantly learn from your and others' successes and failures and adapt your own approach. You will learn to demand much more rigour in the evidence that is presented to inform your decisions.

Development occurs in complex, ever evolving, and sometimes ill-understood systems. These include systems of government, of community, of health service delivery, and of global trade networks. Change doesn't always take the pathway or even the form we anticipate. Results can be unexpected. But learning to distinguish between the intrinsically complex and the unnecessarily complicated will be vital and require enduring attention. There are times when clear, measurable results matter. Such as when you are trying to build a constituency for public funding of social impact. There are times when these results will prove elusive, when the change being sought is long term and difficult to measure, but none the less important (indeed possibly more so).

. . .

Dear younger me, the career pathways and experiences in international development vary almost with the individual. In your case, you will spend much of your time working for government, and with governments, in the context of Official Development Assistance. From here, you will see significant opportunities to allocate resources, incentivise action from a diverse set of stakeholders, and drive policy choices. You will also need to be guided at all times by the domestic, security, foreign, and other policy settings of your own government, which can be an enabling factor but also places limits on what is possible, or elevates certain priorities over others in the competition for scarce resources.

The development world will be subject to significant disruption during your career and the effects will at times be dramatic. Even personal. Some of these disruptions will be widespread, far-reaching, and positive, such as the shift from a narrower focus on ODA to a broader engagement with development finance in all possible forms and from all possible sources. Some will be highly contested across different stakeholders, such as the role of ODA in responding to or shaping the strategic interests and influence of nation states. Your skills will need to evolve to meet these new demands. But at all times, you will be conscious that you are in so many respects an ancillary player, as the heft required to drive real change in any country is always home-grown.

. . .

Dear younger me, you will have children, a family. You will be incredibly fortunate to have a partner that is as invested as you are in all the facets of raising those kids, from the emotional to the deeply practical. You will develop skills in juggling. At times your skills will fail you and something will break (or maybe bounce!). You will accept the fact that your children will never go to school in a lovingly handmade Book Week character costume (which will be due to your complete absence of sewing skills and highly questionable output of anything classified as "craft" as much as general busy-ness) and will survive school hunger pangs on hastily made sandwiches, bananas (the pre-packaged fruit!), and packets of crackers. You will find it much harder to accept the times you weren't there when they fell over/won an award/went to the dentist/needed mummy to sing them to sleep. You will need to compromise to achieve some sort of balance between the demand for stability and continuity (from a high-pitched yet clearly determined little voice) and the demands of your role. I'm writing this deep in the midst of this "muddling through" process so still have my fingers firmly crossed that all will turn out alright in the end.

. . .

Please don't forget to put yourself in the picture. Development is an inherently political process. It requires engagement in the allocation of resources and the distribution of power. In politicised settings, people have agency and you will find that to be true of your own experience. You will need to decide where to place your focus and energy, because it will have a material impact on the results your partners pursue, how funding is allocated, and whether women, young people, and people with disability are able to participate. There will be times when you will try and fail. There will be times when you will wish you had done more (particularly, in your case, on the issue of gender which will increasingly move to the centre for you as a critical domain for change). There will be much that is well outside your scope of influence, and you need to accept that with good humour. Of course, that is easier said than done and some compromises will feel uncomfortable.

. . .

Above all else, my dear, you will laugh with delight (often out loud) at the incredible richness of experience your international development career will bring. You really should try to avoid boring your friends at parties with endless tales of unexpected but delightful encounters with quirky humans, retrospectively entertaining near-misses, and breath-taking natural beauty. Of course, many of the amazing people you will meet and claim as friends will be just as eager to share their experiences. And you will delight in, and learn from, all these different perspectives. You will gain incredible access to ever-so-slightly-more than the usual tiny portion of this amazing world we cultivate and care for. You will be frustrated at your inability to do more to protect its people and its environment but the possibility that one day, in some small way, you can be part of a change for the better, will sustain you.

Regards,
Me
P.S. While we are chatting, can I just say that you should worry less and spend more time outdoors. Just a suggestion . . .

Hannah is a public policy and international development professional who has worked predominantly within government, overseeing bilateral humanitarian and development programs. She has lived and worked in Malaysia, Indonesia, and Papua New Guinea, leading diverse portfolios including governance, social policy, and economic growth programs. She holds a Master's in International Studies from the University of Sydney.

17 Pushing for change

Irina Schoulgin-Nyoni

Dear Irina,

I'm writing you this letter but I'm not sure when, or even if, it will reach you. And if you do get it, I'm wondering what state of mind you will be in. How would you feel about getting unsolicited advice from the outside world? I am aware that the reality you are living now is so intense. Absorbing you entirely. It is in many ways an overwhelming experience, demanding your full attention, your imagination, and your personal devotion – and you are enjoying every moment of it! Yet, I wonder what you are thinking about your survival in this ruthless international setting. I suspect you have now realised that being curious and able to generously share your thoughts and ideas is a talent that will take you places. With your openness and humour your surrounding will give you the attention you crave for and that enables you to gain influence. Because it is still influence you want, right? The last time I checked, that was the revelation that had dawned on you. When you are out there, in "the field", you see so many things that you wish to change – changes that should be easy to secure. And yet, you are repeatedly struck by how often the wrong people end up in the wrong places. How idealism and good will are crushed by cynicism and self-interest. How the decisions are taken so far away. Literally. In every way.

So, the ambition to gain influence is valid and the intentions are pure. To succeed in having a career, so that you can get to those places of influence, you must keep that curiosity that is part of your true personality. You must keep that openness to other ways and retain your genuine interest in people and in building relationships. Be clear and honest, and people will want to collaborate with you. It's true that they may still want that for different reasons, for what you represent or for the fact that you are a woman. Or both. But if you don't connect as a person it will not last anyway. So it is up to you to deal with the macho-men, the backstabbers and the cynicism, without losing your genuine personality and trusting ways. Although it will feel hopeless at times, and you will wonder whether you shouldn't be just as ruthless as some of the people you will meet . . . because, let's face it, 85% will most probably be men. You will be tempted to show them that you are

DOI: 10.4324/9781003260929-21

also capable of playing that game. Don't do it. In the long run it will be your ability to stay true to what you believe is fair and right that will bring you pride in yourself and self-respect. And that, in turn, is what will ensure you can stay genuine. A powerful tool indeed.

I started this letter doubting whether you were open to some advice, but I will take the risk and offer you some anyway. Well, I guess you have picked that up by now in any case. If you want to make a difference you need to stay humble to the complexity of doing just that. When you encounter those who tell you they have found the answer to peacebuilding and sustainable development (and you will meet those people, trust me) be aware! There is no one answer. You can choose to focus on one, perhaps two, fundamentals in which you believe strongly but don't forget that you are surrounded by those who are equally convinced that other ingredients are just as crucial to make the necessary changes.

It is often hard to see the links between your efforts in a certain area and results in the broader sense. That can be the overwhelming feeling when working in the field of human rights and democracy. Intellectually you can argue for it. You can find plenty of "proof" that sustainable development happens when people speak out, demand their rights, and push for transparency or participation. Yet, it is more complex than that. Respect for human rights and democratic principles could be a prerequisite for development. True. They might be non-negotiable too. At least to you. The challenge is, of course, that it is not so obvious to everyone. Or even a priority. What do you do then? You might realise that there are surprisingly few in your surroundings who genuinely try to understand different perspectives. Therefore, this is seemingly obvious, but I still would like to advise you to make sure you reach out and build alliances outside your group of "usual suspects". Seek those who are not your obvious "likeminded" and listen to them. Not that they will necessarily change your mind or position but so that you can understand what arguments might be helpful going forward.

To have a broad network from all regions of the world is worth all the time and effort it takes to build it. It is all about us, the individuals, in the end. When we respect each other, are willing to find honest compromises or sometimes simply agree to disagree, the chances are we move a little bit closer to a place where positive change can be achieved. You will ask yourself if you shouldn't rather be firm and defend what is right to the bitter end. Well, sometimes that might be the best cause of action, no matter how lonely you will be and how that will cost you a possible, although less satisfactory, constructive outcome. Small steps are not your thing. Sure. That expression "don't let the best be the enemy of the good" is really boring, I agree. Still, that might be the smartest course of action at times. Even when it means you will feel as though you are losing face. You will find yourself arguing for what is realistic rather than idealistic. Horrible thought, right?! Well, that might be as good as it gets, in that specific instance. In the slightly longer run, it must make sense though. You give some, you gain some. You can't do it all yourself, you need your alliances, even when it costs you.

Building broad alliances is a must in multilateral settings but it is equally important in bilateral ones. Most people will agree but, as I've already said, far from all act accordingly. I recall the positive surprise that often met me as I took the time to do courtesy calls outside my Western sphere when taking on a new posting. Or when I invited colleagues from other regions to meetings or working lunches and dinners. Sure, it gave me some goodwill and yes, it was generally nice, but mostly it made me so much wiser listening to them! All those different perspectives are important to at least try to understand your surroundings and settings. You don't have to agree, you just have to ask questions and be prepared to share your thoughts openly. That will help you to build trust. It will also offer you a good start in strategising for real. Identify your allies and what to look out for, draft your action plan, and grind your arguments. Not just because it's interesting and challenging and fun, but because it can lead to something real; something that can matter. And that is rewarding. Crucial alliances and successful negotiations, in what ever shape or form, can make that difference you crave for. I remember how I, after many ice-creams on a garden bench with a colleague from a country with diametrically opposed standpoints, managed to get silent approval on a Human Rights resolution that I think actually made a difference outside the bubble that the United Nations can be. Taking time to listen, to discuss, and to build some trust goes a long way. Not always but often enough.

I must, of course, touch upon the subject of feminism. As a Swedish woman you know what that means so there is no need to censor yourself to be polite. Brace yourself though. You will be surprised by how deep the discrimination and prejudice runs. How often you will be struck by the bluntness and behaviour of your male colleagues. The older ones are worse, for sure, but don't be fooled. It is so imbedded in our societies and structures that you might not realise it until afterwards. Men not seeing women. Men agreeing with men. The frequency with which I have seen my ideas and opinions being repeated and hijacked by a male colleague who is then subsequently quoted and patted on the back for the rest of a meeting. By all the other men that is. And they almost without exception outnumber the women. You will shrug your shoulders and decide to let it pass just because you don't really care about the acknowledgement and credit, but rather that things get done. But it will happen over and over again. There are ways of changing things though. One can be that you, ahead of meetings, agree with your (few) female colleagues to take the floor early and always express your strong support for the views of each other. It doesn't sound revolutionary, but I promise that it's effective. Another way is to offer to chair the meeting of course. That opens up a whole array of opportunities. One of my favourites is to be a hard but fair time-keeper. Because giving all participants equal time to speak is of course fair and reasonable. It is also almost always to the women's advantage since we have learnt to get to the point and to be clear and fast when finally getting a chance to speak. The difference in outcome can become painfully clear, at least to those who are the slightest bit willing to see it. Anyway, you will find your own ways, I am not worried about that. A lot is changing, and I am hopeful that the drive towards equality between women and men is happening. It might still have some bumps ahead but there is no stopping it.

I am so proud of you for taking the leap into the unknown and, let's be honest, dangerous field in which you are working. Looking back at it now, after having worked in different kinds of headquarters settings, I am not sure where I actually made the most difference in the end. Yes, it's undoubtedly true that advising political decision making is more likely to succeed when you are actually at the headquarters where those decisions are made. In a multilateral setting you can even work at getting other countries to join you in a common cause that can influence the lives of many. Or . . ., it can also mean absolutely nothing at all. Suddenly the distance between the "decision-centre" and the field can be just as hopelessly long! Especially as you come to realise that the majority of the "headquarter people" have no clue about the realities they are busy influencing. There are just as many wrong people at the wrong place there. Well, OK, I obviously don't know it all. I can only hope I stay humble to that fact. So, watch out for those who claim to have understood it all and have come up with the one solution and, of course, never let yourself be put down by those men who still can't treat you like an equal. That fight you cannot walk away from wherever you are.

Irina is currently the Head of the Africa Department at the Ministry for Foreign Affairs. She brings experience from several postings in Africa, most recently as Ambassador to Mozambique, Eswatini, and Madagascar, and as Deputy Permanent Representative at the Swedish Mission to the United Nations in New York and Minister Counsellor in Geneva. She has additional experience in multilateral contexts from her field experience with the United Nations missions in both the Côte d'Ivoire (ONUCI) and Angola (UNAVEM III).

As a diplomat in Luanda, Brasilia, Harare, and Monrovia, she gained experience in Swedish security policy and development cooperation, including Swedish participation in various peacekeeping operations, peacebuilding and post-conflict development processes. While at the Swedish Embassy in Zimbabwe and Angola she was also responsible for bilateral development support to the human rights and good governance sector.

18

Be what is needed, not what is expected

Jeffrey O'Malley

Apparently, one's sense of right and wrong emerges from a complex interaction of several different regions of the brain. It seems that serotonin has an impact as well, enhancing your negative feelings when you see that other people are being harmed. Whatever the neuroscience of it all, it seems that you had a heightened sense of moral outrage from quite a young age.

When you first tried to come out as a young gay man to Mom and Dad when you were 16, you didn't think you were being subtle. You left copies of *The Body Politic* lying prominently around your bedroom. Subtitle, "A magazine for gay liberation". But neither Mom nor Dad said anything. When you finally brought up the subject directly after your seventeenth birthday, they explained that they thought it was just "another of your causes". Supporting Steve Biko, the Sandinistas and the feminists. Condemning corporate polluters and the death penalty. Even supporting the queers, apparently.

It's 1982. You're twenty-one years old and serving as the first openly gay President of your university's student union. Now you're even making some contributions to *The Body Politic*, with your first column challenging their discourse about homosexuality in the Third World (or lack thereof). A few months ago, the American "Centers for Disease Control" published some reports about a mysterious disease attacking the immune systems of some gay men in Los Angeles.

You call yourself a socialist, and you're flirting pretty heavily with a few fringe far Left groups. But your hedonism will save you from that – your love of getting laid, getting high and getting down. You haven't yet read Amartya Sen, but when that book eventually comes out in 1999, its title will say it all: *Development as Freedom*. You're no Marxist. You're a liberal with a social conscience. You know that the world's riches and humanity's ingenuity should together be able to ensure that nobody is destitute or totally disempowered. And once every person's basic needs are met, individuals should be able to leverage their creativity, intelligence, resilience and ambition to build the lives they want, without arbitrary obstacles like their place of birth, their family's class or caste, their race, gender or sexuality.

DOI: 10.4324/9781003260929-22

Whether you are helping to build a social movement, participating in more formal politics, or contributing to organizations and institutions that are trying to advance "development", you are actively interfering in other people's lives. You know that already, so while you fervently believe in creating platforms for people to express their needs, priorities and ideas, you also know that the very processes of facilitation, participation and platform-building are themselves interventions, shaped by the values and biases of the facilitators as well as of the other participants.

At this point in your life, you pay a lot of attention to who is winning and losing in different kinds of economies, and why. You will keep caring about that, and it matters. But following up that Centers for Disease Control report, you're about to be hit by something much more personal and overwhelming.

Increasing numbers of gay men in the United States and Canada were getting sick with unusual cancers and lung diseases, and sometimes both at once. Illness seemed to progress rapidly and many were dying. It was first called GRID – gay related immunodeficiency. Nobody knew the cause of the disease, but patients often seemed to be connected by sexual networks, so there was a good chance that sex might somehow be involved. Over the same few months in 1982, small groups of gay men formed in both San Francisco and New York, to try to figure out what was going on and how to respond. Each group came up with the idea of reducing risk through use of condoms or avoidance of penetrative sex, promoted in pamphlets called "Play Fair!" and "How to have sex in an epidemic: one approach". Drawing on legacies of feminist organizing for women's health, these groups invented safe sex, an incredible accomplishment for which they were never awarded Nobel Prizes.

You're plugged into gay activism and gay media in Canada, so you're aware of these developments in real time. You start using condoms. By 1984, GRID will be renamed as AIDS, and you will work with a friend with a first generation MacIntosh computer to start producing your own safe sex promotion pamphlets. Handing out pamphlets, condoms and lubricant in bars, you will be met with a mixture of hostility, indifference and occasional appreciation. And despite these early prevention efforts, it won't take long for AIDS to enter your life, first through friends of friends, then roommates, and then your lover. In the meantime, your NGO work life will mix advocacy and solidarity work focused on Third World development with refugee resettlement. And some of those refugees from Haiti and Uganda will start showing up in Canada with AIDS – and they won't even be gay.

Friends and colleagues from university and work will warn you to not be so open about your homosexuality, as it will certainly be a barrier to get work in the development sector. The stigma in Canada is bad enough but no NGO would ever send an openly gay man to Africa. When the stigma of AIDS was laid on top of that, you would definitely be committing career suicide. And indeed, as your AIDS activism continued, with refugees as well as gay men, you would soon find yourself unemployed. Your warnings that AIDS wasn't just an issue for gay men – that it would end up being a serious epidemic in places like central Africa and the Caribbean – would fall on deaf ears.

AIDS will make you sad and depressed, but above all, it will make you angry. Angry that this disease seemed to hunt out and strike down the most marginalized. And even angrier that so many people in development and public health work seemed dismissive of it all. And that anger will fuel your energy, creativity and determination. All of a sudden, your solidarity with developing countries, your intellectual interests in development and poverty eradication, and your personal life would merge. Development work would no longer be about you somehow trying to help very different people, very far away. It would be about bonding with people sharing similar challenges, learning across borders, and mobilizing for action. So be confident. Your politics will be challenged from left and right, and you will often feel out of step with most others around you. Be confident when prioritizing the most marginalized, when truly believing in the universality and indivisibility of human rights, when arguing for choice for all. These are your values, they can guide you even when you find yourself in rotten institutions or processes, and nothing else will give you more strength and clarity of purpose.

Be aware. You're a white man from the Canadian middle class. Your father had a steady job (and then a steady pension) from the military. You were educated in good quality public schools, and you enjoyed swimming lessons, boy scouts, and summer vacations at wilderness lakes. Decades from now, there will be a lot of nuanced attention to privilege that goes beyond wealth – white privilege, male privilege. You benefitted from both of those, but above all, you benefited from Canadian privilege. Growing up in the 1960s and 1970s in a country where anything seemed possible, for almost anyone. Don't apologize or be defensive about your privilege, but be aware that most people in the world come from very different circumstances. While you work hard for your success, you started further ahead.

Be brave. Making progress requires taking risks. Success is born from multiple failures. For many people, life is too precarious to quit their jobs, to choose activism over security, to start up organizations, to tackle unpopular issues. But remember all those privileges you have. When you fall, you will fall back on your education, your family, your hometown, and if needed, on the Canadian welfare state. You can take risks that others can't. So you should.

Be impatient with people in power. Be patient with the poor and the marginalized. Force yourself to slow down and truly listen. But stay impatient in the face of injustice, especially when people in power deny their own privilege.

Be humble. Can you be confident, brave and impatient while somehow being humble at the same time? That will always be your biggest challenge, so force yourself to cultivate relationships and stay close to people who will challenge you, correct you, help you to learn and listen and change as needed.

Be yourself.

Jeff has worked at the intersection of public health, human rights and sustainable development for over 30 years. He is presently Senior Advisor, LGBTI Inclusion, Africa for the United Nations Development Programme (UNDP). Based in South Africa, he works in countries across Africa supporting efforts to promote social inclusion and human rights for sexual and gender minorities, contributing to public health and social protection.

19 Don't listen too carefully

Johannes Oljelund

Dear Johannes,

I'm writing to you from October 2020. I believe it's 1988 where you are. That is strange, isn't it? A letter from the future. A letter from your older self. A version of time travel is now possible. Albeit through the mail. When I first heard Botswana Post had come up with this possibility, I couldn't believe it. Letters through time? It must be a hoax. But as they say at Botswana Post, "We deliver, whatever, wherever".

The very existence of this letter proves that the world can change. It is a reminder of a very important lesson – that fundamental change is possible; very few truths remain forever. The world has changed enormously between where you are in 1988 and where I am in 2020.

On the grand geopolitical stage nations have come in to being and ceased to exist. A large number of new or reinstated states have emerged in Europe and central Asia, with the dissolution of the Soviet Union and Yugoslavia. South Africa is, in many ways, a new country since 1994 when Mandela won the first free election. Sovereignty over Hong Kong has been transferred from the United Kingdom to China. The European Community became the European Union in 1993 and grew in the coming years to include 28 member states. The United Kingdom then dropped out. The Soviet troops left Afghanistan in 1989 but the troubles in that nation are far from resolved. The Sudan remains but there is now also South Sudan. Germany went in the other direction and reunified in 1990. Namibia has gained its independence. East Timor has gained its independence. Western Sahara remains on the United Nations list of Non-Self-Governing Territories.

The economic shifts have been equally big. China is projected in just over a decade to surpass the United States as the largest economy in the world. It might be good to caution that accurate projections are hard to make (it would be great if someone from 2050 could send me a letter!). Looking back is easier and doing that we can see that the economic development in China in the past 30 years has been impressive. This contributes strongly to the decrease in poverty you will see as you grow up. In the 25 years from

DOI: 10.4324/9781003260929-23

1990 to 2015, the extreme poverty rate dropped, on average, by one percentage point per year – from nearly 36% to 10%. Many other indicators on global poverty are also showing a strong move toward a better world. The global under-five mortality rate declined by 59% between 1990 and 2019, from 93 deaths per 1,000 live births in 1990 to 38 in 2019. Maternal mortality dropped 43% between 1990 and 2015. Africa has been declared free of wild polio. Literacy is up, child labour is on the decline, life expectancy is rising. There are a lot of things indicating huge improvements to people's lives!

On a more personal note, there have been some pretty dramatic changes too! You are married and have three kids. How about that?! In 2020 your oldest daughter is the same age as you are 1988. She's interested in foreign policy and development, and possesses an inquisitive and sharp mind that will challenge you. Her younger sister is, to be blunt, way smarter than you. The youngest is a boy – a great soccer player. He bends it like Beckham. I know you don't know who Beckham is but when Beckham comes along and makes a name for himself, you'll see how your future kid will curve his freekicks. Having kids is a great change to look forward to!

While you grow up, reach adulthood and gain your first grey hairs you will see very positive developments for millions of people. Yet many challenges remain. In 2019 alone, roughly 14,000 under-five deaths occurred every day. Child deaths are largely preventable: 14,000 under five deaths a day is completely unacceptable. The correlation to poverty is very strong. In Niger in 2019 the death rate of under-fives was 80.4 to 1000 live births. In Norway that figure was 2.4 to 1000. Other indicators tell the same story. While a lot has improved, poverty-related challenges remain at unacceptable levels. It is unfortunately too easy to make long lists of examples: in 2018 more than 400,000 people died from malaria; 785 million people lack a basic drinking-water service; 60% of girls in Bangladesh get married before the age of 18. The list goes on.

In the field of humanitarian support, developments – if that is the right word – are particularly worrisome. In the five years leading up to 2020 the number of people in need of humanitarian support doubled to 170 million people. That curve shows no sign of flattening out. This is driven not least by the complex and long-lasting conflicts in Afghanistan, Syria, Yemen, Somalia, South Sudan and the Democratic Republic of the Congo (you will know it as Zaire, where your sister was born). The global refugee situation in 2020 is as bad as it was at the end of the Second World War. Or worse.

On top of this when I'm writing you from 2020, we are in the midst of a global pandemic. Something called SARS CoV-2 – a coronavirus – causes a disease called COVID-19. More than a million people have died, and the disease continues to spread. The fear of the virus, the lockdowns and the other containment measures are having a huge impact on societies around the world. Vulnerable, often poor, people are being particularly negatively affected. The World Bank estimates that the pandemic will push 100 million people into extreme poverty during 2020. The UN sees a tremendous spike in the number of people needing humanitarian support. There is genuine fear of a hunger pandemic in the footsteps of the COVID pandemic.

The point I'm trying to convey is that, yes, we have seen in the past decades that it is possible to make great strides in wellbeing. There is reason for optimism. At the same time a lot of challenges remain. We have to keep pushing.

I don't think change comes by chance. In development cooperation a lot of thinking goes into trying to establish how to drive positive development. There are principles, agreements (usually named after the cities where they were entered into), experimentation, research and a lot of anecdotal, often rather vague, evidence. Parts of the development community call for more data, but they are often hard to get. Others emphasise deeper dialogue, yet it is not always clear who the dialogue should be between or the conditions upon which this dialogue should be based. Some focus on "shaping the narrative", some pin their hopes on "innovative" solutions. Many of course mix these approaches and countless other ideas and methodologies are also tried.

I don't want to pretend that I have the recipe for success. I don't of course. I subscribe both to the need for better data and deeper dialogue. I believe we have to push ourselves to be innovative and I see the merits of being part of "shaping the narrative". The way I see it we need a combination of drivers to push for change. First, facts, knowledge, science. We must know what the problem is and what factors can change that. Secondly, traction. Traction in the sense that there must be a public and political push around a challenge for it to be addressed. Here of course media, civil society and such institutions are key. Thirdly, leadership. Good, brave, political leadership that dares address those controversial issues that will make you as disliked as appreciated. All these interact with each other. Rarely do we see one of the factors alone yielding any results.

These observations are not, as they say, rocket science. Nonetheless they might be meaningful for someone wanting to work with development cooperation. There are many different angles and possible entry points into that line of work. My advice would be to choose wisely. Think about where and how you can best contribute. I work in government as a civil servant. I thoroughly enjoy it. I get to be "in" on, and part of, very interesting conversations and I get to support the shaping of political agendas for change. Like any civil servant around the world, I must also try to balance different agendas. If you are happy with that I thoroughly recommend following in my footsteps. If, on the other hand, it is of great importance to you never to compromise and to consistently advocate for a cause you believe in maybe it's a wiser choice to work for a CSO. Or maybe you should focus on research – to allow yourself to dig deep into the facts and to truly try to understand the complexities of a challenge. I vouch to listen to you whatever path you choose.

As the years pass in a career you tend to move up. At some point you find yourself in a place where people read a bit more carefully what you write and listen with a little more attention to what you say. Herein lies danger. Beware. You run the risk of talking about what people need rather than talking to people about what they need. Development organisations, including ministries such as the one I work in, often also run into that problem. People listen to us and that tends to yield self-confidence. We must be careful not to be too confident that our own perspective is the right one. We must be careful not to become prescriptive rather than supportive.

In that vein, my best advice might be to be a little bit cautious should you ever receive advice from some old person who claims to be writing to you from the future.

Best,
Your future self

P.S. Climate change. Embarrassing to add this as a PS but I couldn't fit it in. You should really look climate change up. Some scientists are talking about it where you are in 1988. Even some political leaders. Not enough though. It isn't a major issue in your time. Yet. But it's a big thing. I don't really have the space in this letter to explain it but basically, we are heating the world using fossil fuels. And we are really messing things up. As per usual the poorest are the most vulnerable to the terrible consequences of climate change. Climate change must be mitigated, and we have to adapt to prevent the worst consequences, especially for the poorest and most vulnerable populations. Study that and how to affect political change. The world will need you where I am in 2020! And where you are now.

From 2016 to 2021, Johannes was the Director-General for International Development Cooperation at the Swedish Ministry of Foreign Affairs. He earlier served as the Head of Office for the Minister for International Development Cooperation and, before that, Coordinator to the Director-General for International Development Cooperation. In March 2018, Johannes was appointed a member of UN's Peacebuilding Fund Advisory group by the UN Secretary-General. He is currently the Swedish Ambassador to the Netherlands and lives with his family in the Hague.

20

Driving forces in an international development career

What's the X factor?

Suresh Nanwani

Dear Younger Me,

Introduction: reflecting what was and what is

When you were 16, Suresh, do you remember Ms Doreen Thambiayah, our teacher at Raffles Institution Singapore, saying you are a reflective person? Her observation was acute, and still rings true today. I am now 64 years old, and when I reflect, I am very happy with the path taken and my 30-year career as an international civil servant.

Suresh, when I think of our younger days, it was obvious we had naïve notions of an international development career. In my cocooned world as a teenager in Singapore in the late 1960s, I vividly remember my father's tenants from Japanese bilateral aid agencies who worked on a development project in Singapore. Of course, at that time, we would not have used the word "bilateral" – instead, probably something akin to a big assistance company from Japan! However, my meeting them opened my eyes to the far, far bigger world that lay beyond mine. Development had, in my mind then, to do with improving Singapore. In 1965, Singapore was a newly independent country that lacked infrastructure. Many people lived in *attap* houses (the traditional housing of *attap* palm found in villages or *kampongs*), public infrastructure was basic, and people got about on tricycles and buses. Do you remember walking through *kampongs* of *attap* houses as a short cut to the main road or hailing trishaw riders in *kampongs* to reach the bus stop to catch the bus to school?

During our teens, we had a growing realisation. We stood out like a sore thumb from our other siblings in the family. We were the only one who would pursue undergraduate and postgraduate studies. Our other siblings were into business, office secretary or housekeepers, and none pursued tertiary education. Our father was a businessman and the one thing we were sure of was *not* being one. I recollect with horror when he asked us to take care of a business deal in our school holidays when we were 15. I still remember the sheepish feeling of entering his office, to report on the outcome. We informed him that we had not closed the deal, saw his disappointment, and

DOI: 10.4324/9781003260929-24

realised that we had failed him as we did not have the business "flair" that was pervasive among his other children. Our father was part of the Sindhi diaspora with the partition in British India during the 1940s and had not attended primary school: he ended up in Singapore and, after hard work, became a successful businessman. With no business inclinations, we knew a different and unchartered journey lay ahead for us in pursuit of a university degree to improve our education and to work for a company or an international organisation. We would try to make our parents proud. We would be brave and show we could do something worthwhile. Our "dream" was to work in an international context on development ever since we were a teenager, using an education in law as our springboard.

Daunted but not out, be brave and learn more

After graduation, we practised law in Singapore in a modest-sized law firm before moving to the Asian Development Bank (ADB) in the Philippines. That was the beginning of our new chapter. There was excitement at meeting people of diverse nationalities and cultures, working with them, and being part of a big organisation. The downside was something we did not expect: the internal dynamics when working collectively as a team which required collaboration and acceptance of divergent views, and importantly having to navigate the power plays (economic, political, and cultural). Do you remember our two colleagues who encountered difficult times with their supervisors, which resulted in their leaving and returning to their home countries (one went back to his work in his national development aid agency and the other worked as a general counsel in a big private firm). This tense atmosphere, together with the bad experiences of my dear colleagues, made me feel uneasy and unsettled. No small wonder that after the first four years, Suresh, you said to your friend Jerri that you would give up your development career and go back to Singapore to practise in a law firm or work in any other company for that matter!

On hindsight, Suresh, I am glad you did not leave even though working in a huge development organisation with thousands of staff of different nationalities and cultural backgrounds is daunting. You stayed on with international development institutions (IDIs) and retired in 2016, aged 60, after about 30 years! It takes time to understand the pulse of the organisation and to match your passion with the institution's development mandate. Suresh, at the age you are now – 32 – you saw the world through rose-coloured glasses: you will need courage to understand how development works in a bureaucratic organisation. You will need time to adjust to the new environment and to understand just how true is the adage that "patience pays". You will learn the value of courage and your passion for development will allow you to reach new heights after the frustration and trials of the initial years. Courage and passion are your core values: your driving force to overcome any barriers, and provide the flow in being creative and positive at work.

You will learn courage from your mentor, Eisuke, in the legal department of the ADB. I remember he asked you in 1989, when you were 33, to clarify with the project team leader whether the provision of vehicles in a road project could be considered *baksheesh*, i.e., a bribe – an inducement or sweetener for the project. As the project lawyer, you were embarrassed that there could be talk about bribery, and indeed it was a formidable experience for you to question your experienced team leader. But it made you aware that it was best as a lawyer to postulate and incorporate standards to ensure project integrity (notwithstanding that the Bank did not have a formal policy on anticorruption until 1997). Your team leader was surprised by your question, and clarified and confirmed that there was no *baksheesh*. He appreciated you raising the issue as it demonstrated an enquiring mind, and exercising diligence to ensure project integrity, which made him more conscious of good project preparation. You learnt an important lesson from this, Suresh: to have an inquisitive mind with proper reason; to have confidence in oneself; and not to be intimidated by power. This was a very important beginning for you, Suresh, from which you will gain confidence and find increasing satisfaction over the years.

No turning back on development

One golden thread runs through our story, Suresh: we never turned our back on development. In ADB and other IDIs, such as the World Bank and the European Bank for Reconstruction and Development (EBRD), development continues to be a pathway to improve the infrastructure and other needs of developing country borrowers. I have been thrilled at the opportunities to travel while preparing and appraising projects, to review projects and connect with people on the ground, and to work with colleagues from all parts of the world. I have realised what I learnt in my postgraduate studies were purely academic perspectives: it was the actual practice, the commitment, the passion, and the collegiality that mattered most in working in an international environment. Practice that what works on the ground requires a human approach in applying rules and regulations, and Bank policies and procedures.

Suresh, at the age of 38, you will be working on a rural water development project in a remote semi-arid area of Pakistan which required the Bank to monitor concerns raised by the community. It so happened only male voices were to be heard, due to the constraints placed by the male village chief and his coterie of male councillors that women could be met only by women! Your team leader devised ways and means to engage with the "other half" (the more important other half, I would say) of the village community – the women with their children who were side-lined behind curtains without a voice in decision-making. The solution? To have more female project team members and female facilitators who could listen to the other half voice their needs and concerns. The women in the local community were empowered in having their views heard and thanked the project team for enabling them to participate.

Later, when you have progressed to leading your own teams at 43, you will continue to put people at the centre of projects. As part of an initiative providing a legal education to students in the newly established law school in Maldives, more females than males had graduated at the end of the program. This was, to me, the most successful part of the project (apart from providing legal education for the first time in the country). We empowered women who would not otherwise have had the opportunity to study law: they obtained legal education and pursued careers they never dreamed possible, including a graduate who ended up with a Master degree from the US! I still recollect the joyful tears of many female graduates passing from the Diploma course, telling me how elated they were with the opportunity that had been provided.

Suresh, these two projects will provide you with new insights on the meaning of development: that it is not just physical infrastructure development but also social and economic development, and that community involvement and inclusion is a central component to this. Development is listening and not prescribing, and starting conversations with "tell me" is an effective way to start communicating with the community as it shows listening and empathy with the teller. The women folk in the rural villages and the aspiring female student graduates all needed to be heard for their voices to be included in development. You will help these voices to be heard.

The journey gets more riveting with added meanings of development

Over the years, "development" has taken on new meanings. The Banks themselves have had to change in response to specific agendas, including on anticorruption; responsive accountability mechanisms; harmonising policies and activities for better delivery of results; safeguarding policies on social and environmental matters; the inclusion of climate change objectives into operations; and since 2015, pursuing their commitment on the implementation of the UN Sustainable Development Goals. On anticorruption, the chilling statement of the World Bank President Wolfensohn made in 1996 still echoes: "Let's not mince words: We need to deal with the cancer of corruption." The battle continues to this day, Suresh. Twenty-four years on, in 2020, the IMF Managing Director described corruption as a corrosive force that hits the poor and the vulnerable the hardest.

Suresh, in the 1980s, careers in international development were limited, but nowadays, there is a wide range of opportunities. So you can look outwards beyond working in IDIs. International development can be in policy and research, designing and implementing projects, teaching and researching, and other forms through bilateral agencies, governments, civil society organisations, think tanks, universities, foundations, and the private sector. The opportunities are many, and entry points can be through internships, volunteer work, assignments, young professional programs, or scholarships.

Competition is keen, so placing a foot in the development door is a step in the right direction as you can then move on to the more specific aspect of development that you prefer – as a development practitioner, policy maker, advocacy group, or in the government as executing agency in development projects.

We chose a career in IDIs, and then subsequently taught development in universities, engaging with students, academe, and practitioners. It has been a rewarding experience to touch lives in diverse ways. My best present in teaching international development was when a female postgraduate student from UNSW law faculty informed me after my course she had returned to Vietnam and was employed as a junior legal officer in the World Bank country office there. She found a job she loved, was back with her family, and was very happy be part of the development process in her country. I also heard from another student who, after graduation, went on to work in Moscow for three years, and is still holding on to my notes from the course that she took with me. Development to me, with all these 30 years' experience, is best focused with a human-centred approach to improve improvement: at the heart of development, it's people that matter most.

Conclusion: passion and courage prevail on the road to development

I always wanted to work in international development. What started as a job resulted in passion, belief, and courage to further my journey. In the last 15 years, I have embarked on a parallel road of writing and teaching on international development. And in my last eight years, through the Society of International Economic Law I have worked with research students, academics, practitioners, and government officials to promote and facilitate networking and debate in trade, investment, and finance. I vigorously pursue these roads to enhance my development experience. Additionally, three years ago, aged 61, I studied Organization Development (OD) and completed my PhD degree in OD. So it is never too late to learn, and it was a beautiful journey connecting the dots from my childhood to adulthood, my work in development, my teaching at universities, my learning more about students and people, and in the process, myself. Reinventing myself means (re)learning myself and also nurturing others along the journey.

So, Suresh, for me, international development has been far more than a career: it was passion coupled with courage that drove me along the track. The route was not immaculately palm-tree lined; it will have its ups and downs, but the humps will make the journey memorable and fulfilling. There are and will be sceptics, as in any area fraught with geopolitics. But as a person focused on development, if you arm yourself with inclusiveness and accountability to stakeholders, and distance yourself from politics, the path is both exciting and challenging.

Courage is what matters in the journey: belief in oneself and the will to do what is right is most important. It was a challenge to break away from the pathways followed by our siblings; to question superiors about possible bribes; to ensure the voices of all stakeholders should be heard in decision-making process at IDIs for inclusive development. The *attap* houses in old Singapore are no more, and have given way to modern housing, along with higher standards of living, education, and other infrastructure for the majority of Singaporeans. It has taken courage, passion, patience, and continuous learning: the result is the development from a low-income to high-income country, which would have been unthinkable 50 years ago.

From Suresh, the Older Me

Suresh has 30 years of development work experience with international development institutions (IDIs) including the World Bank, Asian Development Bank, and European Bank for Reconstruction and Development. He has written widely on themes that include IDI governance and accountability, the Belt and Road Initiative, and Organization Development theories like appreciative inquiry. He co-edited The Practice of Independent Accountability Mechanisms: Towards Good Governance in Development Finance (Brill, 2019) and authored Organization and Education Development: Reflecting and Transforming in a Self-Discovery Journey (Routledge, 2022). He has a PhD in Organization Development. He is Professor in Practice at Durham University, UK, and teaches on IDIs, governance and accountability at universities in Australia, China, India, Japan, Peru, Singapore, South Africa, Spain, and the UK. He is subject expert consultant on environmental law and international law at the Green Climate Fund's Independent Redress Mechanism. He is an Associate Certified Coach accredited by the International Coaching Federation. He lives in Manila, Philippines.

Section IV

Social entrepreneurship and change making

21 From a Cold War to a warming Cold War?

Arthur Wood

Dear younger me,

This letter will no doubt come as some surprise. I write to tell you of a journey into development that right now, working as a US Aerospace defence analyst, you probably do not anticipate. It was Churchill, Confucius, and Santayana, Burke, and Marx who all noted that to forget the lessons of history ensures we are doomed to repeat them. As I write this, I do indeed wonder what we have learnt from the past, and if indeed it is possible for us to do so. If we can, you will have the added advantage of this letter to help you do so.

I recall what is currently a recent memory for you, May 1989, and the Royal United Services Institute event that, as a young defence analyst working in the City of London, you were invited to. The Iron Curtain has just been breached in Hungary and the Cold War is at an end. For the first time General Galvin, the Supreme NATO commander, shook hands with his opposite number, the Head of the Warsaw Pact, Marshall Petr Lushev. The event was held in the Banqueting Hall of Westminster, on the ceiling of which is the magnificent painting by Reubens on the Supreme and Divine right of Kings, commissioned by Charles I. Just above where Marshall Lushev and General Galvin shook hands is the window that Charles I must have reflected bitterly upon as he walked to his imminent beheading. I suspected that perhaps someone planning the event in Whitehall had a sense of humorous cynicism; both events signified the collapse of systems.

Writing to you now, after 30 years of a career spanning the public and private sectors, I must admit to feeling the same acute sense of systems failure when entering the UN Palais des Nations in Geneva, the second largest building in Europe after Versailles. Walking in one sees due homage to cost-cutting; the lifts, escalators, and fountains are all frequently turned off to save money. This, I can but think, is a harbinger of things to come, and of the financial systems failure that we/you will attempt to confront. History is in the throes of doing a full circle to a new Cold War 2, to one potentially defined by the dividing line of carbon action or inaction. You will become a passionate believer in the role of finance in creating real systems change, as it has done throughout history. You will attempt to do so by helping to pioneer

DOI: 10.4324/9781003260929-26

the idea of impact investment, noting that the development financial tools that helped win Cold War 1 will not be sufficient to win Cold War 2.

Somewhere in your future you will become a key conceptualiser of the so-called "Social Impact Bond/Development Impact Bond"[1] and Blended Value Model, and will sit on the World Economic Forum (WEF) and Organisation for Economic Co-operation and Development (OECD) expert panels on these issues. When you get to where we are now, you will look aghast at the world's reaction to the existential threat of climate to our children and the continued failure of progress on the current global initiative to build a better future for our planet – the Sustainable Development Goals (SDGs) – by the very intermediaries tasked with solving these issues at the United Nations Conference on Sustainable Development in Rio de Janeiro, Brazil, 2012. The SDGs and climate will become a particular concern of yours. I will tell you why.

The first step to solving a problem is recognising you have one

The 17 UN SDGs aim to produce a better, fairer world by 2030 and they are intrinsically tied to climate. The existential risk to humanity. Much of the global growth in the next 30 years of your life (and the growth in carbon emissions) will come from Asia, Latin America, and Africa. So, unless we provide just social conditions for these communities, the marriage of the pressure for a better life and the vested interests of the fossil fuel and banking industry will push emissions ever higher.

This is unfolding as we speak, despite Bloomberg Energy noting in March 2023 that 70% of Global GDP can be covered by renewables. The next two COPS (I will explain what these are in a moment) are to be held in the United Arab Emirates and then Saudi Arabia, both of which have pledged to further substantive increases in oil and gas. Investment is in place to take us to 2.5 degrees by 2050 (and we are already close to that over the Artic poles). Yet investment in blended value models has recently fallen and what *is* being invested is increasingly going into *adaptation*, not *mitigation*. This will mean that poorer countries will be less likely to be able to get funding to adapt. The consequences for vulnerable countries such as Bangladesh and Kiribati, for instance, are truly dire but so too for vast swathes of Italy and Spain where droughts increase. Yet the banks can continue to make money by funding carbon industries on the one front, while on another securing subsidies to help create adaption. And in Western capital markets? In the very week of the opening of the last COP in Egypt, Total and Shell announced record profits. Like all the oil majors they did not increase investment in renewables but returned capital to shareholders as share buy backs and dividends – why would they unless the negative externalities (the damage) they create are priced into their business models?

I hear regular proclamations of "progress" on the SDGs and see numerous publications from the WEF, Foundations, the Global Steering Group on

Impact Investment, governments, and UN agencies alike. Some continue to note the funding gap to solve the SDGs is $2.5 trillion *per annum* or 3% of global GDP. This figure is actually taken from United Nations Conference on Trade and Development from 2015/17. Most others are using the figure of $5 trillion from 2018, i.e., before the outbreak of COVID-19 (a recent global pandemic, long predicted and ill prepared for). However, if you look at recent McKinsey and International Finance Corporation research on the impact of the failure to mobilize capital every year and the impact of COVID, *the real gap* is now 8% pa of global GDP by 2030. And that's a conservative estimate. It is perhaps also worth noting that the trends were well in place before COVID, with each year's failure compounding the problem.

The bottom line is that as a sector if we add up since 2015 all the expenditures of the Bretton Woods System, the Development Finance Institutions, Global Foundations, and the claimed $1.16 trillion from Impact since 2015, then we have spent well over $3 trillion (and here I ignore the claimed trillions in ESG alignment). The outcome? The climate is well en route to a 1.5 degree increase, SDG investment is 20% below where we started in 2015, and inequality has widened. In plain English, the more we have proclaimed progress and impact, the further we have gone backwards.

So, younger self, how does one square the realities of your future and the decline in SDG investment, the climate crisis, and rising iinequality with the statement from the Global Impact Investing Network (GIIN) that impact investing has gone from $285 bn to "nearly $1.16 trillion" in the three years to 2022,[2] or the claim of the Global Steering Group for Impact Investment (GSG) that "Impact" has reached $2.3 trillion?[3] If we take the GIIN figures, this implies mobilization of 150% of the global budget of the entire Bretton Woods system. Or three times if we use the GSG figure. These represent growth rates of 62% to 82% per annum from 2009 and, if believed, they have continued in the time of COVID: a period of time when foreign direct investment has declined sharply.

At a closer look, there appear to have been changes of methodologies, and in one case, it looks as though historic domestic development expenditure by Chinese and Indian Development banks has been lumped into "Impact". It is surely simply Old Wine – with notoriously unreliable "bouquets" of impact – packaged as New Wine.

Let's look at the Government side. Again, there are divergent or inconsistent claims. For instance, how does one reconcile the recent claims by one large global development institution that Blended Value Models – a financial model where philanthropic or governmental money is used to price out risk of a social investment to crowd in private capital – have achieved leverages ratios of nine times, with one think-tank's view that most of the financing by DFIs (development finance institutions, usually government funded) have achieved leverages of 0.7 to 1.14? The recent Convergence Report on blended structures notes around four times leverage but goes on to note that only half of those funds have come from mobilzaton of private sector funds.[4] And let's also not lose sight of the fact that even at nine times if you could get 100% agreement and allocation of subsidy – a political and practical unreality given that would cannibalise many existing programs – you would still be short of the 16 times leverage that is actually required to fund the SDGs and necessary climate measures through these instruments. It is perhaps starkest if we give an example: Total Official Development Assistance (or "ODA") sits at around $170bn pa, of which Water, Sanitation, and Hygiene gets about 10%. However, SDG 6 (WASH) requires an estimated $1.6 trillion of investment.

Those used to spending time on football pitches will attest that this is likely a case of widening the goalposts. We are systemically underestimating the problem and over-egging how much capital has been raised or could be raised. Of the $3 trillion plus we have spent since 2015, the reality is the major benchmarks of Climate, Capital aligned with the SDGs, and Inequality have all gone in reverse. The date we will achieve the SDGs continues to retreat. Might it now be the next century?

The latest G7 impact report by the Global Steering Group leading the charge on aligning Private capital to development – published in December 2021 – requires a similarly critical lens;[5] the model remains focused on a venture capitalist vision, which at worst compounds the siloing problem, coupled with a "blended" approach where there is simply not enough subsidy to go around. To be clear these financial tools are, of course, part of the solution; but to depict them as *the* solutions feeds into the fragmented and siloed mindset of our sector, which is half the problem. The institutional, sectoral, and practitioner silos in which we operate create, at best, a lack of economies of scale and hence a clear limit to the financial tools that can be applied. The problem and opportunity here is not just innovation, but is also the *incentive to collaborate and scale*. They are not there, and this is killing our chances of making any material progress toward the SDGs.

The GSG/G7 impact report again focuses upon and argues for measurement, which is of course a no brainer; it then, in three sub-reports, fails (or fudges) or is simply wrong on several critical issues:

1. What it proposes measuring (and critically, the implications of what it does *not*) and to whose *benefit* and *detriment*.
2. Ignoring the opportunity of applying systems approaches with technology, which by aggregation has revolutionised every other sector of the economy, including mainstream banking.
3. The danger of politicisation of the multilateral system and the lessons of the documentary, "The Social Dilemma", being played out in development.
4. Where the best practices in governance are in line with best financial regulatory practice and independence/separation of duties.
5. And in our rush to catalyse and engage the needed capital, should we really be assuming that the "Business" agenda is the same as "Society's" agenda?

The bottom line is that if the margin lies in the structural inefficiency of the sector and the future cash flows generated by sequenced collaboration, then who is measuring that and to whose agenda and benefit?

Perhaps worst of all, the report focused as it is on venture capital models is silent on the role of catalytic capital to mobilize other main stream capital sources, and the legal and regulatory policy processes we need to apply to mobilize Billions to Trillions.

Younger self, you will soon witness the first Conference of the Parties (COP) to the United Nations Framework Convention on Climate Change in Berlin in 1995. You will see these international climate meetings being held on an annual basis to much fanfare. Yet it will perhaps sadden you to know that nearly 30 years on we are still struggling to find funding solutions to achieve the lofty goals that we aspire to for the world's population. The world listened to the variable outcomes from COP 27 in 2022; we heard of the finance community coming to the rescue with USD $130 trillion, but as Hiro Mizuno, the former head of the world's largest pension fund and now the UN Secretary-General's Special Advisor on financing the SDGs, noted in December 2021, that figure is simply the funds *they already have under management*. Unless they produce actual plans for aligning this capital, it will go down, as he noted, as "the biggest greenwash in history". In reality, we are still waiting for this strategy.

Young people are so much more prone to calling out bullshit, aren't they, younger self? Perhaps with age we become enthralled with our vistas of naked emperors who don't get called out on their machinations for their silos.

Let's pause for a moment to consider the growth of youth populations across the developing world; a group of people who are increasingly conscious of today's world through their use of social media (something you have yet to discover) and which fuels migration. Let's juxtapose that with aging populations in the West and China, all with huge unfunded, unaccounted domestic pension and health liabilities (40%+ of most government budgets). We have the ingredients for a perfect storm, even ignoring Black Swan events like COVID or anti-microbial resistance (thrown in for those who thought COVID was bad).

Younger self, let us recall the quote by Machiavelli in 1528 that to create change is the most difficult thing to do as the existing status quo does not want to change and those who would benefit, given human scepticism, will be lukewarm supporters compounded by fake news and alternative reality, married with vested self-interest at play, as our old Yorkshire father would say, "there is nowt as dumb as those that want to be". But it is a challenge we must accept.

And it can be!

Do you remember, as a rookie broker at Merrill Lynch, meeting in the lift the Merrill CEO who was doing his speech to our NY training course that morning? You asked him what his speech was going to be about, and he tapped his Mickey Mouse watch, noting, "have something people don't expect and follow the money".

I have taken his advice concerning the trillions that must be aligned to mobilize funding for the SDGs and Climate. The good news is the fact that catalytic capital is not the issue. Nor is it innovation. So, what is the issue?

Let's start with the *status quo social sector* bankers. One could argue that much of the mostly unaligned $2 trillion+ held by the global foundations runs contrary to their stated social function as the tax code ensures only 5% pa is actually mandatorily aligned. Come to think of it, perhaps we should ensure their tax break or credit should be a function of the social impact created, not just in the front-end act of giving. Lest we lose faith in humanity, there is precedent for all three – there are foundations (Heron, KL Felicitas) that align 100% of their portfolios; a tax regulatory code (ignored in both G7 impact reports) which promotes impact investment that could be more broadly applied (the PRI code passed by Congress in 1967); there is even an accounting policy that could track how effective a government subsidy is (the Congressional Budget Office – annual review of the Community Reinvestment Act) which could be adapted. Perhaps the chief cooks in the kitchen would do well to take a harder look at their larders.

Described as a "no brainer" by the UNSG's former special adviser on Financing Sanitation there is good sense in using the $3 trillion+ in local currency pension funds in the developing world to deliver their own essential sustainable development. Instead of convening endless seminars about how bonds can be done in product silos and over-egging the leverage attainable as noted.

Instead, how about creating a Western guarantee entity (on a proven model where $41bn of structures has been done in the developing world) to those entities in the developing world where at the systems level $250 million could leverage $100bn in ten years by guaranteeing local currency pension funds invested locally, which by currency matching in the process takes 70% of the risk out of development funding by negating much of the Forex risk? Coincidentally with an estimated 20% pa return. This is, of course, is not necessarily in the interest of some, including those who would even argue that it is the banks and rating agencies who hold the key. Yet, is the track record of global lending in hard currency to soft currency projects an exemplary and, more critically, a sustainable one, in the face of the climate challenge? I posit my response: no.

How about doing exactly what the bankers do – and that the rest of the economy has done – and aggregate markets? Ride on the back of the technology and legal revolutions to create a transparent, technically robust and trackable multi-sided aggregation of development markets i.e. cities and their hinterlands, water basins, First Nations, Small Island Developing States, or small-scale farming communities (40% of global employment)?

On the cost side, moving away from continual reinvention in product and geographical silos – the opportunity of "plugging and playing" financial and entrepreneurial solutions (already created) and driving cost efficiency of scale into development – exactly as happens in current capital markets, this would allow a much wider range of financial tools and capital to be applied. Even an intellectual property regime that could fast-track the profiling and value-capture of ground-level innovations would go a long way towards monetising and scaling models that otherwise "don't travel", for lack of funding. Both could sit in a process that also transparently tackles corruption, by empowering communities as consumers and auditors of social goods. We'd have plenty of options when it comes to systems-planning technology platforms empowering communities with the tools they need, which peer reviewed research at the World Bank has estimated could reduce 45% of the cost from the SDGs.

On the revenue side, reputed players like McKinsey, the World Bank, Accenture, and Stop TB, in issues as diverse as health, road safety, education, and WASH have all calculated that if stakeholders worked together in a systems approach, and did so in a data frame that can marry competing "theories of change" predictively, this would generate markets worth hundreds of billions annually.

In good news, the reality is that the capital and the legal and technology solutions we require are all there to solve the problems we face. In development, since McKinsey, World Bank, and Accenture and others have priced the externalities (Negative, Positive, and Sequenced), we even know the potential returns of up to $50 per dollar of investment. Let's turn an unfinanceable problem and instead recognise this as future economic value created for all humanity and the economic benefit that an alternative to the carbon economy can provide.

It is the same process that we have seen throughout history, from the 12th century with the Templars; the first pan-European bankers in the medieval struggle between the powers, temporal and spiritual; to the drivers of the nation-state by the bond markets from the 14th century onwards; from the 18th century, the dominance of the Anglosphere built on central banking, capital markets, and efficient taxation. All finance innovation with political impact is leveraged by technology and legal innovation.

As ever, the question is: *by whom and for whose benefit*? But since climate is an urgent, existential threat to all humanity, we cannot cynically shrug this time, noting that the poor have always been with us, as you will come to hear shockingly at a private bank meeting to justify slow development. We need to ensure our system mobilises enough capital and quickly enough for all humanity, and not just indulge in a reallocation of a shrinking subsidy pool that is not working. What is crystal clear is that the current strategy cannot mathematically solve the problem – there is simply not enough subsidy in the current strategy; if we don't acknowledge this problem, we are effectively engaging in a massive betrayal of future generations.

Whichever way we go, it is clear a new system is needed and, as we move to the construction of the new cathedrals of development, this must be driven not by today's legally siloed hierarchies but with the use of open, networked technology and legal systems, which you dear younger me (today) will grasp and understand intuitively. It has ever been thus.

Arthur is the Founding Partner of TOTAL Impact Capital and Equity4Humanity. He is a recognised pioneer and innovator in social finance/impact investment, having held senior positions in both financial institutions and in "socially driven organisations", including Ashoka. He lives in Geneva, Switzerland, with his wife, children, and black Labrador dog.

Notes

1 Although called a Bond they are more like derivative structures where payment and return is contingent on the social impact generated.
2 Hand, D., Ringel, B., Danel, A. 2022. *GIINsight: Sizing the Impact Investing Market 2022 Global Impact Investing Network*. October 12, 2022.
3 The Impact Taskforce. 2021. *Time to deliver: mobilising private capital at scale for people and planet.*
4 Convergence Blended Finance. 2022. *The State of Blended Finance 2022: Climate Edition*. Convergence Report.
5 The Impact Taskforce. 2021. *Time to deliver: mobilising private capital at scale for people and planet.*

22 Everyone a changemaker

Bill Drayton

Dear Bill,

There are some things that I would love you – the younger me – to know. First, you can and must be a changemaker. As you come to realise this, you will also come to know that your path lies in helping others to see themselves in this way too. There are also some things that I want to share with you that may help you on this journey. Things that I now know to value after having walked the life path that you will take.

You have been lucky enough to grow up in New York, an incredibly diverse and cosmopolitan city – a city of immigrants. The bustling energy and drive of those who came to the city as migrants, as your mother did from Australia, have helped make the city unlike any other in America. The people and the institutions of New York, their history, and the culture they have given rise to, will leave their mark on you, a huge gift.

You are also lucky enough to have an empowering education. The principal at the elementary school you attended in New York made room for you to be different, to be confident, and not just to conform to societal norms. You have the same gift now in high school at Phillips Academy, which also allowed you to develop in your own way. For example, it cheered you on as you founded the Asia Society, which improbably became the school's largest student organisation. These are formative years, and what you have learned about organising to drive change and the deep inner confidence this gives you will serve you well in your career and life in general. And you will be helping many of your friends and classmates grasp the changemaker's superpower by your model and by helping your team members.

Don't worry that Latin, French, or maths seem less relevant to you. You will get serious about your studies, and you will do well. Now your energy is directed where it should be, into building things. Never forget the importance of the environment that supports this, in which you are lucky enough to find yourself. You will continue to build things, to help people help themselves to find solutions to problems, be they local or global. Remember your journey began here, in a family, school, and city that tolerated and supported a culture of change making.

DOI: 10.4324/9781003260929-27

As your path unfolds, you will help others to know this simple truth. That we all can *and must be* changemakers for the good – and that must start when we are young.

To have a dream, to build a team and to change your world should be the norm, an experience *all* young people have. This will be your vision – what you must work to make a reality for everyone. To have a life in the everything changing new reality requires the power to be a giver, which is only possible if one is a changemaker. To deny others this power is unethical.

Your views will be shaped by the struggles for social justice that are being fought around America and across the world. A struggle led by individuals with a passion and vision for a better society. Their determination and self-sacrifice will capture your imagination and help you to better understand what it takes to transform society for the better. The civil rights movement will impact so many in your generation and then, shortly after that, the women's rights movement. And don't forget how central the national liberation, anti-colonial movements have been. This reform wave is growing and growing – and it always talks, especially to young people. It's a perfect fit with, and reinforces, their core values, and it opens lifelong patterns of learning. It will be this way for you, and it will help you to understand how to help others change their world. Engaging with historic movements is deeply satisfying. And empowering.

Give yourself permission to pursue your dream, to build your team, and, put simply, to change the world. Many will tell you that you can't achieve what you set out to do. What that usually means is that the person discouraging you didn't do what they wanted to do. When they see you doing something that they didn't, it raises uncomfortable questions about how they have lived their lives. When they therefore tell you that you can't, be kind and polite, but firmly nonetheless give yourself permission and press ahead. Anything you care about; you can find a big opportunity to make things better. Please . . . be persistent – despite all those people who keep telling you that what you want to change is difficult, too complicated, et cetera. One day they may be less afraid. In the meantime, be firm and give yourself permission to dream, and to work with and inspire other dreamers/changemakers.

A word on change. You should realise that there are three very different ways of bringing about change, each with its own methodology and measurements. The first is *direct service*; in which, for example, one needs the teacher in the classroom and the engineer out digging wells. Second is *systems change*. This second level is where entrepreneurs kick in and change the whole pattern in whatever field they are playing in. Here you will need to work across boundaries and identify and leverage connections to bring about system-wide changes at scale. The third level has the biggest impact: *framework or mindset change*. This is where the paradigm changes, where everyone comes to see the world differently in terms of what can and should be done to build better, more equal, and just societies. Understanding this difference and deciding clearly, case by case, at which level you decide to play will give you great power.

Once you've given yourself permission and are committed to the good, your experiences and ideas on how to bring about society-wide transformations can make you a social entrepreneur. Knowing this about yourself is magical. Of course, you can drive positive, big social change! Once you have a vision and desire to transform systems and frameworks to make people's lives better, you'll want (and be able) to act like and be an entrepreneur. This is not at all as daunting, although it does come easier for some. Change requires action, and everyone has the power to change something. Being able to see a problem is where it starts, and helping young people to organise and motivate and collaborate to realise change will help them to cultivate their ability to act as changemakers and then social entrepreneurs.

This, they will learn, is a superpower, their superpower. Once you know you have this superpower, your life and you need never be common.

Your social entrepreneurship power enabled you to help *everyone* to have a good life. And the essence of everyone having a good life is being able to give, because giving brings health, happiness, longevity along with confidence, power, and learning. Without giving, we can't play – a short circuit for humans, who are social creatures. Leaving anyone not able to give is unbelievably destructive.

Because the world has jumped from organising around efficiency in repetition (think assembly lines and bank lending) to its *opposite*, a world of accelerating change and universal connections, many are left behind. This is the "new inequality". It is unethical and is dividing us bitterly. You will have to help lead this final fight for equality. Giving is central to our happiness and wellbeing and nothing is more life satisfying than giving the power to give – to all.

You, of course, must develop your own power as a giver. In the new reality of an everything changing and connected world. This means constantly becoming an ever more effective changemaker for the good.

The foundational first ability you must have and constantly grow to do so is "conscious (cerebral cortex) empathy (mirror neurons) based living for the good of all". One can no longer be a good person by diligently following the rules: they are more and more not there. This requires steady, both reflection and very active and loving work to understand others and the now ever-changing and larger and larger contexts. The best way to grow this power is, of course, to help others grow theirs. Every time you lead or organise is a brilliant opportunity to do so – as well as for you to grow your own understanding and empathy power.

Travel and living with those who are different is revelatory and brings deep growth, especially if it is beyond your home in Western culture. There you will be able to tell what is cultural and what is universal.

Settle down in a traditional village and make friends. Most people have these roots. Those friendships are bridges that will always be with you – opening real understanding and providing guaranteed antidotes against ever looking down on anyone.

Every time you help any person or group get their giver superpower, these people will see you as a trusted friend. You will learn far more than you give – and that friendship is another antidote against your slipping away from a life of love and respect in action – which is what will give you a truly great, happy life.

Once you have thus given yourself the core power of a changemaker for good, you will of course grow a series of associated abilities. How to work on many interconnected teams in many and changing roles. How to envision a new solution for society and then (1) invite the right team of teams; (2) develop the right organisational and communications structures so that each colleague is playing as a powerful and collegial changemaker – and helping all the other team members grow as changemaking players.

The key, of course, is to jump in. Have a dream, build a team, and change your world (be it a school or faith community or town or bigger). It could be a virtual radio station, a program to challenge older people, or a tutoring service. Whatever is your dream.

Once you do this, you have your PhD in life. You will be what the world more and more urgently needs – a changemaker.

Regards from a permanently changing world,
Warmly,
Bill Drayton

Bill Drayton is a social entrepreneur with a long record of founding organisations and public service. As the founder and CEO of Ashoka: Innovators for the Public, Bill Drayton has pioneered the field of social entrepreneurship, growing a global association of over 3,900 leading social entrepreneurs who work together to create an "Everyone a Changemaker" world. Ashoka Fellows bring big systems-change to the world's most urgent social challenges. Over half have changed national policy within five years of launch.

23
Finding solid ground

Dias Rahwidiati

Dear Dias,

I've often wondered what you would think if you could see me now – the you I've become in 18 years. Would you be proud of what we've become? Would you wish I had taken a different fork in the road? Would it surprise you to see that the hardest fights to fight are with the demons within? Is this what you imagined your future would be like?

I am writing this to you in the middle of a pandemic – I am pretty sure this scenario was not in one of your imagined futures. It feels like the entire world is in chaos, sometimes, and to be very honest with you, I often find it hard to summon the willpower to get out of bed and start my day. Some days feel like such an uphill battle to even get through. Words and sentences which come so readily to your fingertips often fail to come to mine, and I feel their loss deeply.

This letter was written in stops and starts; on sticky notes and random journal pages; on voice notes to capture fleeting thoughts. I think of you, facing your first day in your first real paying job in a sector that will captivate, thrill, and frustrate you for the better part of the next two decades. I know you can't hear me right now, but if I could go back in time to share with you a few things that I have learnt along the way, this is what I would say.

The things that you're good at aren't necessarily the things that give you joy. Take, for instance, public speaking. We're good at it, you and I. We're lucky that we're able to articulate arguments clearly and persuasively, that we have a pretty good sense of timing, as well as a sense of what would appeal to which audience. What I've come to realise recently is that this is not without cost. The anxiety tying your stomach in knots days and days before you're scheduled to speak; the sleepless night before; the cold clamminess of your hands just before you step up to a microphone; the insidious fear creeping in that you'll stammer and stutter and say all the wrong

DOI: 10.4324/9781003260929-28

things; and after it's all over, the obsessive analyses and endless replays in your mind of every single word you've said, wondering if maybe you should have said something else. These are all costs, and I've learnt to recognise them as such.

You shrug this off as a weakness, I know, and you think you need to toughen up. I think what you need to do is give yourself ample time to recuperate. Should we continue public speaking when it exacts that kind of cost? You're damn right, we should. Many times in the next 18 years you will be in spaces where mostly white men are giving their opinion on what needs to happen for the "development" of your country – and at times, these opinions will be based on faulty assumptions or thin evidence. Speak up and use your voice bravely, especially in these times. Just make sure to leave ample time to recuperate afterwards.

You know what else is interesting? Leading teams. People have told you since you were in kindergarten that you're a natural leader, and I know that at this point in your life, you aspire to someday lead a large organisation of your own. Over the next 18 years, you will get glowing feedback from both your supervisors and the people you manage, attesting to your competence as a leader and a manager. Some of your team members will become your friends for life. So why, I asked myself two years ago, do I feel so miserable leading a team of 30 highly intelligent, creative, passionate people who are working on issues that I deeply care about?

I think I'm still working on the full answer to this question, but I do have a couple of reflections. The first is that being in a senior leadership position, even in an organisation that I love, requires performing administrative duties, managerial tasks, and representation[1] that are crucial to keeping the organisation afloat. However, these obligations mean that there is less time spent doing things that do give me joy and were the reasons I joined the organisation in the first place – things like helping people map out problems and work through potential solutions; synthesising information and pulling out insights; and identifying cool, context-appropriate practices that could potentially be adapted elsewhere. The second reflection relates to what I perceive a leader to be, in a professional sense: someone who can create a conducive workspace for their team to thrive and shine bright; someone who can secure ample political coverage to enable the team to work independently; someone who can buffer the team from external shocks and stresses so they can get on with their work. Perhaps this aegis-like conception of leadership was borne of admiration of the many leaders that you will encounter in the next few years. What I've grossly underestimated was the emotional toll it would take. Like public speaking, I don't think we should stop leading teams. I think I probably need to reconfigure my conception of what leadership entails and have a better gauge on the emotional cost of such an approach. (And maybe manage smaller teams.)

Our need to achieve is most often driven by fear. A while ago, a good friend of mine forwarded an article on high-functioning anxiety. One of the things that caught my eye in the article was how it explained that, for some people, achievements are driven not by the ambition to succeed, but by an intense fear of an adverse outcome. Think about it – the competitions you've won, the awards you've collected, the grades you strived for, how did you feel after achieving each of these? If you were honest with yourself, I think the answer would be that you felt relieved. I think you felt like you could take a breather from being afraid of not meeting expectations, being afraid of losing affection, being afraid of not being able to make your parents proud. You have a brief respite from wondering whether you've tried hard enough, or whether you are enough. In time, this fear-driven approach to getting things done will cost you your wellbeing, my love.

I truly wish that you could hear me right now, so you can start finding motivators other than fear. I've learnt that excitement is a good one; joy is another. The tips of your fingers will become warm instead of cold, and instead of that tightness in your chest, there will be a light, sparkly feeling that pushes good ideas to come through. Take note of these moments, for they are when you work with joy.

Listen first, then speak. I know how anxious you are to prove yourself. Again, this is something driven by fear: the fear of being underestimated, of not fitting in, of being thought to be a total fraud. You wonder whether people think you deserve to be here, so you take every opportunity you can to convince them that you do. Instead of taking every opportunity that presents itself to speak up and make your opinions heard, try being quiet and listen for a bit. Try and understand where people are coming from. What are their motives, do you think? How are they feeling? How are they acting? What are the power dynamics that are going on in this room? What do you think is not being said?

A few years from now, you will be in a position where you have influence over how development programs are shaped and how resources are allocated. It is imperative that you develop the ability to listen, especially to the people these programs are meant to benefit, in order to ensure that when you do use your voice, you use it well.

I promise that this is my last piece of unsolicited advice, after which I will bid you well as you venture on your path. I am writing this on the eve of Mum's birthday. I know how sharp the pain is this year – your first year without her. I know how much you miss her, and I know how complicated things must feel because there were so many things seemingly left unresolved. I am sorry to tell you that the grief of losing her does not lessen over time – the pain just morphs into something less jagged and sharp.

I know there are things you longed so much to hear from her, though. So, let me say this to you now, in the hope that some echo of my voice reaches you back in time: Dias, you are loved. You are enough. It's okay to fall, because I know you're strong enough to get back up. My love for you is unconditional. I am so, so proud of you.

Be kind to yourself, and take care.

With much love,

Dias

Dias is passionate about grassroots innovation, and especially interested in the thinkers, doers, and fixers that create positive change across Asia and the Pacific. She is also interested in how knowledge is socially constructed and how ideas spread across different spaces. For the past 20 years, she has worked with multilateral organisations, bilateral donors and other agencies to design, manage, and implement development programs.

Note

1 See above notes on public speaking.

24 What an elephant can teach a girl about physics

Frannie Léautier

Dear 1987 Frannie,

It is hard to write to you today. A landslide has disconnected Lushoto from the rest of the road network. Heavy rains have caused the hills, now bare naked from deforestation, to just give up and slide down to the valley. Fortunately, our cell phones still work, else we would be cut off entirely from the world for several days.

I have been rummaging around to find your notebook from your days as a student at the University of Dar es Salaam. I am looking for the translation you did of the standards for designing mountain roads. Armed only with a French-to-English dictionary and an old French Swiss Road Design Manual, you put in a lot of hours of tenacious work. You didn't speak a word of French at the time but you wanted to solve a major problem.

That week, more than two decades ago, when you undertook the tedious work of looking up word by word for the English meaning, a whole village had been swept away by landslides. An entire mountain slope broke off from the heavy rains. I didn't know it at the time, but have since learned how affected you were by that and why you toiled so hard to find a solution to building resilient roads in mountainous regions.

Well, it has happened again. A whole mountain side has come tumbling down but luckily with fewer injuries and no deaths. It turns out that the road design that came from your translations held very well. In fact, the road is intact. You should be proud of that. Yet not all is well. The trees that held up the slopes years ago when the road was built have all been cut for firewood and charcoal. The slopes simply cannot retain the heavy rain we are seeing these days.

Today, it's true, thanks to that translation work, a paved road runs from Mombo to Lushoto and there hasn't been a severe landslide in a decade. You solved the road design problem but not the climate-change induced heavy rains, nor the deforestation born from the need for cooking energy. So here we are. Cut off for several days.

Looking back, you should have thought more holistically, and not just focused on the road design. Sort of what you learned to do when you followed

DOI: 10.4324/9781003260929-29

the streaking of light down the Infinite Corridor as you walked to class early in the mornings in Cambridge Massachusetts. Your being admitted to that school is as improbable as your ending up as a top decision maker in the world of development finance. But one common wisdom permeates all your choice points: seeking solutions to the day-to-day problems facing you and your community.

That's why you studied engineering but applied your problem-solving skills to development finance. Just like you did in justifying the economic value of financing public infrastructure. You see, I travelled to the future, and have been reading one of your old memos – the one that argues for investment in rural roads in Ccorca, Peru. There, you were successful in translating engineering language and concepts into terms economists and bankers would understand.

That memo set the standards for assessing the value of public expenditures in infrastructure. Do you remember your motivation for arguing in a language accessible to non-engineers? It was the farmer you met going down the treacherous hills of the Cuzco region with a bag of potatoes on his llama. Understanding how much he fetched for those potatoes and the time he spent going up and down that rough stony path gave you the idea: how could you value such effort and what would a paved road do to his income, and hence the value of that investment for him and millions like him? That was *presencing*, as Otto Scharmer would call it in his Theory U thinking.

Do you remember the first time you tackled a problem using presencing? When you were five you spoke "dog", translating what your puppy was saying to your siblings. And it wasn't just the dog you spoke to. Your siblings thought you were weird when you told your Mom what the rooster was saying as you collected the eggs from the hens. And do you remember when you told your sisters that the cow was about to give birth when you were yards away from her? And how excited you were when you first noticed your three-year-old son had the same talent? Your sensing from the field started with animals. Learning their language, empathising with them, and making their needs understood.

This empathetic skill became more refined over time and stretched to other ways of knowing. That's why you listened carefully as your grandfather explained how you could tell the weight of an elephant from its footprints. You learned at an early age to relate signs in nature to concepts in physics and engineering. In fact, that's how you got interested in the study of physics and mathematics – from observing nature.

You learned from the field. You followed the signs you observed, not caring that you would be ridiculed many times, something that happened frequently, being the only lady among 60 men in class to graduate as an engineer. That's what led you to pick up the Swiss Road Design Standards for Mountain Roads in French and translate them into English: you wanted to understand and, in turn, you wanted others to use them so that they could build sustainable roads.

These qualities are your superpowers. Powers of observation and listening to what nature is telling you. Powers of empathy and sensing from the field, including from those whose language you don't speak. Powers of trying and experimenting and doing what's hard. Powers of synthesis and the skill to crystallise the learnings into actions that bring systemic change.

These qualities helped you successfully enter the world of development finance. You were born in Tanzania, in what was a newly independent nation. You observed first-hand the challenges of development through the struggle of your parents. They toiled each year to earn a living as farmers. Their fortunes and quality of life were impacted not by their effort but by the volatility of coffee prices in the global markets. Their annual income was further affected by the type of national policies towards the role of cooperatives, regulation of minimum wage levels, and provision of agriculture extension services and infrastructure. You became critically aware of the impact of good policies on the daily lives of ordinary people.

Do you remember the year the family was hardest hit? That was when facing a triple shock: the collapse of global coffee prices because of a boom in production in Brazil; the loss of half of the coffee harvest due to an attack by the boll weevil; and very heavy rains that washed away the only road that was used to transport coffee to the market.

You were an adolescent at the time and felt totally unable to control the first shock (a commodity price shock), and severely ill equipped to manage the second shock (insect infestation whereby you had to find and crush each boll weevil one by one, coffee tree by coffee tree). But you figured you could help your parents dig earth and carry stones to fix the road and save what little crop they had for the market that year. Along with the strong influence and encouragement of your grandfather you vowed to study engineering so you could at least make sure that you could control what could be done, and you could be of help to your family and their rural neighbours.

When you join the World Bank Group, you will be armed with a world-class engineering education and experience of constructing infrastructure in a developing country setting. At the World Bank, you will see first-hand the value of good policy on the outcome of development finance. But you will also learn how divorced driving development impact from Washington could be in terms of pairing the right policies, the right financial instruments, and the necessary country capabilities.

You will also learn about the huge potential of large multinational corporations to drive impact, if well intentioned. In more than 15 years to come you will leave the Bank to set up your own company. This is a courageous decision but the right one to make: it will help you try to engage closer to the ground, work from home, and have time to walk your daughter and son to school. You believe that by founding a company, you can advise large corporates on risk management and impact investing in emerging markets, and hence attract more financing for development. But advice, necessary as it is, isn't sufficient to attract and direct financing for development results. Capacity is the missing link. Capacity to develop strategy and policy for sustainable results. Capacity to implement complex development programs. Capacity to anticipate future challenges and mitigate emerging risks. You need to spend time working hands-on with policy makers in capacity building, which will shape the rest of your experience on how to drive change on the ground.

What you learned translating engineering standards from French to English when you didn't speak French were critical lessons; they would give you the audacity to think that you could transform capacity building organisations that are far out from your field of specialisation in engineering and infrastructure systems. So, don't be afraid to try, make mistakes, and fail, as what you will learn from failure will help you discover how to succeed. Just like you had to listen carefully to distinguish between when the cow was hungry or in pain.

The landslide today reminded me of a similar moment in your adolescent years that influenced how you would approach investment decisions in the future. I remember you waking up one night as you heard your Mom weep silently. You and she had a conversation which would have a profound impact on you. You discussed how she could start a small business of transforming her eggs into *mandazi* (an East African doughnut), which would allow her to manufacture her own chicken feed, raise the productivity of her egg production, and buttress her income for when global coffee prices collapsed.

That was the beginning of your interest in transforming small businesses and ultimately will lead to your involvement in private equity and impact investing. The time you spend at the African Development Bank will help you further refine the approach to market instruments for financing development and the very critical role of de-risking. These skills will be very useful to you in asset management and investment banking: there you will see the value of clear policies for development that are grounded in sound non-ideological research and thinking. But the building blocks of your decision-making approach started during a sleepless night talking to your mother about transforming eggs into *mandazi* so as to diversify her sources of income and build a resilient business. Remember that when making investment decisions; someone's wellbeing and capacity to execute are at the end of each successful investment decision.

In ending, be courageous and don't be afraid to do the hard things. Hone your empathetic skills of listening to others and sensing from the field. Be audacious; try new ways of doing. Be tenacious in translating what you hear to others who don't speak the same language. And get better and better at crystallising and synthesising what you observe while staying open to feedback.

And in summary, remember the Bantu Proverb: "The road doesn't tell the traveller what lies ahead".

2017 Frannie,

Frannie is a finance and development expert, with long-standing global experience leading and transforming organisations in the private, public, and not-for-profit spheres. Born and raised in Tanzania, she served as Senior Vice President at the African Development Bank, Vice President at the World Bank Group, and Executive Secretary of the African Capacity Building Foundation. In addition to being the Chief Executive Officer of SouthBridge Investments, Frannie is a Board Member, Trustee, Special Advisor, Founder and Member of a number of prestigious international organisations, including the World Economic Forum, United Nations Foundation, Overseas Development Institute, and the Nelson Mandela Institute for Science and Technology. She holds a PhD in Infrastructure Systems from MIT and has taught Masters-level courses at Sciences Po, MIT, Harvard, University of Zurich, and the University of Tokyo. She lives in Washington DC, USA.

25

Nothing changes your field of work like doing fieldwork

Indrani Medhi Thies

Dear younger Indrani,

What an unusual journey you've had! It's been more than 20 years since you were doing an undergraduate degree in Architecture, studying how to design better buildings. Today you're a scientist at Microsoft Research looking at the role of information communication technologies (ICTs) in global development. Of course, I know this, but you don't: this lies ahead of you, yet to be discovered. So, as you embark on your early career let the older Indrani share some wisdom.

Growing up in Assam, India, in a family of educationists, legislators, and Gandhian freedom fighters in India's independence, you always knew you wanted to do societal impact work. But you were good at art from a young age and you went to art school on weekends. You really enjoyed that. Taking up architecture after high school felt like a natural progression, but your department was in a technical institute with mostly engineering programs – computer science, electronics, electrical, and others. From time to time, you felt deeply insecure that your friends in engineering would find better paying jobs in the tech industry more quickly. Initially they will but hang in there. Oh, the social pressure to "get settled early" in middle class India. Be brave! You'll be surprised to know how much your art and architecture training will prepare you for your career in technology research in global development.

Of course, not everything will be easy along the way. As you already know, life away from home in Chicago as an Indian student was a struggle – financially, emotionally. In addition to a full-time master's program that will prove essential for your future career, you needed to work off-campus, at a fast-food place to pay your bills. At times you really wanted to quit. But you were right to hang in there because there are benefits to life abroad that you won't appreciate until a decade later. That time in Chicago builds resilience and will ultimately bring a much-needed outsider perspective to developing world problems. After all, when living in India, poverty and social problems can be so much in your face that it can sometimes be easy to look past them. Having some distance and being outside of a given context for a while helps

DOI: 10.4324/9781003260929-30

see problems better and to feel more passionately about solving problems pertaining to that context.

It is 2005, you're back in India. In Bangalore in fact. You're now an Assistant Researcher at Microsoft's new research lab in India, in the Technology for Emerging Markets group. It's like a dream job you never thought you could have. Technological changes are taking place across the country and the world. Low-end mobile phones are starting to be more prevalent. Conversations abound about how rural kiosks will be the first computing experience for more than 700 million people in the country and will move people out of poverty. All you have to do is translate this transformative technology into an interface that low-literate people can understand. Then it will surely change the world – right?

Wrong. Trust your instincts because your intuition is one of the most powerful tools in sensing what ICT solution might or might not work. Remember that real change rarely comes from technology by itself. This is easily forgotten. When you are surrounded by a brilliant cadre of techno-optimists, even the most grounded of user-centred researchers have a tendency to buy-in to the hype cycle of the latest technology. Only after hundreds of hours in the field will you and your mentor, Kentaro Toyama, amass enough stories of technology's shortcomings for him to write a book titled *Geek Heresy: Rescuing Social Change from the Cult of Technology* in 2015.

Those hours you will spend in the field are the ones that will stick with you the longest. So, keep your feet on the ground, spend time in the field talking to communities you're designing for, and iterate on your designs. As a design researcher, especially one with a certain amount of socio-economic privilege, you'll see that you bring your own biases into design. It is important to identify and address those biases as you design more effective interfaces for underserved communities. In technology design it is very easy to be caught in an ivory tower and have technological utopianism; to believe that technology alone can solve many of the world's problems. If you want to understand real user constraints and sociological nuances involved in good user interface design, get out of the ivory tower and immerse yourself in the field. Fieldwork will help you develop design intuition like no formal academic training can.

Let me give you an example. In 2007 and after some amount of fieldwork and iterative prototyping, you'll have your design prototypes ready. Your "text-free" interfaces use a combination of graphics, audio, and video. You'll have removed all text since people cannot read. Low-literate users should be able to use these interfaces – right? No, not quite. Controlled usability tests with potential users will show that your interfaces are not sufficient to allow people to proceed independently. The lesson? Always conduct rigorous testing of your design prototypes! It might be disheartening to see your designs fail, but better to fail early and fail fast and hopefully make amends in your next iteration.

As you rethink your tech intervention, really design for the cognitive abilities of people who have never been to school. And read up on related cognitive science literature. And explore the joys of interdisciplinary work! Why? Because many low-literate users you'll meet won't have been to school and, even if they had, it would most likely be in a very low-resource classroom where not every student receives individual attention. You'll think at first that non-literacy is the lack of textual literacy but, over time, you'll come to realise the importance of other cognitive processes that are attributed to formal education: the ability to reason abstractly; the ability to follow detailed instructions or have attention to detail in general; and the ability to think in hierarchical organisation. It turns out these have a much bigger impact on low-literate users' approaches to computers and user interfaces. If you keep this in mind you might finish your PhD from IIT Bombay much sooner!!

Technologies come and go, but the people you meet will remain in your heart forever. You will live on the campus of "Samaj Pragati Sahyog" (SPS) in rural Madhya Pradesh in central India, learning about the grass-roots initiative for water and livelihood security in central India. During that time, you'll live in the house of a small farmer family owning less than an acre of land. There will be no phone, internet, or running water. A little too outside of your comfort zone for an urbanite like you but there is so much to be gained by keeping an open mind and enjoying the experience. Never again in the next 20 years will you get a deep dive like this, one that not only gives you incisive research insights but also teaches you important life lessons.

In time you will also come to realise that the closest connections you will find are the ones that come from trusted local partners, like the non-profit "Stree Jagruthi Samithi" (SJS). SJS works with domestic workers in low-income communities in Bangalore. The meetings you will attend will help you understand the context, culture, and practices. Sometimes you'll ask yourself if you're wasting too much time or losing focus from your ICT research; you work in a technology company after all. But keep at it. Technology systems to solve societal problems often require significant work above and beyond an implementation of the technology, with trustworthy human intermediaries playing a critical role in owning and successfully running any services that you might design for communities. And of course, partner organisations are crucially important to run the show; to implement and scale proven technologies.

Finally, a word of caution. When you think of testing your intervention in the field, keep in mind that people will tell you they like your design intervention even when they don't. Because they don't want to offend you! This is especially going to be true when there are large differences in social status between you, the investigator, and your participants. Your collaborators and you will later write a paper about this! ("Yours in Better!" Participant Response Bias in HCI, CHI 2012). Be aware that response bias affects all studies. You will want to dissociate from your design wherever possible; get someone else to do user evaluations for you. Also do mixed methods evaluations – qualitative and quantitative – to validate your data.

In closing, this is what I have to say to you – when you're designing for people like yourself you might have good intuitions, but when you're working in ICT for global development and designing for people who might not be like you, people who have different constraints and challenges than you, it is super important to immerse in the communities that you seek to impact. This is how you'll develop intuition. When you're piloting a tech intervention, doing user evaluations, basically when the rubber meets the road, many of your design interventions will fall flat, or experience challenges that you had not even considered. Do iterative prototyping from the beginning, keeping end-users at the centre of the design process, and involve them in participatory design. Be ruthlessly empirical in testing, refining, and rebooting your assumptions, if you want your tech interventions to have real world impact.

More power to you!

At the time of writing, Indrani was a principal researcher in the Technology and Empowerment Group at Microsoft Research India. Her research interests are in the areas of user- centred design, human–computer interaction, and technology for global development. Over the years, Indrani's primary work has been in user interface design for low-literate and novice technology users. Indrani has published research articles in leading scientific conferences and journals. She has a PhD from the Industrial Design Centre, IIT Bombay, India; a Master's degree in Design from the IIT Institute of Design (ID), Chicago, USA; and a Bachelor's degree in Architecture from VNIT, Nagpur, India. Indrani is also trained in fine arts. She splits her time between Boston, USA, and Bangalore, India.

26 Be kind to yourself and others

Julie Mundy

Dear Jules,

I didn't realise just how hard it would be to write this letter to you: you're 27 and just embarking on what will be your life-long career and passion in international development. Thirty years later, you would think I would have sage advice and wisdom to share, but to be honest, as I get older, I have more questions than answers. But that's OK. In fact, it's essential. You were always curious, and I am pleased to say you will hang onto that curiosity. I have struggled with the validity of me – a white woman who has grown up with all the privileges of a wealthy country like Australia (and only just beginning to understand what that really means) – sharing my reflections on international development with you, at a time when the thinly held status quo is in the balance. I have wondered if my writing to you will have any relevance, as an important new path is slowly emerging. We are still very much at the start of something exciting, inching our way slowly forward, and it will require courage and heart-rending honesty from all for us working in international development to move from a place of historical approaches, good intentions, and cynical geopolitics to a place of equity, where power is genuinely shifted and shared. A utopia perhaps, but this does not mean you shouldn't strive for it. There will always be a need for your grounded optimism.

In the last three years, the world has experienced a pandemic such as you have never seen in your lifetime. It has fundamentally changed this generation's way of being in the world, with lockdowns, deaths in the millions, and no country in the world left untouched. Yet many of the countries you will work in have suffered so much more due to the appalling health inequities that still remain in the world, despite everyone's constant and concerted efforts (including yours with your work in women's health) and billions of dollars of investment. In years to come, and hopefully sooner than I did, you will start to seriously consider the systemic nature of development, the interconnectedness of everything: how the economy, education, income, health, governance, women's reproductive rights, and more are all interwoven in ways that mean a concerted and collaborative effort across sectors and stakeholders is the only sustainable way forward.

DOI: 10.4324/9781003260929-31

Yet for all that complexity, don't let it deter you from your single-minded focus in supporting and strengthening local organisations, headed by local women and men of significance and character. They taught you so much, and were so generous with their knowledge, their time, their patience, and their company. Some of those country directors have become life-long friends: Dr Yasmin Ahmed from Bangladesh who went on to become the Global Director of Asia Programs – you recruited each other really, women of the same age, shouting through the bars at Dhaka airport in the middle of a *hartal* (strike); Nguyen Bich Hang, who has achieved a sustainable women's health services model in Viet Nam, seeing through the country's transition to a socialist market economy (can you believe that you will both have babies at the same time, and they will be crawling about together in Viet Nam while you both developed a kick-ass strategic plan?!); Kamala Thapa in Nepal, possibly the most quietly courageous person I know – establishing 60 women's health clinics across the country at a time of major political unrest with a clear vision to prevent women dying and enable them to choose the size of their families; Bolormaa Dashdavaa from Mongolia, who was able to socially market and distribute condoms by any means possible (including camels!) to help address the country's growing HIV crisis, and is now Senior Vice President of one of the country's largest companies; Atula Nanyakkara and Dr Ramanathan from Sri Lanka, an entrepreneur prepared to challenge the status quo, and a doctor whose life's work was to save women's lives and who taught you to always ask questions and never, never stop learning; Dr Mohsina from Pakistan – a pioneering and sophisticated leader who worked in some of the toughest conditions to bring women's reproductive health services across her sometimes troubled country, wending her way through the cultural mores to always find a solution, as well as getting you out of the occasional civil conflict with grace and calm; Hu Hongtao and Lily Liu Chen, both from China, who met you on your own terms as peers, confident in the needs of their country, and shared more knowledge with you than you could ever return. So many incredible people and role models who will help you become you and will enrich your life beyond measure.

In fact, working with national leaders feels instinctively right to you. You will know that you are a conduit to the support and resources they need to achieve what they know they must. That you will share outrageous laughter, tears, frustrations, and successes together, is such an amazing privilege. At the moment, you think you are "leading from behind" as the regional director. I am here to tell you that in fact, your role is very much *supporting* from behind.

In your late twenties, after acquiring some skills and maturity, you will choose to work with an organisation which was founded in the 1970s by a visionary British man, Dr Tim Black, who is driven by the need to ensure every child was wanted, and works on the assumption that nationals of each country know what the issues are but may not have the resources or experience to address them. It is a great fit for you as an organisation: pragmatic, solutions-focused, innovative, brave, fun. You will be given a lot of responsibility and autonomy, and you will thrive in that environment. Your time off will be spent hiking, walking, puffing up and down hills, and the intensity of that is such an essential way for you to recharge – keep at it!!

You will also make plenty of mistakes along the way, and that's OK too, as long as you are humble, are honest about them, and learn, learn, learn what to do differently next time!! You will have a fabulous and dynamic team about you, and knowing to recruit people smarter and more experienced than yourself, who know things you don't, is key. Trust them to deliver – they will if they can and you can provide an environment for them to succeed.

Over time, as the organisation evolves, expatriates of all nationalities (not just "the north"), will also be deployed to support rapid scale-ups in various countries. However, for you that will feel like a retrograde step and after 17 amazing years, it's time for you to move on, though you never will really lose your love for the organisation, its people, and what it is trying to achieve. You will start to work independently, focusing now on building your skills in an emerging profession, the "how" of collaborations and partnership – that invisible thing that you have always been aware somehow gets in the way of effective and impactful work when it is not done well. You will retrain as a partnership broker and help a wide range of organisations and governments work more effectively together to solve really complex development problems. You will love the challenge and the variety, and the privilege of helping partnerships really thrive. I wish you had had these skills earlier because what a difference they would have made! By the time you reach my age, the nuanced layers of power inequities between partners become a real focus. You are learning all the time, and now growing in confidence, and with experience and independence you are better able to question and to challenge. I would wish that for you also earlier in your career – put aside the imposter's syndrome which many Gen Y women seem to carry (and I mean you!) and hold your space, Jules: inhabit your competence.

I also want to reassure you: from the shock and horror of COVID, some good will emerge, which speaks to your instincts and your drive for equity. When countries were slamming shut their borders, people were locked down in their cities and villages, and the "international" aspects of international development were redefined. The long, slow burning conversation about "localisation", and what this *truly* means, will finally begin in earnest, thrust into everyone's immediate reality. This is a confronting conversation, which is challenging the status quo, bringing up difficult, deeply held detritus to genuinely consider the decolonisation of aid and the deeply ingrained power imbalances between "donor" and recipient, between international NGOs and local organisations, between multinational companies and local businesses. As I write this, we are in the thick of this, resistant and afraid and excited about whether things can really change, whether a true recalibration is possible in a way that honours *all* those involved. But change is hard, and here is where I really need you to lean in, with an open mind, an open heart, and courage.

The coming months and years will be as challenging and upending as your early time in this sector, Jules. Embrace it. Live it. You will feel uncomfortable from time to time, and if you are not, then you're not listening hard enough. I hope for you that you will never stop learning, never stop questioning, never stop valuing the people around you.

But most of all. Be kind to yourself and to others. Be you. It is enough.

Much love to you, Jules.

Julie is an experienced independent partnerships specialist and development practitioner, working extensively with government, international institutions, the business sector, research organisations, and INGOs across the Asia Pacific, Australia, and globally to help build and sustain effective cross-sector and multi-stakeholder partnerships in support of the sustainable development goals. She is Chair, and former Founding CEO of MSI Asia Pacific, and is an Adjunct Research Fellow with Latrobe University Institute for Human Security and Social Change. Julie is based in Melbourne, Australia.

27

Follow your own path, forge your own route

Ken Banks

Dear Younger Me

You're too sensitive, they say. Too quiet, too introverted, too emotional. You probably think about things far too much. You're not tough enough for this world. And yes, back then they were probably right. But rest assured – these will turn out to be strengths, not weaknesses or faults. In a world that will grow increasingly sceptical, divided, and inward-looking, your open, friendly, caring nature will stand out. I know you're going to struggle with what you'll later call "empathy overdrive", and that things are going to be difficult for you on many levels, but you're going to turn into someone strong, compassionate, and, yes, successful. All of your so-called negative traits will make you stand out, give you an edge and a determination to never give up, and will form the cornerstone of a future career in the world of technology and international development, one you will become very proud of – your mother, too.

You won't know this yet, but your safe, ordinary life will be turned upside down by a famine in a far-away country and, of all things, a global rock concert called Live Aid. A world of suffering will open up in front of you, and the armies of international conservation and development workers fighting against the odds trying to solve them, and the images of poverty, suffering, and destruction they all bring into your home will be the fuel that drives you for the rest of your life. You'll later apologise for using the word, but you'll be driven to action by guilt, a sense that you were one of the lucky ones not to live in any of these places, and in your drive to learn more about inequality and injustice you'll embark on travels to faraway lands, not once but many times, and help build local schools and hospitals and, yes, even work with primates. You'll dedicate the majority of your working life to global development, although it won't feel that way at the start. You'll put all your efforts into finding work with an international aid organisation, and disappointment after disappointment will end up driving you to take your own path,

DOI: 10.4324/9781003260929-32

to go it alone, to turn your back on convention and build something alone. The worlds of social entrepreneurship and innovation don't exist yet, but they will when it matters, and you'll be quick to realise the power of driven, engaged citizens in driving social change. Not only that, despite all the odds, you'll become one yourself. All that late night coding on Mr Cooper's Commodore PET computer will turn out to be the most valuable skill of all, and those tiny computer programs you're writing that help students at the local club will be nothing in comparison to the millions your software will go on to help when you have your big idea. And, yes, the text messaging technology you'll adapt to help people the world over doesn't exist yet, but when it does you'll be one of the first to embrace it, and you'll become something of a reluctant leader in the world of ICT4D, or Information and Communications for Development. Mobile phones will become one of the most transformative tools in global development, and you'll be right up there doing your best to help everyone make the most of the opportunity.

Other than the guilt, you never did understand what it was that drove you, but one day you will write a book about it. You'll edit a couple of other books, too, sharing stories of other people who, like you, just couldn't turn their backs on the suffering they saw in the world and who also used their skills to become leading social entrepreneurs. In fact, you'll use your platform to share the stories of hundreds of other innovators doing their own work, their own way, outside of the more traditional global development system, and you'll become something of a champion for community and citizen-led change. In fact, it will end up being the only approach you believe in. You'll write widely about the failings of the international development community, and suggest alternative, more sensitive, better locally-led approaches to problem solving that are completely at odds with the top-down, technology-led (rather than people and problem-led) approach that dominates. And eventually you'll turn your back on an aid sector, which felt more like an industry and not a movement for good. And, this time, you'll seek change not on your own, but back where it all began for you, in the private sector.

Believe it or not, those poems and scribbles you write under your covers at night will lead to books and articles for *The Guardian*, the BBC, *PC World* magazine and guest chapters in all sorts of books, including this one. I know you already are, but be extra grateful to your mother and to Mr King – the only teacher at school to support your writing – for encouraging you. Never be afraid to express yourself in the written word, in whatever form that takes. Storytelling might be underrated to some, but it will go on to become almost an industry in itself.

Don't worry too much that school only seems to measure the things you're not good at. Your creativity and imagination will be far greater assets to you when you're older. Everything else you'll learn as you go along, and that's fine. And don't worry that you're not a prolific reader like some of your friends. You just need the right books, and to find something to be passionate about. That will also come thanks to that rock concert, and the horrors of that famine in Ethiopia.

You won't know it yet, but you're going to become quite the opportunist, taking advantage of opportunities that, over time, will lead you to a much better, happier place. Your inquisitive nature will turn you into something of an expert at dismantling old televisions and radios that you'll buy for next-to-nothing from jumble sales. From there you'll teach yourself to wire your own sound systems in your bedroom – don't worry about getting the odd electric shock – and go on to teach yourself how to program early computers at your local club. Programming will become an early passion of yours, and form one of the cornerstones of your later career. You don't know that yet, so keep on hacking the code, and keep on applying your creativity to make things that, right now, might only live in your imagination. One day you'll build something on the back of mobile technology (which doesn't exist yet) that will make a big difference to the lives of some of the poorest and most marginalised people on the planet. FrontlineSMS will also change your life, giving you ammunition to prove that simple, low-cost, locally appropriate technologies can make a difference, can be successful, and can drive deeper change than the millions of dollars too-often wasted on far less impactful projects by the development community.

If you ever feel lost, or directionless, then I just want you to know that almost everything you do will make sense one day, and that your life will come full circle – often in the most surprising of ways. One example – see that man on the news? That's Archbishop Desmond Tutu, fighting for a fair and just South Africa. Things are particularly bad there at the moment. As you watch in admiration, learning about the kinds of injustices in places far away, it might surprise you that one day you'll end up in South Africa, and that you'll become friends with the Archbishop. He will even go on to write the foreword to your first book, and record a welcome video for your first son, Henry. So keep dreaming, and keep imagining. The impossible isn't always that impossible after all.

Your love of music is also going to grow, and although you'll never learn to play or write music you'll surround yourself with it nevertheless. Don't worry – one day you'll be able to buy your own records. I know how annoying it can be trying to tape music from the radio, but you'll look back on those days with fondness. In a few years, when you get your first car, you'll spend countless hours driving around the island listening to music, and Peter Gabriel will become something of a favourite, although you don't know who he is at the moment. And, in another twist of fate, Peter will not only become a globally recognised human rights campaigner, but will become a friend and admirer of your own work, and will write one of the forewords to your second book. As I told you, life will come full circle for you, even if it doesn't feel like it will right now.

I just wanted to sign off by saying that, despite your successes, your career will reveal a world of disappointments. Your inherent belief in the good of people won't always stand true, and your hope that everyone wants what's best for everyone else won't either. Money and politics and a skewed world order will get in the way of much of the progress you'll strive for, and hope for. Finding solutions to problems will not be enough – the hard work will begin when you try to get them into the hands of those who might benefit most. For a while you're going to believe that the best chance you'll have of helping correct many of the injustices you'll see in the world will be by getting a job in a large international charity. But I can tell you now that you'll soon get frustrated, and the only option you'll have left is to follow your own path, and do things your own way. And you will.

I write this to you, Boyo, almost 50 years on, surrounded by awards and photos and memories of a tremendous few years doing it our own way. I am also surrounded by my own family now, and see traits in my children that I see in you. But now that doesn't worry me. If anything, I'm proud. They have a curiosity and a hunger for knowledge, and a love of people and cultures and the natural world, that you did.

And that didn't turn out so bad, did it?

Ken Banks is a British award-winning social innovator, technologist, and anthropologist with over 25 years experience working in developing regions of the world, particularly Africa, with a focus on technology, conservation, and humanitarian relief. He is a PopTech Fellow, an Ashoka Fellow, a National Geographic Explorer, and the recipient of numerous other fellowships and prizes including the prestigious ACM Eugene L. Lawler Award for Humanitarian Contributions within Computer Science. He is best known as the creator of FrontlineSMS, a globally successful text messaging communications platform, and the founder of kiwanja.net. Ken is also a keynote speaker, mentor, and the author of four books on social entrepreneurship and social innovation.

28
Trust yourself

Petra Karetji

Dear Petra,

I see you, 26 years ago, leaving on a bus from the town in which you've just spent the last eight years of your life; the town that housed the university where you studied, where you made good and bad acquaintances, and where you grew up and had your first real job. I know you are sad to be leaving behind a happy and easy lifestyle and your wonderful friends. I also know that you are wondering if you are making the right choice. Your instincts tell you that it feels right; that it is time to move on.

I'm glad you decided to take this step. Trust your instincts. Your greatest regrets, and worst mistakes, will come when you don't listen to what your gut is telling you, when you meet someone new and work with them, even learn to trust them, yet from the start something didn't feel right. You'll try to rationalise the relationship, argue that you are working to a common goal, and persuade yourself that you are just being paranoid. You'll even chastise yourself for being biased and self-opiniated and that you should look for the positives in others. Trust yourself. There will be other opportunities, new contacts and relationships, so don't try to sustain the ones that start with that feeling of uneasiness and doubt.

On the other hand, identify those who you know to be "constants" – important friends and relationships you know are stable, who find joy in openly sharing their knowledge, and who love to learn from others. You already know some of these: the university professor, and the friends and family who are there for you and who will nurture and critique you. The constants are those who know who they are, and are comfortable with their identity, their self. They are the ones who tell you when they are happy or proud of what you have done, but who will also warn you and are aptly able to argue their standpoint against your opinions and perspectives. Listen to and appreciate those you can identify as constants, as they will provide anchorage and safe haven for you. Learn to measure yourself by your constants, where you have progressed or regressed.

Learn to understand your fears and motivations. Inherently you feel disadvantaged and inferior, coming from a remote region in Papua, yet now

DOI: 10.4324/9781003260929-33

working amongst those with international academic degrees, privileged upbringing, and decades of access to information and knowledge you are only now aware of. You often internalise or personify your work, arguing that you need to be passionate and motivated about what you want to achieve. That same motivation and passion can become a barrier. It can prevent you from seeing the merits of others' perspectives and arguments, because you become resistant to others who are seeking to assist by identifying the holes and weaknesses in your argument. Counter arguments are not personal attacks on your integrity and capacity, so avoid being blindsided by your own fears. Instead, learn to harness your passion, and temper it with strong data and evidence. Once you have your facts right, and are able to gauge rationally with others' perspectives, then don't be afraid to show your enthusiasm and love for the work you feel and know is important.

Much of your anxiety and tension stem from an underlying inferiority complex, coupled with a fear of failure and rejection. You've had to learn to adapt on your own in new environments, ever since you were sent off to a boarding school when you were 11 years old. As your bus carries you further away from the comfortable existence you had, you will need to further prepare yourself for the challenges ahead. Invest in yourself, buy and read books, expand your knowledge, and develop your self-awareness. Don't feel guilty to take time even during your working hours to grab a few chapters. Take notes or scribble in the pages, it helps to reinforce points you like and will help you find the reference you want when you need to quote and drive home your case. Importantly, turn your feelings of inadequacy into a stimulant to better equip yourself. Understand that your background and worldview can provide perspectives for your collaborators to think outside their boxes, and even to create new ones.

A wise person once said in a meeting I attended: "if you know what you are talking about and have a clear opinion or concern, please speak up; if neither – please don't!". You will often hesitate to speak up, to state a counter opinion, as you think you should pick your battles, and your tendency is to look for and nurture allies. This is true to a certain extent, but there will be a time where your presence is to provide a "local" or "South" perspective. Do not waste these opportunities, be prepared, and have your facts – the programs and projects you are asked to review can have real meaning for real people.

On matters and initiatives that you feel are important, take the time to talk with those who are key decision makers prior to critical stop–go junctures. Try to understand and alleviate their concerns and biases. You are more effective working this way, through one-on-one meetings rather than in larger forums, and your knowledge of others' perspectives will give you comfort, as you are often wrought with worry and crippled by nervousness when speaking in large forums.

Importantly, try to identify the underlying agenda of dominant individuals; look to better understand what is influencing their decisions. You've been able to observe "agenda-setters" in university, where some leaders are driven by academic principles, others engage in departmental power plays, and some just seek clarity of purpose to proceed. Use these categories of principle, power, or purpose to read between the lines. Is the person more concerned about whether the topic under debate is misaligned to their principles? Are they worried that the outcome will undermine their authority? Or are they into the minute details of outputs and delivery? Find these cues and use them to shape and deliver your message and responses.

Try to be succinct when you communicate. When you started university, you hoped to become a teacher, but in your work, you can't always try to make everyone understand your viewpoint. You have to stop trying to get everyone on board as there will almost always be dissenters, unwilling to step beyond their own worldview, biases, and preconceptions. Accept this and stick to your main points. Talk to the key decision maker: it is they that you have to convince, not the crowd. Although unanimous agreement is nice, understand that it is not always necessary.

As you progress into a career working on social development, try to find the time to reconnect with those on the ground, particularly those who are facing and dealing directly with issues and challenges. Don't let them become numbers and abstractions. You'll find that this re-energises you and provides you direction and clarity. Use these moments also to reconnect with the teacher in you. Cherish the joy you feel when you are able to share knowledge and experiences with those who have not had the opportunity to experience the same exposure you will gain in your work.

When you do reconnect, don't try to motivate those you meet with general platitudes about the importance of their work. Look for and provide them with specific details of what impresses you. In doing so, you will find you will also learn more, because you have started from a position of appreciation, and this will usually be reciprocated with openness and honesty. On the other hand, if your appreciation does not elicit candour, then you will need to triangulate and dig deeper, as this is usually a good signal that something is amiss.

Try to make conversations with as many people as you can with different worldviews and experiences, from the passionate community facilitator to the chatty taxi driver and the shy mama selling smoked fish – appreciating each opportunity as a meaningful discussion, providing insights on others' lives significant to those they interact with. By sharing what you think you know, you will find that your opinions can be reinforced or debunked. Don't fall into the trap of thinking that you are impactful because of the funds or resources you are able to bring to bear. It is the dialogues you engage in and the knowledge shared and gained that provide a lasting impression for both sides to use to their benefit.

You've learnt to survive in a university setting, with its own style or "code" of communication to navigate academic hierarchies. As you move to take on your new job, you will learn new codes. Learn to code-switch. Different people communicate in different ways. You will find that, working in Western, or "modern" settings, you are required to provide quick responses, to have answers and views, while using the right mix of terminologies and jargon or buzzwords to fit in and be seen as competent. I realised I had fallen into this trap when chatting to a much wiser person who was head of the village I was visiting. We were sitting in the afternoon on one of the beautiful beaches of Padaido island, and I thought it would be a great opportunity to fire some questions at him about the project I was monitoring. I found myself becoming flustered because he did not directly respond, and so I rephrased my questions, assuming that he did not understand what I was asking. This time he just looked at me and continued to chew his betel nut. I decided to stop and, like him, sit back and enjoy the view. After some time, he started to talk. He proceeded to give me a very structured overview about the project, and his impressions and concerns. I realised then how much I had become slave to the code I was accustomed to. Even worse, I was judging others by their ability to communicate in the same manner, not only in terms of jargon, but also in terms of space and time. Learn to adapt and be appreciative of other's codes. Also be aware of the shortfalls of your own dominant code, being fast and responsive does not necessarily equate to being right.

The last point I'd like to share is to be patient and let things flow. Enjoy and learn from the process as much as the result in everything you undertake. Too many times I look back with regret on occurrences where I did not have the patience to allow things to fall in place, so I pushed, and tried to make things happen and force things to completion, counting the proverbial chickens even before the eggs are laid. By all means chase opportunities, but please take the time to chart the pathways, the potential obstacles, the risks, and the possible damage to you and to others. Rather than starting from a position of longing, of wanting to achieve more and be more, try to start by first being grateful of where you are and why you are there. Believe me, the ends do not justify the means, if this means having to go against your principles, risking your reputation, and putting yourself and others at risk.

There's so much more I'd like to share, but a simple joy of life is the day-to-day discoveries about yourself and others. Savour the strokes of your paddle as your canoe of life navigates rivers, lakes, and seas in this turbulent world, amongst the high-powered ships of political and economic interests. By all means get on board when they are going in your direction, but if you do, don't be a passive passenger. See if you can help them avoid crushing other canoes, and don't get so used to the amenities that you're unable to get off when their direction shifts. Give thanks for the life you have and enjoy the anticipation of destinations ahead.

Salam,
Petra

Petra has more than 25 years of professional experience and has undertaken a range of leadership roles. Until recently, he led Pulse Lab Jakarta, a joint data innovation facility of the United Nations and the Government of Indonesia. He is currently Team Leader of a program that seeks to address regional disparities in Indonesia. He lives in Jakarta, Indonesia.

Section V

Researching development practice

29
Ask why?

Deepa Narayan

Dear Deepa,

You will be fine. Don't kill yourself. Don't run away. Not to an *ashram* and not to Bollywood! As soon as you wake up at 6.35 am you will run from your cot in the garden in *Moti Bagh* to pick up the *Times of India* lying on the ground. Your heart is racing. You wonder if your name is the first in the first division of your first year in college? You joined Lady Irwin College, this elite women's college as a joke when you failed to get into medical college after a year of pre-medicine. And now your name is on the failed list. I know it hurts to see failure announced in the national newspaper. It's such a ridiculous practice. Soon everyone in New Delhi will know and the black phone sitting on the table near the entrance will start ringing. You crawl back into bed and cover yourself completely with the white sheet. Nobody had ever failed in our family. Everyone is quiet.

I am from your future, so I know your life will be fine; actually, it will be spectacular – it will be full of all the things your heart longs for, adventures, travels, awards, and yes, lots of books.

I will not give you three wishes but even better, I will give you three pieces of advice to guide you for the next 50 years.

Life is not a straight line.

You are only 18. Your life will take many twists and turns, ups and downs, so don't focus on the future. Focus on now. The way will find you. You are a dreamy girl lost in books. Unfortunately not your textbooks! Ever since that day in Class 7, when Mummy complained that you only got two merit report cards for doing extremely well in two subjects in school instead of the five that your friend Ritu got, you stopped studying. I know medicine is your father's dream but now your defiant decision never to study is hurting you. Think about it.

Do drop the shame of failure, it will stop you from moving forward in life. Don't hide it. And it's ok to feel lost . . . but keep taking action. It is easy to misunderstand what Papa reads to all five of you children on Sunday mornings from religious texts and the romance poets, and even though he laughs a lot, he is actually trying to teach you something. *Action in inaction, vedantic*

DOI: 10.4324/9781003260929-35

wisdom is overrated at your age. Act. At your age, it is important to participate in life. Don't be paralysed by, "Is this forever?"

I promise you, nothing lasts forever, you won't have time to be bored, you will move so many times, maybe 40–50 times around the world. You will study all kinds of topics – textiles and clothing (you fail), nutrition and cooking (you sneer), psychology (research methods will stay), sociology, anthropology (intriguing), child development (not excited), human development, journalism (fun) . . . the only thing you will not study is economics, nobody told you it was a subject, even though your father was a tax guy and will soon become the head of taxation for the country.

Your quiet defiance and stubborn resistance to the predictable future of a girl in India, marriage, will take you to study in the USA in 1975 – the first girl in your extended family to go, you won't know anyone, you won't have enough money, you will experience hunger and also kindness. And men will not bother you on the streets.

Half-way across the world, in a rich country like the USA, while at Iowa State University, you will become curious about poverty. You learn that a person with a fridge and car can still be poor. When you visit a poor black woman in her home in Ames Iowa, you learn she is totally isolated and has to spend hours constantly proving that she is poor enough to get some government benefits to take care of her children. When she gets a job at Target, her benefits are taken away, and when her benefits are taken away, her job is not enough to feed her children. She lives in limbo between Target and Social Services. You write an article about her poverty trap and the silly please-do-not-escape-poverty-policy for the student newspaper. It is six months after your arrival.

When your full-page article questioning the wisdom of the government policy program is published in the student newspaper, you are proud, especially as Americans are constantly surprised that you can speak English at all! Your major professor in Child Development, a tall skinny blonde lady, calls you in. There is no praise or encouragement. There is no policy discussion. There is no discussion about the black woman in the article. She just looks you up and down, and her glance – it's the glance given to servants in India. You can't make sense of it. You don't understand racism. It is too early in the promise of a great country.

You will change not because of what you study but because of your father's readings about goodness that becomes your thick inner skin that cannot be scratched, dyed, torn, or traded away. Those Sunday morning readings will flip the switch one day half-way through Graduate School and you will say to yourself, "I come from a poor country: I must work on poverty".

This will be the impact of "brown bag lunches". It basically means, please bring your own lunch to the meeting. In India you would never sit around a table and eat your own food without sharing, it is so shameful not to share. The lunches are held every Wednesday at the Foreign Student Office on campus. They feature experts on development, including returned Peace Corp Volunteers. You love these talks because you start to see your experiences in India through foreign eyes, the answers to so many questions they study are so obvious to you; but some others not obvious at all. You learn to become an insider–outsider to your own culture.

You find your purpose at a brown-bag lunch. For the rest of your life. Yes, there will be many more turns and twists, but you will always address some poverty and power puzzle and inequality. You will borrow concepts and research methods from different academic disciplines and you will be inventive, because in your wanderings across subjects and remote villages you escape the ideological indoctrination of places of power and the elite universities of the world.

Speak up! You are a brown girl, this will never change so don't wait. It will be hard to be brown in an infinity of white, a woman, a woman from the other side of the world with an accent and a strong mind, someone who constantly questions and challenges. *Stop trying to fit.* Believe in yourself and speak up. Communicate, communicate, communicate.

You are now 26. You are waiting outside for Dr Damaris Pease, the Head of the Department, to come out and tell you whether you have passed, if your doctoral dissertation has been accepted. Your mind drifts to all those conversations in churches and schools at talks in Ames, when people said, "If only poor people did not have so many children, they would not be poor". Tired of this dismissal of the poor, you switched your research topic to examine statistically the perceived costs and benefits of children to parents, and the links to fertility in villages near Lucknow, India. You really wanted people, including your professors who had never been outside the US, to understand the realities of poor people in India, so you screened a slide show of beautiful photographs you had taken during your field work to explain poor people's choices.

The door of the conference room opens and Dr Pease comes out and says, "We now understand why it is rational for poor people to have so many children, you have passed, congratulations Dr Narayan".

You are spunky. In Botswana, one day in 1980 you walk into the office of the Head of Ministry of Commerce and Industry in Gaborone and ask Mr Klaus why there is no rural industrialisation policy and you convince him to finance your organisation to do research in rural areas to inform a national strategy.

Strangely, the districts are run by young white Canadian volunteers, college kids who live in small houses, but their bodies swell up when they sit in their offices or drive their Land Cruisers with the "clear the roads for me" swagger of past white masters. Is it even possible to be humble when you come from a modest home in the West, with no job experience, and are suddenly put in charge of administering an entire district? You are overwhelmed by the power of two white 25-year-olds who wash their hands of the study even though there is no other. You can't speak up. Your heart breaks. Don't be heartbroken, racism is coiled tight in every framework and sexism inside its every molecule; it will bite you often, but your work and impact will grow. In Botswana your open-ended methodology to understand rural resources and work preferences, including asking poor school children their dreams for their future, will be replicated across the country after your departure.

I know it's easy to say, speak up. You do speak up. But you don't yet know how to overcome fear and speak up when there is conflict. Your mother's voice, your aunt's voices, your teacher's voice, your father's voice, men's voices, all tell you not to be argumentative or stubborn. To be good. You must learn how to resolve conflict, how to negotiate with others and how to stand up for yourself. Keeping quiet does not change the world.

There is one other way to gain strength – the power of numbers, build a community, a circle of support. You don't have to be alone, have some fun with others. Not knowing is wisdom of the sages. Always question, don't become a brown neo-colonial. Your special power is to constantly ask, why? Probe deeply and widely.

To avoid becoming a brown faced neo-colonial, you have to look at problems, theories, and assumptions with fresh eyes. Grapple with and identify the core problem. If the problem is improving sanitation, don't assume flush toilets are the answer; if the problem is getting girls to school, don't assume parents are the problem; if nutrition of infants is the problem, don't assume giving mothers extra food is the solution; if hand pumps don't work, don't assume technology is the solution or even that water is a problem. Find out more, observe, learn, and talk to those most affected and those who hold the power over those affected. Constantly be aware of how power is distributed in local communities, in districts, and in organisations you want to change. Understand the geography, history, politics, and social organisations.

You will learn by working in villages for a decade. Probing the desires, interests, choices, power, love, geography, and social life of different groups will yield new insights. Whether you work with small NGOs or large multilateral organisations like the World Bank, the problem of knowing the solution before deeply probing the problem is the same. The only difference is that mistakes made by large organisations will have much greater negative impact.

It is very seductive to want to join large organisations like the World Bank or the United Nations or governments or large civil society alliances, because whatever you achieve is multiplied many times. But with great opportunity comes great responsibility. So don't join big organisations very young – get into the field and learn something, do something, solve problems in the real world, make your mistakes, fail on a small scale so you don't contribute to spectacular harm on a large scale. Develop a point of view of your own.

Beware of ideologies in small and large organisations that swing and change every 5–10 years . . . "shrink the public sector", "privatise everything as quickly as possible", "the poor must pay for everything", "make willingness-to-pay God", "social entrepreneurship" . . . Ask basic questions. Question assumptions.

You will take on complex problems and with others you will question poverty measures, gather voices of the poor, create terms like community-driven development, probe social capital, empowerment, call for a new FeminismX, argue a lot, and be fulfilled.

There are so many big questions we need to answer:

- Are the basic assumptions of economics right? Individuals and competition? Where are kindness, sharing, collectives?
- What does it mean to be a man, woman, or person of any gender, race, caste today?
- Can we achieve gender equality by only focusing on women's empowerment and ignoring what men do?
- Why are women still being beaten up or raped all over the world?
- Does white feminism serve the globe?
- Where are poor people's ideas and desires in the policies to reduce poverty and inequality?
- Why do organisations spread themselves thinly when they haven't even changed one state or one country?
- Can we change food production systems quickly enough to survive?
- How can we get global consensus and financing for climate change, will we survive, for how long?

Always ask why, why, why?

You are amazing! Brilliant, smart, thoughtful, kind, original, unique, and yes – beautiful. Own all of it. Completely. Don't believe anyone who says anything contrary, they are just beings lost in their own hurt. Your life will turn out just fine, you will be fine. Make that your mantra when you feel lost, when your dreams crash. Don't run from them. Do the opposite – pull them inside you, keep them close to you, so your heart and mind remain open for the next adventure.

I am always with you.
Mama

Dr Deepa Narayan is the author of the ground-breaking book, Chup: Breaking the Silence about India's Women. She has over 25 years of experience working at the World Bank, the UN, and NGOs on poverty, gender, and inequality in development.

She was Senior Adviser at the World Bank in Washington D.C. and wrote the influential series Voices of the Poor based on 60,000 people in

60 countries. She has written 17 books and is the recipient of many awards, including being named as one of the 100 most influential global thinkers by Foreign Policy Magazine in the USA as well as one of India's 35 Great Thinkers by India Today. Dr Narayan spent many years living in village communities. This led to her focus on "people first", and local community-driven approaches nested in social and political processes. She lives in Delhi, India.

30 My development decades

Gabriele Köhler

1960, schoolgirl

Khrushchev bangs his shoe at the UN General Assembly. I realise from the radio and TV news that there is this important gathering of all countries, called the United Nations, and that they want peace. So do I, and name my new kitten Nikita.

1974, student

I sit in a German university library reading two UN resolutions on a *new* international economic order – the NIEO. They call for correcting inequalities, redressing existing injustices, and eliminating the widening gap between developed and developing countries in a system which perpetuates inequality. They recommend codes of conduct on the transfer of technology and on transnational corporations, and measures to address the unbalanced terms of trade. This politicised approach to economics is different from my detached mainstream macro-economics textbooks. And it totally resonates with our extracurricular reading and protest marches – and with the idealism and excitement that the economics professors at Regensburg university instil in us. So, I decide I would like to work where a just international economic order is the underlying principle.

1983, young professional

After some detours, I eventually pass the UN entrance exam and start work at the UN regional office for Asia and the Pacific in Bangkok. All my bosses are from so-called developing countries. Most are upper-class privileged-caste men. But they are also the offspring of the generation of anti-colonial independence fighters, and intellectually left wing in their economics. Many perceive this woman from Germany as a post-colonialist agent, with "NGO-ish" views on development strategies. Or feel that a wife and young mother belongs in her home, not in an office. So, I am challenged: on

DOI: 10.4324/9781003260929-36

the job, there is the agency's commitment to economic and geopolitical justice, but social and gender equality is not on the vista.

1992, mid-career development economist

I move on to Geneva to join UNCTAD – birthplace of the NIEO. But while I am in the throes of moving back to my home continent, under pressure from the US, UNCTAD adopts its Cartagena commitment – turning to market forces and away from equalising regulatory measures such as commodity funds. Transnational corporations are re-cast as "engines of growth", the codes of conduct on business are abandoned. The WTO prevails over UNCTAD – all the developing and least developed countries scramble to join and throw open their economies to foreign investors, with little negotiation on the socio-economic safeguards for their societies. So, it is a difficult decade.

2002, senior-ish UN official

I am in Latvia, which is about to join the European Union. I help to close the UN's development programs in Latvia, handing all the portfolios back to the relevant ministries and agencies – human rights, gender and youth participation, judicial reform, environment, HIV-Aids prevention, export diversification, and many others. Research on human development and human security is anchored in Latvian policy and academic discourse. So, I am happy: this is the situation every development economist dreams of – a country is "graduating".

2020, retiree

I talk and write a lot about the UN's agenda 2030. I support how it reframes the concept of development: all countries are developing countries. Many countries acknowledge, and promise to address, their income inequality, gender disparities, inequities in the access to decent work, health, education, water, energy, the digital divide, and global warming and planetary destruction. New generations are broadening, and questioning, the concept of development. So, I ought to relax: a good share of the public discourse is progressive.

Instead, I am despondent. The promise of "development" is unravelling – peace, justice, social and economic justice, a safe planet, and even just universal access to health services appear more out of reach than ever before.

And onwards?

My website still calls me a "development economist". Mainly out of habit and convention. But I mean it to be understood in that new sense that all societies – and all individuals including myself – need to commit to continuously develop!

Gabriele Köhler studied economics and Chinese in Germany in the early 1970s. She worked as an "economic affairs" officer with the UN for two decades, and later as a UN resident coordinator/UNDP representative in Latvia, and a UNICEF regional advisor on social policy in South Asia.

In 1994, she published a volume of essays "Questioning Development".[1] *In it, she queries the overbearing notion of development, and muses on the parade of development paradigms that shape development interventions in the Global South. A follow-up piece is "Seven Decades of Development – and Now What?".*[2]

She is currently affiliated with Women Engage for a Common Future – an NGO devoted to climate and gender justice, and with the UN Research Institute for – Social Development!

Notes

1 Co-editors Charles Gore, Utz-Peter Reich, Thomas Ziesemer, Marburg: Metropolis 1994.

2 *Journal of International Development*. 2015. https://onlinelibrary.wiley.com/doi/abs/10.1002/jid.3108.

31

Transforming opportunities and challenges into a career in gender and international development

Leith Dunn

The Sankofa bird flies forward while looking backwards. Looking back on your life, I can see the events, factors, and lessons that have shaped your 30-year career in support of development policies, programmes, and practices. Opportunities will emerge for you to work at national, regional, and international levels. Like an onion with different layers, each phase of your life will prepare you for the next. Of course, you don't know that yet: you are only 19 years old, preparing to graduate from university. You want to "have it all": to get a job, get married, and start a family. So, let's start with what you do know.

Looking back on your adolescent years, you knew you wanted an exciting career that included travel, transforming lives, and promoting equality and development. Of course, your grades in the science subjects at St Hugh's High School for Girls made you less confident of coping with a nursing curriculum, so ruling out a pathway taken by many of your peers. So, with your adventurous spirit, your love of foreign languages, and inspired by having a Cuban-born mother, you manage to convince your parents to sponsor your one-year student exchange to Brazil between 1971 and 1972 with the International Christian Youth Exchange (ICYE).

If I were to tell you that the year in Brazil would prove to be a major milestone and "tipping point" in your career in international development, you might not be surprised. You might also recognise that it has shaped you as a person (and will continue to do so). Yet you will only fully realise how much of an impact this student exchange will have with the passage of time. There, only two years ago, you learnt Portuguese. Brazil opened your 17-year-old eyes to new social, economic, cultural, gender, racial, and political inequalities.

The Episcopal church, which hosted your visit, provided you with opportunities to support their social work and literacy programmes in the *favelas* of Rio, to attend high school and, later, to spend a semester at Rio's Catholic

DOI: 10.4324/9781003260929-37

University. Your exposure to Paulo Freire's "conscientizcao" method of teaching literacy was an eye opener! His method of teaching literacy was not only to equip people with reading and writing skills, using examples from their everyday lives, but also to make them critically aware of the structures of power and inequality that oppressed them.

Brazilian friends also taught you how to dance samba. "Samba is in your blood", they said, as your body responded to the rhythm of the drums of your African ancestors. The year in Brazil also showed you that, despite censorship, people can use their cultural creativity to communicate and protest against oppression. Remember the musical genius of artistes such as Chico Buarque, Caetano Veloso, Milton Nacimiento, and Gal Costa? The double meaning in their musical lyrics communicated protest while meeting the constraints of censorship imposed by the government of the time. In later years, you will draw on this knowledge, to convince Christian Aid's Grants Committee to support a communications project for campesinos in Peru during the war with Sendero Luminosa. Using disposable cameras, they captured images of the violence they were experiencing, and mounted photo exhibitions in public spaces. The pictures "spoke" volumes: they "silently" communicated crimes that could not be verbalised for fear of death.

Your time in Brazil not only made you critically aware of inequalities and human rights abuses, but the potential role that international development assistance can play in facilitating or inhibiting people's development. Among the valuable lessons were the importance of people's participation in their own development and the diversity of strategies that can be used to support change, transformation, and the right to resources to meet their basic everyday needs: food, water, shelter, education, health services, and employment. These experiences made you realise that development policies and programmes must both serve the needs of people and respect their right to identify their own needs and priorities. You will also learn the importance of how gender roles and responsibilities ascribed to males and females as family breadwinners and family caregivers, shape their daily lives; how the intersection of factors such as age, ability/disability as well as socio-economic background, can affect access to opportunities as well as the outcomes.

In Brazil, your participation in the Episcopal Church's outreach programmes in Rio's *favelas* provided many valuable lessons. Little did you know that your accompanying Elizabeth Daniel, the North American Social Worker, to the *favelas* would help to build the foundations upon which you would support international development assistance programmes in the years to come. Residents of Rio's *favelas*, many of whom are Afro-Brazilian, taught you about people's resilience; their survival skills. Their poor housing (shacks precariously perched on hillsides overlooking affluent communities), the lack of proper sanitary conveniences, and the limited access to potable water were all infringements of their basic human rights. Yet, you were also struck by their generosity in sharing the little food they had, and by the women's ability to care for their children and maintain standards of beauty so typical of Brazilian women. Important lessons from these visits confirmed that, despite the misery associated with a lack of access to potable water, basic sanitation, and jobs, as well as overcrowding and violence, many people survive; they have hopes and dreams of a better life. People like Raquel, your Afro-Brazilian friend from the Rio *favelas*, who took you to Cidade de Deus, a new government low-income housing scheme, pointed to the role of education in behaviour change, for example in the use of an inside toilet. This was a major change as they were accustomed to throwing plastic bags with their human waste outside their window. Socialisation is learnt behaviour and new contexts require resocialisation.

So, that much of your journey you know; so now let's look ahead. In the months to come you will delight in landing your first full-time job – with the Caribbean Conference of Churches (CCC) – after graduating from the University of the West Indies. You will be responsible for supporting development projects and programmes of CCC member churches in the Northern Caribbean and Central America, giving you a chance to work with youth, women, and community development organisations. In time, you will be recruited by Christian Aid to work in London. As Christian Aid's first black, female Project Officer you will cover Peru, Bolivia, and the Caribbean, allowing you to build on your diverse experiences to promote gender equality, cultural and racial diversity, environmental awareness, and disaster management and response. Work with the British Council of Churches will also provide opportunities to share perspectives on development from the Global South, to challenge historical norms and practices, and to learn about development challenges in Africa and Asia.

Career highlights with the Commonwealth Foundation and Commonwealth Secretariat will see you co-author the Foundation's *Non-Governmental Organisations: Guidelines for Good Policy and Practice* which will be translated into ten languages, and serve as a Commonwealth Observer for tripartite elections in Zimbabwe, Zambia, Rwanda, and Malawi. Your posts will provide opportunities for gender awareness training with Caroline Moser; exchange visits between the UK and the Caribbean; advocacy on Fair Trade for the Caribbean Windward Island's banana farmers; dialogue on development between theologians and academics; visits of black British youth to Jamaica; resource mobilisation for Caribbean disasters, as well as environmental awareness and solidarity with marginalised communities in Haiti and the Dominican Republic. Visits with project partners in Peru and Bolivia will provide opportunities to support NGOs working with indigenous communities, women's organisations, trade unions, miners, and farmers. Watch, listen, and reflect closely: all these experiences will provide lessons about what works and what doesn't in development. They will also inform your PhD thesis at LSE on Women Organising for Change in Caribbean Free Trade Zones, and subsequent work on mainstreaming gender in trade as well as promoting labour rights and standards in global value chains.

This sounds so positive. So rewarding. It is, of course, but as I see you now, just starting out on your journey, you have yet to see the politics and the contradictions and gaps between policy and practice. These will arise time and time again in many of your jobs, including your spell as UNFPA's Assistant Representative for the English and Dutch-Speaking Caribbean. In your future roles you will wrestle with the gaps between the ratified human rights conventions and agreements on the one hand, and the practices of international, regional, and national agencies on the other. You will observe the gaps between commitments of industrialised countries to provide 0.7% of their GDP for international development assistance projects and programmes, and their actual contributions.

The political economy of international development assistance will be an eye opener. History lessons have taught you that the causes of global poverty are rooted in centuries of exploitation of human and natural resources, enslavement, and unequal trade and financial systems between industrialised and developing countries and, of course, "Third World Debt". You will recognise that the development assistance from donor countries and agencies is the result of decades of exploitation. You will also learn about and experience the impact of "tied aid". You will see that development assistance is not altruistic; it is linked to the political, economic, and ideological interests of the donor. You will observe the process of international consultancy companies bidding for contracts to provide technical assistance to developing countries. You will also note the structured inequalities in these relationships, such that consultancy companies of the donor communities are more likely to be awarded the contracts than local consultancy companies, but then rely on local consultants to share their knowledge and expertise . . . and at much lower rates of remuneration. You will also be challenged when placing Canadian "cooperants"/volunteers to provide technical assistance to Caribbean governments and national development agencies. Undoubtedly, local agencies benefitted, but perhaps the volunteers more so, as they looked to "sell" their experience as they advanced their careers as international development experts. The politics of international development assistance has many facets.

Over the years you will teach, research, write, and publish work that seeks to bridge the gaps and contradictions. As you read and learn and observe the inequalities that deny millions of people their basic rights in industrialised, developing, and emerging economies, you will return time and again to issues centred on the unequal access to power and decision making, and the patriarchy structures and institutions that privilege a few and deny the majority access to resources to meet their basic needs. You will learn that, when you remove your "rose-coloured spectacles", the distance between political power elites and ordinary citizens contributes to persistent inequalities.

As ordinary people become conscious of their human rights and organise for change, the political economy of development assistance can change. Development policy and practice will change, from "top-down" to "bottom-up" participatory models that reflect a rights-based approach to development. Governments as "duty bearers" will be held more accountable to citizens who are "rights-holders". There will be demands for greater accountability and involvement of citizens in their own development. Gender mainstreaming will come to play a central role in your career and in development policies and programmes. Learning how the socially constructed roles and responsibilities ascribed to males and females as family breadwinners (males) and family caregivers (females) can affect their ability to access resources to fulfil their life goals. These gender mainstreaming skills that you first learnt while you were at Christian Aid will enable you to collect and analyse data disaggregated by sex and other factors, identify the differential needs of various social groups, and use this information to develop polices, programmes, and strategies that take account of the needs of each group.

Much of what you will learn about development around the world will be facilitated by new technologies created by the convergence of telecommunications and computers. Expansion of the Information, Communication and Technology (ICT) sector will enable you to access, use, and share on-line data and keep up-to-date with international development issues. You will become a news "junkie", taking full advantage of communication tools that you could not have imagined during your adolescent years. So, be open to learning and the rewards will be amazing.

In fact, as your career progresses, you will find that your interest in learning will evolve: you will decide to focus on human resource development and capacity building so that younger people better understand and address gender-related inequalities. You will focus your future work on mainstreaming gender in development policies, programmes, and strategies in various sectors, again closing the gap between policy and practice! Of course, you don't know this yet, but in 2006 you will be appointed Head of the Institute for Gender and Development Studies Mona Unit at the University of the West Indies Mona campus in Jamaica. There you will implement a new BSc degree in Gender and Development training, thereby "passing the baton" to a younger generation, while allowing you to instil your passion for research, advocacy, and gender equality and sustainable development.

So, what advice should I give to 19-year-old Leith and other adolescent girls in developing countries who are seeking a non-traditional career in international development? Use each day's experiences as opportunities to gain knowledge. Read widely; think critically and creatively; be true to your values, beliefs, and conscience. Be open to new ideas and embrace technologies as they evolve. Pursue not only formal education but also the knowledge and skills learnt by adapting to opportunities that come your way. Embrace the philosophy of lifelong learning to continue building your capacity to respond to emerging global and national development issues.

As you search for your career niche, go on-line and learn about the policy and programme priorities of international development agencies. Be brave. Be willing to seek opportunities for employment or collaboration anywhere in the world. However, as you search, find out about the institutions. Are they committed to gender equality, diversity, and social justice? What value can you add and how can they help you grow? Be realistic and recognise that organisations are run by human beings who, like you, have strengths and weaknesses. No institution is perfect! If you are given the opportunity for employment, learn how to manage conflicts creatively and to close the gap between development policy and practice.

Volunteer, if needed, to acquire valuable development skills and experience. It's not always about the money. There is satisfaction and reward in supporting change processes; providing opportunities to meet needs; transforming lives; and protecting human rights.

On your journey, work hard but also learn to rest and reflect on the lessons around you. Remember: self-care is important. Working in international development jobs is physically and intellectually demanding. It may require long hours. Unhealthy lifestyles among international development workers lead to stress, "burnout", and can shorten life expectancy. Women, as a significant demographic group working in these agencies, face what Gender and Development Planner Caroline Moser calls the "triple shift": paid work which is very demanding, unpaid care work for their families, and unpaid community management work.

Take courage! The good news is that you can survive the journey with the help of supportive work colleagues and family partners. So, choose a life partner with similar values and goals who will help you fulfil work commitments, while raising small children to adulthood. Your experiences of balancing work and family life will have a positive impact on their lives as they too will find their own niche in the struggle for sustainable development. Enjoy the ride . . .

Leith, a Jamaican Sociologist/Gender Specialist, has a PhD in Sociology from the London School of Economics and Political Science. She is currently an Honorary Research Fellow and was Head of the University of West Indies Institute for Gender and Development Studies (IGDS) Mona Unit (2006–2020). Her 25-year academic and professional career spans teaching, research, and publishing, human rights advocacy and mainstreaming gender in development policies and programmes. Leith previously worked with regional and international development agencies, including UNFPA, Christian Aid, and CUSO. She has served as an Advisor to the Commonwealth Foundation and as a member of four Commonwealth Observer Missions for Tripartite Elections: in Zimbabwe (2002), Zambia (2006), Rwanda (2010), and Malawi (2014). She is currently based in Gaborone, Botswana. She currently resides in Botswana and is a Research Affiliate with the Sociology Department, at the University of Botswana.

32

Start where you stand

Lina AbiRafeh

Dear Little Me,

I see you, 14 years old, sitting in that classroom. You're in the back, wondering what this is, what you'll learn, and why you're there. You were drawn to this subject instinctively – years before you actually found the class.

You were an annoyingly enthusiastic kid, with an insatiable curiosity and a desire to see, do, and taste everything. You invented adventures, building comforter-and-pillow forts in the living room, knowing that you were bound to go places.

Little girls around you dreamed of white dresses. You, little girl, you dreamed of white Land Cruisers.

At age 5, a family friend asked you what you wanted to be when you grew up. "A flight attendant!" you announced, "because I just want to travel!"

And indeed, you will live a life in transit.

You were born into it, after all. You're part-this, part-that, and have the complicated privilege of renegotiating your identity at every turn. You are the product of a Lebanese–Senegalese father and a Palestinian mother – both of different religions who managed to escape war and dodge laws that forbade them from marrying. And you were raised first in Saudi Arabia and then in Washington, DC. You have always been comfortable with extremes. And conflict.

Your parents fuelled this fire, in ways they did not realise at the time. As a child in Saudi Arabia, you watched your mother put on her *abaya*, the black covering she was required to wear whenever you left the isolated bubble of your expat compound. "We do this because we are here", she used to say, "but this is not how we are". She was your first feminist, filling your Saudi childhood with stuffed animals and Legos – gender-neutral toys.

Your father was no different. Every few days, he would quiz you with his favourite question: "What's the most important thing for a woman, Lina?" and you would parrot back: "Financial independence", just you had been trained to do.

And then you moved to Washington, DC. Shortly thereafter, you woke up.

DOI: 10.4324/9781003260929-38

There you are, Little Me, 14 years old. An immigrant geek in a liberal all-girls school, the brown girl in the back of the room. What you're about to learn will blow your mind – and change your life. The class, Comparative Women's History, will tour the world through stories and images of violence against women. There, you will see a bound foot, female genitalia after it had been cut, a widow on her husband's funeral pyre, a woman's broken ribcage after tightening a corset, acid burns of domestic violence survivors, and on it will go. You will be haunted by those images. And you will swear to dedicate your life to this.

You will learn that one in three women worldwide will experience some form of violence in their lifetime. Everywhere in the world. Almost every woman. Including you. And that violence is made far worse by conflict, disaster, and poverty. Violence against women is the most pervasive human rights violation in the world. Every culture, every society, every religion, every time period – even now. No one is immune – and we are all responsible.

You will feel responsible. You may not know what to do, but you know that you must do something. To undo violence. Or at least try.

You will study, you will watch, and you will wait – wondering if you'll ever be able to do the work you're dreaming of. Be patient – it will happen. The minute you can get to the field, off you shall go! You'll be 22 at the time – just a pup, really. A few years later, you'll start working in humanitarian emergencies. Afghanistan, 2002. You never forget your first, they say, and the naïve enthusiasm (and fear!) that will fuel you.

You'll land in Kabul, armed with $20,000 and a plan to establish the Afghanistan country office of Women for Women International, an NGO supporting women in conflict. Looking back, you will call those years the most exciting/exhausting/exhilarating of your life. You finally will be doing the work you are only just starting to dream of now – and will continue to visualise for over a decade until it actually materialises.

Afghanistan will surprise you. It will capture your attention for four years. While there, you'll start to examine your own work, thinking of ways to do more, and to do it better. You'll start a PhD so that you can "bitch constructively", as you'll call it, giving yourself a lens through which to understand what "development" really means for the women you want to help.

And so you'll become an accidental academic, publishing books with long titles and colons in the middle. Later, your degree will be useful in response to inappropriate questions like *Mrs or Miss?*

Neither. It's Doctor.

One day, a young Afghan man will tell you this: "The world thought they could bring freedom to Afghan women, but freedom is only won from the inside". And there it will be – the most important line you'll hear. This is how you want to work – supporting women "from the inside".

At the time, you will not think that this may also be about you, and your own freedom from the inside. So you'll plough forward, doing more, working harder, travelling farther. You won't look back.

Little Me, you will go places! You'll cover over 20 countries – places like Central African Republic, Haiti, Mali, Papua New Guinea – armed with an extra-large passport filled with stamps you won't be able to read, a supply of chapstick, and a bottle of hot sauce. Trust me on the hot sauce.

And ever so naturally, your life will become "the field". All your friends will be in the field. All your partners will be in the field. All your strange ailments will come from the field. You'll no longer know how to have a life on the outside. You won't be able to draw a line between work and life. There was no line. Connecting with family and old friends will become awkward – how could they understand the life you'll live and the choices you'll make?

You'll defend these choices forcefully. It was never a "choice", anyway. It was a calling. You'll know from those early years, from the first day in that class, that you had a duty to do this – and you sensed that you'll love it, and you hoped that you'll be good at it. All of those things will be true.

For a kid whose identity was always "other", you'll finally find your place. You'll feel at home amongst a family of eccentric characters with multi-ethnic backgrounds and last names even longer than yours. You will not be an outsider here – this is where you belong. You'll find your tribe.

But more than that, you'll find your identity. A hyphenated identity is really more about the hyphens than anything else. You could get lost in the cracks. Countries and religions have always been meaningless to you. Borders were arbitrary, religions were oppressive, and all other identity markers were only used to divide people. You cared about none of these things. Starting today, you'll connect only with your identity as a woman. And in that you will find your purpose.

You will desperately want to do good. For women. You will carry with you the constant frustration of never knowing if you'd done enough good. Or any good at all. This baggage will become heavy – be careful about how much you allow it to weigh you down. And how much you expect to achieve.

You will call yourself a one-trick pony, committed only to ending violence against women – or at least to making gains – in your lifetime.

"Dig me from the grave", you will say, "and let me know when we've succeeded!" You will say that often, despite your desire to be cremated. After all, you know the fight will be long, and hard won. But you want to have one small part in making that happen.

You will use the barometer of women's safety to better understand how to help. "Are you safe?", you will ask, knowing the answer is likely no. "What will it take to make you feel safe?", you will say. And that is where you will hear women's voices, and women's choices. You want to help make those choices a reality. But often it will not be within your power to do so. And it will become harder and harder to accept this. The frustration and sadness will accumulate, bit by bit, creating a hole in your belly that will become harder and harder to ignore.

You will also come to realise that, while you are trying to do good for women, the problems are bigger than you. And the solutions are too few. It's about resources – and you will always be angry at the world for short-changing women. You will see that rhetoric fails to match reality – and that money never materialises, reducing women to having to beg for rights to their own bodies and lives. This anger will stay with you, and eventually you will learn to use it as a force for change.

At the same time, your life will begin to look like a good CV – and eventually that won't be enough. You are more than just a piece of paper with a list of accomplishments! You will begin to think of balance, of home, of partnership. And you'll wonder if you are too late for those things.

You will decide that the Nepal earthquake in 2015 will be your last emergency. After Nepal, you'll build your TEDx talk around a graffiti message you'll spot on a wall in Kathmandu: START WHERE YOU STAND.

You'll go on to do just that – work where you stand, and do whatever you can with whatever you've got. This will lead you to Lebanon – a "home" you had never known. You park in Beirut, at the intersection of comfort and chaos, taking up the position of Executive Director of the Arab Institute for Women at the Lebanese American University. The Institute is the first of its kind in Lebanon and the Arab region – and among the first in the world. A virtual unknown, in need of a champion.

Just for one year, you'll think, while you plan to reflect on where you'll stand next. Unexpectedly, you'll fall in love with this little place. Perhaps it was expected. After all, you were destined to be there. You'll learn that you're the third generation of women in your family to work at this university. Your late grandmother (on the Palestinian side) graduated from the school in 1938 and went on to serve the Lebanese American University for 20 years. Her eldest daughter, your aunt, wrote the Bibliography on the Status of Arab Women for the Institute in 1980.

You'll learn from the young women around you, inspired by their fire. You will hear one young woman ask you if, in her lifetime, women's rights will be a matter of *fact* and not a matter of *fight*. You will tell her that you are fighting now, for her, so she won't have to.

In this part of your story, you will see that you'll come full circle. And you'll be taking one step closer to understanding what balance is, and where home might be. You'll spend four years in Beirut, and then you'll come to realise that you need to go back to the US – back to where you started. After a two-decade absence, you'll feel a bit like a time capsule – from a different era. Did the store always have this many bodywash options?! Why does everyone order everything – from socks to sofas to sex – online?!

Don't worry, you'll figure it out.

You'll leave Lebanon just before civil unrest, a government vacuum, an economic collapse, and a massive explosion that rips through Beirut – with your old apartment being ground zero. Had you stayed, you would not have survived. You'll arrive in New York in time for a brief taste of what normal life might be like, and then you'll be locked down again, along with the rest of the world, trapped by a global pandemic that erases every bit of normal – the normal you had barely begun to enjoy.

You'll leave the emergency – but it will follow you. You'll work so hard to keep women safe – what about you? You'll talk of resilience – where's yours? Think of the Afghan man's words, and find your freedom from the inside. Do it while you are young enough, and carry it with you.

You'll eventually try to date – clumsily. You'll be a bit late on the scene, but you always do things in your own order anyway. It is hard for people to understand what you need because they have not had your experience. Be patient – and stop saying it's too late. It's never too late for what's right. I can't promise that you'll have the life partner that you will later hope for, but I can tell you that you'll never regret your choices. Pay attention now – and understand what you will gain in making those choices, and what you will miss.

You'll spend the first half of your life chasing chaos. In the next half, the hard part is learning to stand still.

Little Me, listen up. What I want to tell you is this: you're a work in progress – just like the countries you've lived in and the women you've worked with. A mosaic, formed out of disparate bits – broken up close, but beautiful as a whole.

Stay in that classroom. And you'll see that it's all worth it. Let's do this!

Love, Me

Lina AbiRafeh, PhD is a global women's rights expert with decades of experience worldwide. She is a writer, speaker, advisor, and the former Executive Director of the Arab Institute for Women at the Lebanese American University. Lina completed her doctoral work from the London School of Economics and published "Gender and International Aid in Afghanistan" and "Freedom on the Frontlines" based on her work. She is currently working on her fourth book. Lina publishes and speaks frequently on women's rights and has been featured on CNN, BBC, TEDx, and Good Morning America, amongst others. Lina is among the Gender Equality Top 100 worldwide in 2018 and 2019, and has won numerous fellowships and recognitions for her work. She is a Vital Voices Fellow for outstanding women leaders, a Women's Media Center Progressive Women's Voice, and a Women in Power Fellow.

33 Learning to work in Lesotho

Mark Moran

It was 1987 in London. You were at the end of the great Australian wanderlust, readying to return home, expanded but still at a loss for a career direction. You chose engineering at the end of high school because your older brother did, and you were too young and lost in the late '70s in suburban Brisbane to know any better. As a graduate at the age of 21, you were soon consumed by the long hours and pressure with little meaning. You were desperate for something else. When you saw that little ad in the *Guardian* newspaper for a water supply engineer in Lesotho, you took the jump. A close mate had volunteered, and you loved his stories. You had no idea.

You were fortunate to be replacing Stuart Bland as the District Engineer with Village Water Supply in the mountainous Qacha's Nek. Stuart was a tall, gangly Brit who had worked hard over the past five years to establish the district headquarters. He had also built the house that was to become your home for the next two years. Even now, 30 years later, I clearly remember the calming view of grassy valleys, bands of sandstone cliffs, and those ubiquitous Lesotho mountains. Fortuitously, it had hot water, which ensured a regular stream of visiting volunteers. You met your future wife, Joy, a Peace Corp volunteer.

Stuart was fluent in Sesotho (the language the Basotho people of Lesotho speak), teaching himself from scratch. His were big shoes to fill. You learnt so much that had nothing to do with engineering. You loved it immediately.

It was the late 1980s, Nelson Mandela was still in jail under apartheid South Africa. The South Africans were the bad White guys, and aid workers across the border on the Lesotho side were the good White guys. It was old-school community development, building village water supply systems before private enterprise models irrevocably took over. Any problem was resolvable via a public meeting. You did spring measurements in the middle of the winter, at the peak of the dry season, trekking and scrambling up the sandstone slopes. You learnt how to ride a Basotho pony. You didn't realise it then, but this will be the best job you will ever have.

You read, and read, and read some more. You gave away every book and traded for more. I remember you being amazed by Tolstoy. How could he be so true to human nature in the present when writing of one hundred years

DOI: 10.4324/9781003260929-39

ago, and in absence of modern technology? How could the John Irving's *World According to Garp* contain such life wisdom? And the sad reality of anthropologist Colin Turnbull's *Mountain People* of how development had so terribly dehumanised the Ik people. And Steve Biko's *I Write What I Like* and its uplifting political manifesto for the Black Consciousness Movement. It was Biko who then led you to read Paulo Friedo, and his *Pedagogy of the Oppressed*, a commonly used university textbook, but far flung from the reading lists of any engineering course. On and on your reading went, each book leading to another.

You also made your first forays into the international development literature. You struggled your way through Sandy Cairncross' research on water supply and sanitation in Lesotho, which would be later recognised as seminal in the global movement from water supply to WASH (Water, Sanitation and Hygiene). It will take you two decades to work this out, but you were actually in Lesotho at the same time as one of your latter-day heroes, James Ferguson, who wrote his hallmark critique, depicting foreign aid as the *Anti-politics Machine*. You did not know any academics then.

You realised in Lesotho that your university degree was more vocational, than educational. You began a learning journey that would take you well beyond engineering. But you did not know then – you could not have known then – that this would lead to your PhD, and eventually to a Professorship of Development Effectiveness at the University of Queensland, in Brisbane Australia, where I now live. You would have laughed at the prospect.

You will call yourself less and less an engineer, but will remain true to your training, of designing and incrementally working your way through problems. But from your first day in Lesotho, the scope of your problem definitions expanded exponentially. You realised the importance of culture, history, social organisation, politics, and most importantly, to slow down, to connect with people, and pay attention to the milieu of knowledge beyond that needed for an engineering solution.

At this young stage in your life, you are still struggling with being too sensitive, with taking too much on board. By degrees, you will eventually embrace this as a strength of your nature. Your sensitivity makes you a good listener, a good student of people and places, and adept at unpacking what is holding them back. Thirty years later, you yourself will teach students that there are three basic things to effective development practice: to *listen* until you understand; to *respect* that people know their situation better than any outsider could ever presume; and to *deliver* once they then invest in you and entrust you to do something. You never talked like this back then, but you did this intuitively.

But there is much that you missed. So now some words of advice, from me 30 years later, to you 30 years ago. I would tell you that learning a language is one of the keys to understanding culture – but as hard as that is, it is not enough. Culture can be frustratingly unfathomable, but then again with respect and persistence, you will find you are more alike than you are dissimilar.

And there is no need to be so judgemental of other stakeholders. You were the self-righteous aid worker. Being so sure of yourself and your ideas was one thing, but you needed to not be so judgemental and damning of others'. Almost all stakeholders come from a rationale position, and everyone understands development differently. Aid work is a job that blurs the personal with the professional; people bring their values to the table, and take things personally. They are mostly well intentioned, trying their best. So, you will get further by helping them to express themselves, to get their ideas and theories of change onto the table, and then to move the conversation towards collaboration. You yourself will learn more in the process, shining more light on the problem.

Do not be naïve of politics, especially the power that you yourself wield. There is no escaping it, even within the most caring and bottom-up community-based organisations. You will be good at sensing and negotiating the many forms and layers of privilege. But it will take you many years to realise just how important privilege and autonomy is to yourself, as you struggle with hierarchies that contain you. Accept your privilege and use it well, as convening power to bring marginalised people to the table – whether by status, gender, disability, class, or otherwise – in ways that allow them to participate equally. When given genuine decision-making powers, marginalised people engage in surprisingly direction-changing ways for the better.

Forget about transplanting solutions, regardless of how well something worked elsewhere. Context is everything. As you know from Lesotho, to understand a place takes a long effort and personal investment in language and relationships. So, be of wary of expert's claims that they have the solution and their eagerness to scale up. Their claims of evidence are inescapably politicised. You too played this game, but you will learn better. In the future, your forays into evaluation science will teach you that proving impact, in light of alternative causal explanations, is something of a holy grail. Whatever the external forces you help muster, it is usually internal forces around culture, gender, markets, and youth that drive or resist change, and they often have little to do with any aid assistance.

You struggled then to deal with the unknown, change, and daily chaos. Get used to it. The ability to adapt to complexity is central to development. Change usually occurs through informal processes, which are not immediately evident from the start. When you reach that sense of humility, the beginning of knowing what you do not know – the known unknowns – you are as close as you will ever get to understanding a context.

You will pick your first fight with a funding agency, challenging the power they yield from their capital city offices. Although it was an honourable cause, you failed badly. Funders will never be waiting on your local knowledge, nor your new discoveries. They have their own ideas and they will be busy building their careers on them. Aid fundamentally involves financial transfers, with strings attached.

I am proud of you standing up though, at such a young age. You will remain rightfully outraged by the mismatches you observe between policy and practice; people's delusions when faced with massive implementation problems, and their capacity to keep going when things are so blatantly not working, to hit the next milestone and the contract deadline. You will invest a lot of time trying to fix the system and become frustrated and annoyed in the process. Give yourself a break, and look instead for people, policies, and organisations that enable practice, tolerate adaptations, and reward innovation. They will be out there, looking for you too.

As you pack up to leave Lesotho, at the end of 1990, you will be stumped by something that you never anticipated. On the plane home you were so chuffed with what you had achieved, and how you would be unstoppable back in Australia. Skillshare Africa, the volunteer agency that sent you, did so much to prepare you for your arrival – but nothing to prepare you for the return home. Their presumption was that you would struggle with adjusting to a new culture, but you readily took to that. Quite the opposite, it will be the return to your own culture that will drop you. You will become the most depressed of your life. Unemployed, not understood, you will finally find your way to a remote Aboriginal community called Doomadgee, beginning a whole new chapter of your life which will come to be as important as your career in international development.

I'm glad you never lost what you gained from that deep dive of learning and understanding in that one place in Lesotho. You were living it then. You will go on to live in remote Aboriginal communities and working in villages in rural China and then in Papua New Guinea, but never to the same depth

Always remember, you will be most effective when you have the authenticity of local voices and knowledge behind you, which will simultaneously elevate and ground you, as it should. With time, you will set out to describe effective development practice, through your research into the intercultural spaces where "outsiders" interact with "insiders", and the mismatch between what policy imagines, and practice requires. You will become a collector of practice tools and frameworks, to help you with teaching.

From those days in Lesotho, I wish you had written down your stories of success and failure; the magnificent hopes and tragedies that played out each week. Fortunately, you posted many handwritten letters, which I was able to collect from your friends and family who received them. They helped me to write this now.

Looking back to you now, I can't finish without recollecting what you knew better then, things that I have somehow lost. You would tell me to take weekends off, and to have more fun. To not work so hard, lest no one can replace you – how there is something in our efforts that displaces others. That our life choices should be about what expands us, rather than fighting against what limits us. That the more secure we are, the more insecure we feel. Back then, you were much braver than me now.

We would both agree though, that to do this work well, is to understand yourself. It will forever challenge our values and ideas and ego and force us to confront ourselves, and what is holding us back. That was how it was then, and how it still is now, 30 years on.

Mark's background includes both social science research and applied development projects, in a career spanning academia, non-profits, government, and consultancy. His cross-sectoral career has sought to forge new collaborations between academia and development practice, and blend work between international development contexts and remote Aboriginal and Torres Strait Islander communities in Australia. Until 2021, Mark held a Professorship in Development Effectiveness at the University of Queensland (UQ). He now works as a freelance development worker, researcher and author and lives in Brisbane, Australia.

Afterword

Dear next generation

Lina AbiRafeh

Dear Next Generation,

You've made it this far. I hope you'll indulge us a little further.

People entering the field, this is for you.

Will these letters change your mind? Of course not. They would not have changed mine, if I'd had the chance to see them when I was starting out more than two decades ago. But that's precisely the point. I saw no letters. I was told no "real stories". So we share these with you because you can now decide for yourselves, with far more information than we had.

We, the letter writers, are a diverse cast of characters. We comprise several dozen nationalities and stem from a rich mix of backgrounds, sectors, organisations and experiences. Here's what we share, though: motivations to make a difference, aspirations to drive positive change, successes – often small – in making the world a slightly better place, and failures to do better or achieve more in the face of massive setbacks. We try to be better, but, at times, the world seems to conspire against us.

We recognise now what we can – and cannot – control.

We, the humans behind the letters, share our lives with you. We now leave it to you to decide what's meaningful – and what's missing. As I see them, they are honest, brutal, and inherently human accounts of what it means to work in this sector. They do not romanticise the field. Instead, they expose our lived experiences and, at times, our dirty laundry.

Next generation, you've got a lot of what we did not – the technology and the skills and the protocols – to get this work done. You can find that stuff elsewhere – in courses and certifications and practitioner-based programs and academic degrees and online tools and giant tomes telling you to "do no harm" and laying out what a "duty of care" really means. All that stuff is there for you. Is it perfect? No, but I think our generation had to make it up as we went along!

These letters are not tools and how-tos. No. They are the *spirit* and *soul* of the work. The stuff no one told us. So that is why we decided to tell you.

Yet even with these insights, you have formidable challenges before you. The world faces unprecedented levels of emergency, protracted crises, multiple disasters, funding shortfalls, humanitarian fatigue, the tyranny of the urgent – and a hell of a lot of crap to grapple with in the world. I hope you will see us as a resource, as support, and – more importantly – as cheerleaders for you, as you set out to finish what we could not.

Too often, we write ourselves out of the story, like anthropologists from the 1950s, or scientists in a lab, examining bacteria under a microscope. As if we are passive observers. *As if*. And yet we seek to support, advance, sometimes even fast-track processes of social change. How can we be objective? How can our presence *not* have an impact? As if we're invisible forces at work. No.

In this field, there is no "objective". There is positionality, perspective, perception. All of these things matter.

And "us" – whoever we might be – being "there" – wherever "there" is – can never be neutral. We affect these processes of change just as much as they impact us.

And when we choose to enter this line of work, we do so with the knowledge – hopefully! – that this is not just a job. This is a life choice. This is not an office where you switch off the lights at 17:00 and go "home". For many today, the lines between "home" and "field" are indistinct. We live where we work. We live with those we work with. And too often, we live *for* our work. And when we write, we write ourselves out of the story.

So this time, we *are* the story.

Does the next generation really want to hear it? We should ask ourselves.

This is not a sermon or a summary of our sacrifice or a recitation of our too-full CVs or resumes. This is not a barefoot-in-snow-walk-to-school type of story.

Is this the stuff you even care to hear? I asked my friend whose life in the sector is still young.

Let me at least be honest about what's useful, I thought, rather than pontificating from on high while you all snooze!

"People enter this field thinking they're gonna make a difference," she started, "thinking they're gonna make some real change."

Yes, we all do.

"But the more I learned and studied and experienced, the more cynical I got. There's so much to change. Where do we even start? There's so much wrong with everything."

Yes, there still is. And perhaps there will always be.

"And then someone said to me, you just have to have hope. And I thought 'Are you kidding me?!' But honestly, I've never heard anything truer. You just need to have hope. Because if you don't have hope, what do you have?"

I hope these letters provide some of that hope – despite the hardships?

"A lot of people forget hope, or it gets lost along the way. Especially if all we have is manuals or programs or processes and systems of work. It's just very sterile and I think that gets confusing."

Yes, I saw some of those manuals too. Maybe even helped in writing some of them. They make it look easy, clean, formulaic. In a world that is anything but.

"But what is missing is the human side and the emotion and the soul – that's what is missing."

Yes, I feel that too.

"And where do we go to get the authenticity? The human side? The personal stories and personal experiences? That's a critical part of it all. Critical in keeping a person centred."

Centred, yes. A feeling I too often went without.

"Not only does it remind you of why you do it and why you're in this job, it reminds you that the whole point is to help other people. And if you take the human element out of it, how can the response be human-centred?!"

Are we centred – as humans – and are we human-centred? Different stuff – but both critical. The connections between theory and practice are often missing. All too often the messy, sometimes contradictory and often uncomfortable lived experiences of development workers are "sanitised" in academic writing. Personal stories, such as those in this book, allow us to look behind the curtain. They tell us what lies behind the scenes. They tell us what the data doesn't. They move us beyond the sterile language; the buzzwords. So human experience speaks to the lived impact. What goes right – but also what goes wrong.

That kind of honesty is not easy. It is not easy to read, but neither is it easy to write, because it means facing yourself on the screen – failings and all. That's what personal stories do. They offer honesty.

And more. We operate with a mandate to "do no harm", but don't we strive to do more than that? Surely we should be holding each other to account, holding a mirror up to our pledges and behaviours. Surely we should demand more of ourselves and of each other? Not just doing "no harm" – but actually doing "good". And doing good not just by our own standards, but by the standards of those we set out to serve. These stories are also about accountability – the accountability we have, and the greater accountability we need.

I hope those things can coexist. In this book, they do.

There's chaos in this coexistence. And situations that appear chaotic in the moment can sometimes make sense with the benefit of hindsight. Even if we can't imagine it at the time. In this line of work, there's always room for the unexpected. How do we plan for chaos? How do we react, and how do we move forward? It's about how we build from it. How we learn and how we adapt.

As my friend observed, "Sure, you can always try to be prescriptive, but these letters open the door for something different; they make room for something real".

In a world full of turbulence and transformation, the best we can hope for is hope. That hope is built on people – those who drive change forward – or aspire to do so. The people who aspire to make a real difference in the lives and wellbeing of others. This book is *about* those people, *from* those people, *for* the next generation of those people.

This book set out to offer the real story, told with the benefit of hindsight. "Wisdom born from experience rather than knowledge derived from academic analysis", we said in the introduction. Both are important, but the former is rare. The need to both share and make sense of our experience. We write for you – and for us, too.

How do we make sense of our experience? I look back on 25 years of this work and ask myself this every day. And, how to make *use* of this experience? After over two decades and over 20 countries, I now live in New York (a "field" of a different sort), looking for ways to continue to make a meaningful impact. Supporting the next generation is one of those ways. *This book* is one of those ways.

I write this as a former aid worker, author, advisor, academic, activist. I write this as a woman in what remains a male-dominated field. I write this as an Arab woman in what remains a Western-dominated field. I write this as an Arab-American, a Lebanese-Palestinian, and perhaps many other seemingly-contradictory and hyphenated things. I went into this line of work firstly because I couldn't *not*. I saw injustice at a very young age, and in having done so – I could not unsee it.

I was 14. Violence against women. You know the story . . .

I never spoke of "other women, over there". No. These women were all around me, all the time. I was one of those women, too. I still am.

I never spoke of "charity" or "beneficiaries". No. These women have agency.

Looking back now, I wonder if I was able to give as much as I got from the experience.

It is not often that we are given the opportunity to self-reflect, to be honest about our experiences – and their impact. To assess our own performance. To examine our own lives. I say this not in a navel-gazing self-indulgent sort of way. I say this as someone who, at age 14, promised herself she would do something – anything. What do I say to 14-year-old me today?

These are the uncomfortable questions we should all be asking ourselves, all the time.

When I was approached to write a letter, I was both attracted and afraid. Could I summon the courage and candour needed to make this meaningful?

What will you share? What will you withhold? What stories will you choose to tell? There are stories in the silences and omissions, too.

Will you tell the story of being sexually harassed by a colleague in the field – although you were, ironically, the "gender advisor", charged with eliminating those very things?

Will you tell the story (stories!) of being sick in the field – of feeling so ill and so isolated that you'd howl dramatically: "I just want to die at home!"

Will you tell the story of the project you managed being taken from you because "how would it look to the government" to see a young person, an Arab, a woman, in a leadership position?

(I know how it would look: *Honest.*)

Will you tell the story of struggling with self-care (a word that is now a mantra to the new generation) so much that you'd collapse in a deflated heap, with no energy to care for yourself or anyone else?

Will you tell the story of how, as a woman, you would have to tolerate sexist jokes, macho attitudes, toxic masculinities, cowboy culture, emergency junkie behaviours, and still be grateful that you've got a job "in the field"?

Will you tell the story of seeking out senior women in the field who might mentor and support you – women who could have, potentially, "had your back" – only to be told "you will not take my job from me!"? *How could I*, I wondered? I was 20 years her junior.

Will you tell the story of locationships – field "relationships" based on location – that left you feeling horrible and hollow, while watching "development guys" seduce newly arrived "development girls" without even taking off their wedding rings? *Yes, I'm single*, they'd say. *Geographically single.*

Will you tell the story of the frustration and total defeat when a moment of calm between fighting ends too abruptly, with masses of people on the move, and instability and insecurity once again the norm – in a country that has hardly had a chance to know peace?

Will you tell the story of having to be your own security, of – as one example of a bazillion – being "forgotten" at N'Djili International Airport in Kinshasa and wondering how you might find some safe and reliable transport at 02:00 to a hotel that they had "forgotten" to book?

Will you tell the story of the devastation you witnessed, the horrors you saw, and the crimes you heard – the times you realized you could do nearly nothing to help? Instead you were a helpless spectator to the tragedies of others.

Will you tell the story of reporting security concerns, or suggesting alternate (read: safer) travel plans to superiors only to be told that "maybe you're not tough enough for the field" and "there might be a 'safer' job for you in Geneva or New York"?

Will you tell the story of colleagues who would roll their eyes when you walk into meetings, prepared to fight you for the scant resources to implement projects they deemed to be "more important"?

Oh look, it's the Gender Advisor. Again.

Will you tell the story of coming "home" only to sleep for an 18-hour stretch, straight through Christmas, barely able to answer questions from family and friends?

How was [insert country x]?!

Fine, fine.

Was it, though? Anyway, why bother answering? Why tell the truth – that it was far from fine, in fact. It was a disaster in every sense of the word.

And I worked for six straight weeks without a day off only to watch my work undone by those who didn't think that preventing sexual violence was a priority.

Should I have said all those things?

Maybe then I would have built more honest relationships with those I left behind. Instead, I did my best to attend weddings, congratulate them on babies, and hear stories of the summer-they-spent-refurbishing-the-deck.

How did you spend your *summer*? They'd ask.

Should I have answered honestly? Should I have said: From my base in Senegal I covered Mali, Niger, Mauritania, Chad, Democratic Republic of the Congo, Central African Republic . . .

When would they have lost interest?

My summer was busy . . . fun. It went by fast.

Yup, it sure did. I spent the summer in transit. On an airplane. Bouncing from country to country – from warzone to warzone – to places too many people had not even heard of.

Which stories will I tell?! In the end, I told you what I would tell myself – my little self. My unbearably enthusiastic it's-the-field-or-nothing little self. She will encounter the ugly stuff and figure it out. What work is free of those nasties anyway? Surely, we have a very specific style of crap that we have to contend with, but that's the stuff that makes us tough. Or so I'd like to think.

That's the real stuff. The gross and gory stuff.

If I'd heard it, would I have been deterred? Hell, no.

At the same time, I had to figure out too many things on my own. I had no mentor in the field. I told my younger self that I would compensate for this "when I was older" by being a mentor to others – I would support anyone who asked, speak with anyone who sought my advice. In some ways I resented that I had no mentor. But it makes me a better mentor now. We build our own systems of solidarity and support.

This work isn't easy. Or fun. Build your safety net. Your people will help you. And so will we – the "old people"!

Sure, there's a lot "wrong" with this field. The processes, the politics, the power. But there's so much that is right. I've had the pleasure and privilege to work with some incredible professionals, whose dedication to this work is inspiring, whose integrity is exemplary. Contagious. People who raise the bar, even as it pushes them down.

The people I've known did the best they could with whatever they were given, often going beyond what they thought possible in order to get things done. There are more setbacks than successes, surely.

What drives us – *you!* – forward is the shared passion for positive change. If we don't believe it is possible, what are we doing?! There's not much glory in this work, after all. No one would do this unless they truly loved – and believed. Here you've seen what we love and believe. Here you've seen who we are and why we do it. And what we leave behind.

Here you've seen the real story – not the stuff from academic textbooks or ambitious development plans. We trust that our actions have had an impact. We hope our words will have an impact.

Dear Next Generation, take these letters, go forward, and make your own choices. We're here for you. We're cheering for you.

MIX
Papier | Fördert gute Waldnutzung
FSC® C083411

Kolibri 360 GmbH
Ferdinand-Jühlke-Straße 7
99095 Erfurt, Deutschland
produktsicherheit@kolibri360.de